Surviving

Advance Reviews

'Clearly and gracefully written, *Surviving Capitalism* presents an interesting and fertile thesis about the nature of capitalism and how different societies have learnt to cope with it. Pursued in theoretical terms in the first part of the book, the argument is developed with a cogency and subtlety that is rarely found in books in this subject area. The historical sections display broad erudition and abound in relevant and memorable examples. Perhaps most surprisingly, given its potentially deadly subject matter, the book is also consistently enjoyable to read.'

John Gray,
Author of *Straw Dogs: Thoughts on Humans and Other Animals*
(Granta, 2002)

'Surviving Capitalism presents a highly literate cost-benefit analysis of the history of capitalism. Yes, capitalism will survive. Given its benefits, it may even be inevitable. But we survive the costs of capitalism only through an extensive variety of coping mechanisms, including the family, community associations, guilds and unions, religion and the welfare state. What does the author mean by surviving? Simply this. He means retaining our humanity, because the central cost of capitalism is to undermine it. So he argues. The books is fresh, fascinating, relevant, and, yes, humane.'

Jeff Madrick,
Editor, *Challenge Magazine*

Surviving Capitalism

how we learned to live with the market and remained almost human

ERIK RINGMAR

Anthem Press

Anthem Press
An imprint of Wimbledon Publishing Company
75–76 Blackfriars Road, London SE1 8HA
or
PO Box 9779, London SW19 7ZG
www.anthempress.com

First published by Anthem Press 2005

British Library Cataloguing in Publication Data
A catalogue record for this book is available from the British Library.

Library of Congress Cataloging in Publication Data
A catalog record for this book has been requested.

1 3 5 7 9 10 8 6 4 2

ISBN 1 84331 175 5 Hbk
ISBN 1 84331 176 3 Pbk

Typeset by Footprint Labs Ltd, London
www.footprintlabs.com

Printed in Great Britain

Contents

Acknowledgements

Thanks to Khun Prathomporn, Khun Lek and Khun Malee for making our stay in Thailand into such a memorable experience. Thanks to Mr Powell for fixing me up and LOL to DMP.

THEORETICAL
PRELIMINARIES

1

The Inevitability and Inhumanity of Capitalism

During the last ten years or so there has been a lot of talk about the coming of a 'new economy'. Different authors define this amorphous entity in slightly different ways; some focus on new technologies, others on new styles of corporate management and ways of working; or perhaps it is rather a product of a scaling-back of the state or perhaps a consequence of an ever more globalized world.[1] Although the items on this list, or on some longer list like it, may appear quite disparate, what they have in common is an emphasis on the logic of the marketplace, on the interplay between supply and demand. What is new about the new economy, in short, is an emphasis on market forces. Economic markets, we are today constantly told, must be given freer reign – we must 'get prices right' and stop pampering and mollycoddling the inefficient, the unproductive and the merely lazy. Only in this way will we survive in the new and vastly more competitive world in which we live; only in this way can we achieve economic growth and lasting happiness.

We are in this way invited to participate in a gigantic social experiment. According to the engineers who have drawn up the plans, our societies are to be reorganized ever more closely in the image of a market. Efficiency, rationality and productivity are to characterize ever more of what we do, and what cannot be justified in such terms should disappear, or at least receive less of our time and attention. This is the future, after all – we do what everyone else is doing, and if we fail to conform, we are doomed. And even though the benefits of the experiment may be slow in coming, and it sometimes seems as though we are becoming poorer both in material and in social terms, we are assured that the day eventually will arrive when all the sacrifices of the present will be justified.[2] Just as once Communism, capitalism will bear its greatest fruits in the future. Meanwhile we should take pride in the fact that we have history on our side and that we live according to its fundamental principles. The new economy is thus above all an idea – it is an idea that requires boundless idealism and commitment.[3] *Fiat* capitalism *et pereat mundus*.

We have of course been here before. The proponents of the new economy sometimes talk as though they are the ones responsible for inventing economic markets and as if no one previously has understood their benefits. But markets have been around for thousands of years. In China there were thriving markets in both consumer goods and factors of production even before the establishment of the first imperial dynasty in the third century BCE, and in Europe markets have existed continuously since money was reintroduced sometime in the eleventh century.[4] And as far as a committed defence of market forces is concerned, our contemporary social engineers are merely the bleak shadows of the real revolutionaries of the eighteenth and nineteenth centuries: economists like Adam Smith, David Ricardo and Nassau Senior. It was on their recommendations that market forces were unleashed from the fetters of mercantilism and traditional privilege. Markets, after all, are not natural beasts but created ones; the free markets of the nineteenth century were products above all of actions undertaken by the state.[5]

This historical context holds a lesson for us. The nineteenth-century combination of industrial production and *laissez faire* policies led to unprecedented levels of economic growth but also to unprecedented levels of human misery. The problem, to put it briefly, was that subsistence farmers were deprived of their land and forced to sell their labour in markets that were completely glutted. Once the value of a human life is determined by market forces and once that value sinks sufficiently low, a situation is created which is highly unstable. As a victim of the market you need to do something in order to save your dignity and improve your conditions. Some people protested and put political pressure on governments to institute pro-labour legislation and social reforms. Others decided that markets had to be abolished, and others again turned to fascism. In fact, most of the politics of the twentieth century was taken up with attempts to deal with the direct and indirect consequences of nineteenth-century industrialism and *laissez faire*. Hence the social strife, the revolutions and many of the conflicts and wars.

And now we are thus invited to do it all over again. We should liberate markets, we are told, and see what happens. Of course the situation is not the same as one hundred years ago – we are richer now, better educated and prepared – yet the parallels are there and the prospects are troubling.[6] Once again the economy is likely to grow rapidly in the aggregate while the market becomes the arbiter of our lives. There will be new victims, and while we are likely to be better off economically, we are also likely to be more humiliated and debased.[7] Capitalism, in short, is inevitable, but it is also inhuman. It is inevitable since there is no other system that produces comparable levels of prosperity, but it is inhuman for what it does to human beings and to the societies in which we live.

The question is thus not how capitalism can be replaced with something else – there is nothing else that can replace it – the question is rather how its negative consequences can be avoided. In fact, ever since markets were first introduced at the very beginning of recorded history, people have tried to come up with various ways of coping. Although capitalism is very good at breaking down social structures, human beings are very good at rebuilding them. This book is about this interplay of destruction and recreation. The aim is to briefly go over the history of capitalism and to look at some of the ways in which people have sought to deal with its destabilizing effects. What we want to know is what capitalism does to individuals and societies, but also what individuals and societies do in order to protect themselves. This book is a work in historical sociology, but it is written with a certain sense of urgency. Before the new economy comes down on us in full force we need to know more both about capitalism and about how to survive it with our humanity intact.

The Power of Markets

Capitalism has always had a way of shaking things up. Capitalism has undermined traditions, eroded the power of well-established authorities and made, in Karl Marx's famous phrase, 'all that is solid melt into air'.[8] Normatively speaking, many of these changes have been for the good. The expansion of markets has brought about economic development, leading to prosperity for some and a far better standard of living for the many. Economic development in turn has made it possible for people to leave their hand-to-mouth existence and lead proper human lives. As a result there is more time for rest and recuperation, for social interaction, for cultural and intellectual pursuits. Although the evidence here is far more contested, there also seems to be a connection between economic development and a number of other long-cherished goals including peace, social justice and democracy.[9] If nothing else peace, social justice and democracy are far more difficult to maintain when people are poor and the economy stagnant.

And yet capitalism has also had a number of consequences which normatively speaking have been quite disastrous. The expansion of markets has forced people to specialize on ever more well-defined tasks, and as labour has been more finely divided, so has the fabric of social life. Over the course of the last 200 years capitalism has continuously broken up social relationships and destroyed communities and established ways of life. Facing new economic imperatives former farmers and farmhands have suddenly found themselves factory workers in cities where they have had few connections with other people. In the course of the nineteenth century, the Europeans were uprooted in this fashion, and today farmers throughout Southeast Asia are going through much the same process.

In addition the expansion of capitalism has meant that more and more of our lives has become subject to market forces. Things have become commodified, as it were. To 'commodify' something is to turn it into an object that can be sold in a market at a price. As a result of this process we have come to adopt an increasingly rationalistic attitude to our relationships with others and to ourselves. At the same time other non-economic ways of understanding the world have become more difficult to uphold. Values have been replaced by prices, and prices as always are determined through the interplay of supply and demand. In this way, even though the expansion of markets makes sure that resources are becoming increasingly efficiently allocated, we become increasingly impoverished.

Capitalism, finally, seems to make our lives more and more alike. When subject to the same market forces, societies, products, and even human beings start to resemble each other. In part this is a consequence of the spread of the new market rationality. When we all apply the same standards to our actions and our thoughts, we increasingly come to think and act in similar ways. But convergence is also a consequence of ever sharper competition. Everything else being equal, the bigger the market, the larger and fewer the companies that supply it, and before long a few enormous companies will be selling ever more standardized goods to ever more people. If nothing else, such homogeneity is terribly boring. But homogeneity is also a threat since our very notion of an identity presupposes the ability to draw distinctions and to create boundaries. There must be something about us that is uniquely ours if there is to be a point to our lives. In a fully extended market society, it is less and less clear what that could be.

Both pictures are consequently correct. Capitalism is simultaneously both inevitable and inhuman. It is inevitable since there is no better way to bring about economic prosperity together with all the cherished social goods which prosperity produces. It is inhuman since capitalism undermines our communities, our values and our ability to determine who we are. As inevitable, capitalism has to be encouraged; as inhuman, it has to be controlled. The all-important question is how we can simultaneously respond to both of these conflicting imperatives.

Political discussions over the last 250 years have more than anything concerned precisely this issue, and the various views on the matter make up the familiar left-right scale according to which political positions are conventionally classified.[10] The traditional right-wing of the *anciens régimes* was anti-capitalist and defended time-honoured values and hierarchies, whereas the left-wing was pro-capitalist and revolutionary. Once the left seized power in the course of the nineteenth century, however, the positions switched. The new right-wing praised the virtues of capitalism and sought to make sure that nothing would restrict its reach. The new left-wing emphasized the negative consequences and looked for ways in which capitalism could be controlled.

Important as these debates have been, it would be a mistake to think that the conflict between competing imperatives can be settled entirely through political actions. There is certainly a role for politics here but it is more limited than we commonly imagine. The conflict between competing imperatives is too tangible, too pressing, too everyday, and none of us can afford to wait around for the political debate to run its course. What we do is instead to rely on a kind of infra-politics, a low-level, barely visible politics which we all engage in, whether we know it or not, whenever we take steps to protect ourselves against the negative impact of capitalist markets.[11] As it turns out, there is an entire repertoire of social arrangements we routinely draw on to assure such protection. There is nothing left-wing about these instinctive actions and they are not undertaken in order to make a political point. In fact, even the most vocal of market fundamentalists end up protecting themselves in much the same manner.[12] They too are human beings, after all, and they too have to defend their humanity against the encroachments of the market.

The result is best described as an uneasy compromise. Far from conquering all of social life, markets and societies have reached a kind of *modus vivendi*. Since capitalism is an unrivalled source of prosperity, it has been retained, but since it is also destructive of social life, it has been contained. There is the logic of the market, but there are also alternative logics that are non-market-based. Within the market, supply and demand reign supreme, but outside of the market, supply and demand are reined in. The combination is not without its problems, but most of the time it works reasonably well. In the end this is how all successful societies have survived capitalism; we all have our various ways of remaining human.

Our first task in this book is to provide a more detailed investigation of some of these threats.[13] The strategy here is similar to that employed by many economists. Instead of talking about the actual world, what economists typically do is to talk about the version of the world they have created in their theoretical models.[14] Whereas the actual world is messy and full of awkward facts, the world of the model is neatly organized in accordance with a few basic principles. Economists are regularly ridiculed for this hopelessly academic way of proceeding, and yet it is often the only way to make sense of highly complex situations. Proceeding like an economist, therefore, the question is first what the social consequences are likely to be of the development of capitalism. Only once this logic has been described is it possible to say something about what we have done to protect ourselves against it.

Division of Labour

Consider first what happens when markets grow wider in scope. Markets grow in width, we could say, when they come to include more people and larger and better integrated geographical areas. The widest possible market is one that includes absolutely everybody and in which prices and qualities are determined through the same processes. Everything else being equal, wider markets are characterized by a higher degree of division of labour.[15] Instead of everyone making everything they need for themselves, people come to specialize on whatever they are relatively better at producing. By trading with others who similarly specialize in their comparative advantages, the division of labour will spread. Before long, work will be divided into ever smaller and better defined tasks, and in the end we will all be doing just one unique thing.

The economic benefits of this process are incontrovertible and they were the reason why the classical economists were such strong advocates of free trade.[16] Specialization makes people vastly more efficient. By focusing on a particular task we soon become far more skilled at what we do. By leaving each task to the person who is best qualified to perform it, and by trading with each other, everyone benefits. In this way it is also far easier to introduce technological innovations. Instead of having a person perform the same tedious task all day long, we can have a machine do it. Before long the machine can carry out the work and the workers can focus on attending and servicing the machine. Hence the factory.[17]

For individuals the division of labour has a number of obvious benefits. When labour is divided, new kinds of jobs and new opportunities present themselves. Seizing on these, people are given a chance to break with their previous lives. Those who are poor and otherwise disadvantaged are in this way able to improve their lot.[18] A striking example are the medieval serfs who decided to run away from their feudal obligations.[19] As customary law stipulated, after having lived in a town for a year and a day the runaways were declared free; *Stadtluft*, as the medieval German saying went, *macht frei*. Understood figuratively, city air is still liberating. It is easy to imagine the exhilarating sense of freedom experienced by nineteenth-century European farmers, or by peasants throughout East Asia today, when leaving the soil and the animals for new lives in faraway megalopolises. It is not irrational to prefer the unpredictability of city life to the all-too-predictable drudgery of the countryside.

And yet it is also possible, and equally correct, to describe the very same process in far more negative terms. The division of labour brings not only new opportunities but often also too many, and too many unwanted, changes. Increased specialization not only allows us to change our lives but it *forces us to do so*. We are compelled to change whether we like it or not, and to live and work under conditions that are not of our own choosing. In this way the division of labour is constantly undermining the fabric of social life together with the social positions and the identities we have acquired. We can no longer be who we are and live the way we are used to. The result is likely to be alienating – meaning that we suddenly feel estranged from the familiar, well-established contexts through which we make sense of our lives.[20]

The Industrial Revolution in England at the end of the eighteenth century provides the classic illustration. Here work was for the first time separated from the home, family members were separated from each other, and one's own time was separated from the time owed to one's employer. When all family members were forced to specialize in their comparative advantages, it was not long before fathers were sent down into mines, children were pushed up chimneys and mothers were left washing and cleaning for others rather than for themselves.[21] And because the factories could be run more profitably around the clock, there was no natural end to the working day. Deprived of their land, former peasants were forced to sell their labour – and because the number of people looking for work was next to endless, their wages fell to around or below subsistence level.

Compared to labour on the farm, labour in the factory represented an unprecedented regimentation of daily life.[22] In the factories people were bossed around in a way they never previously had been. Workers were supposed to emulate the efficiency and rationality of the machines they worked at, and before long they ended up being treated like machines themselves. The term 'factory', Andrew Ure reported in his *Philosophy of Manufactures*, 1835, 'involves the idea of a vast automaton, composed of various mechanical and intellectual organs, acting in uninterrupted concert for the production of a common object, all of them being subordinated to a self-regulated moving force'.[23] 'Many mechanical arts', the Scottish political economist Adam Ferguson pointed out already in 1767, 'succeed best under total suppression of sentiment and reason.'

> Manufactures, accordingly, prosper most, where the mind is least consulted, and where the workshop may, without any great effort of imagination, be considered an engine, the parts of which are men.[24]

Coming across this passage in his readings, Karl Marx wholeheartedly agreed.[25] Since factory workers see only a small part of the production process, they are never in a position to properly understand the rationale for the actions they spend most of their lives performing. Industrial production, Marx concluded, means that people are alienated from the fruits of their labour. Compare this situation with that of the medieval craftsman who had control over all stages in the production process and who worked in his own time and for his own profit.[26]

Although the nature of factory work has changed dramatically since the days of Ferguson and Marx, its consequences are not necessarily all that different. In contemporary factories, rather than supervising machines, workers are increasingly supervising computers which in their turn supervise machines.[27] All you need to know as a computer operator is how to press a few buttons on digital displays which are becoming ever more user-friendly. From the point of view of occupational health and safety this represents a vast improvement, but at the same time computerization has continued to drain work of its meaning. Much contemporary factory labour no longer requires any particular skills, and it is for that reason not something to take much pride in. Work is increasingly something that you do while daydreaming of a more authentic, perhaps a more glamorous, life elsewhere.

But alienation can also be understood as a society-wide process. The division of labour forces us to give up unprofitable occupations, to retrain and reskill ourselves and to look for new jobs elsewhere. Often this means that we are forced to move to cities, perhaps to other countries, leaving our families and friends behind. To seize on new opportunities is too often to turn one's back on an entire way of life. Before long specialization has divided not only labour but also societies, and distanced and alienated people from each other. As Peter Gaskell noted in his survey of the effects of the factory system, *The Manufacturing Population of England*, 1833, the discontent of the workers had less to do with wage issues than with 'the separation of families, the breaking up of households, the disruption of all those ties which link man's heart to the better portion of his nature, viz. his instincts and social affections'.[28]

There are plenty of historical illustrations of such effects. From the introduction of a monetized economy in the Middle Ages to the industrial revolution of the nineteenth century, the expansion of markets has produced great waves of migration, growing larger in each successive stage. In the course of the nineteenth century, no fewer than 85 per cent of Europe's population moved; some 70 per cent within the borders of their own countries and the rest abroad, to the Americas in particular.[29] Outside Europe the expansion of markets has had the same consequences, especially once the process of industrialization got under way in the twentieth century. In the 1910s and 1920s, large numbers of Japanese farmers began migrating, and in two frantic decades cities like Tokyo, Osaka, Kobe and Nagoya doubled in size.[30] In China and much of Southeast Asia the corresponding migratory movements began only in the 1980s and 1990s. This was when cities such as Shanghai, Guangzhou, Bangkok, Jakarta and Kuala Lumpur suddenly exploded, creating sprawling ghettos where new opportunities were mixed with new forms of human misery.

The social costs imposed by these migratory movements have been substantial. While the initial excitement offered by city life soon wears thin, the challenges become ever more pressing. After all, life in the city is entirely different from life in the countryside. In the city there are far more people around, but also far fewer people who know and care about each other. Often the new immigrants lack both emotional and material support, and without friends and relatives nearby the feeling of rootlessness can become overpowering. Thus London of the eighteenth century was, according to a contemporary description, a 'social wilderness' in which 'everyone is indifferent to another'.[31] Likewise the Tokyo of the 1920s, as the author Yanagita Kunio observed, was filled with people who were 'not attached to anything, anywhere'.[32] There was a 'general thinning out' of social relationships. Similarly, contemporary Thai society is subject to 'the dangers of extremely rapid social mobility that alienates people from their roots, even forcing them to seek new names and new identities with which they do not feel at ease'.[33]

Moreover, by moving to the city people necessarily become far more exposed to the vagaries of the market. Life in the countryside was no idyll, to be sure, but most challenges were presented by nature and people had their time-honoured ways of coping. Subsistence farming guaranteed a reasonably stable environment. In the city by contrast most challenges are man-made, unpredictable, and new arrivals often have no idea how to cope.[34] Fully exposed to market forces they live in constant fear of sickness or a recession that might ruin their businesses and their livelihoods. And even those who do well for themselves, such as the prosperous merchants of eighteenth-century London or twenty-first-century Shanghai, find that the intense competition of the new and larger markets constitutes a perpetual source of anxiety.[35] On average, people living in cities are not only better off economically than people in the countryside, but also a lot busier and far more worried.

Such feelings of rootlessness and anxiety have had profound existential consequences for the individuals concerned. As many have come to realize, with fewer people around who know and care about you, there are fewer people to turn to for social and emotional sustenance. As a result it is more difficult for individuals to gain recognition for the self-descriptions they come up with. This is a particular problem in new urban environments where previous, well-established, identities have lost their meaning. No one can be a farmer in a city, after all. Eventually, to be sure, people will cobble together some new identity for themselves and as a result they will gradually come to feel more secure, or at least their children will. Yet the transitional costs involved in this move from one identity to another are often substantial, and for the people who have to pay them it is little comfort that most likely, one day, everything will be fine.[36] Moreover, in a society in a continuous state of transition, transitional costs of this kind do not only have to be paid once but continuously.

Commodification

Markets are not only growing wider, however, but also deeper. The depth of a market refers to the range of goods and services it has to offer. A shallow market is one that encompasses few goods and services, and a deep market is one that encompasses many. In an ever deeper market an ever larger range of goods and services are being bought and sold. The deepest possible market is one in which absolutely everything is for sale; it is a market in which everything is commodified.

To be fair, let us first remember that commodification too has a number of positive consequences – again above all economic ones. Everything else being equal, the deeper the market, the more efficiently the resources of society will be distributed. The reason is that things which were previously badly allocated can now be allocated with the help of the interplay of supply and demand.[37] Instead of simply accepting the way resources have been distributed by nature or by luck, markets move things around to where they are more productively employed. Instead of traditional elites hogging all the prestige items – the women, jewels and cult objects of a society – they become available to whoever can afford to pay for them. The outcome is not only more efficient in economic terms but arguably also more just.

If markets really are a good idea, there is no reason not to extend them ever further. Yet when everything is eventually commodified, instead of living in a society we live in a gigantic shopping-mall. It is easy to see this shopping-mallization becoming reality before our eyes as many things and activities previously thought of as off-limits to markets are now touched by them.[38] There is for example an illegal but growing market in body parts such as kidneys, and there is a black market in children, ostensibly paid for in the form of adoption fees. The internet provides a new outlet for previously off-limit items ranging from prescription drugs to sexual services and stolen Tibetan works of art. Political power too has recently become commodified since electoral success can increasingly be bought with the help of advertising. There are still things that are not marketed – reproductive success, for example, or eternal life – but recent advances in gene technology may yet change that fact. The day is surely not far off when we can buy the babies we want and live as long as we can afford to.

Market fundamentalists see no reason to stop this process. In fact, they view it as perfectly benign. And yet once they start talking about 'markets in babies' or 'the economics of rape', most of the rest of us will have had enough.[39] It is not that we doubt the possibility of efficiency gains in these areas too, rather we are worried that whatever economic gains that materialize are more than offset by non-economic losses. Not everything is a commodity, after all, and not everything is reducible to utility calculations.[40] By allowing the market to take over we deny the existence of alternative principles of distribution and thereby also the alternative values they embody.

This argument applies with particular force to attributes associated with our own person.[41] A kidney or a love life, most of us would conclude, have a value in and of themselves; they are not commodities that can be disposed of if the need arises but are instead intrinsic parts of what and who we are. To sell them is demeaning and it is to do violence to our sense of self and thereby to our standing in our community. An analogous argument applies to children who as human beings have an intrinsic value and who as members of a family are integral to the identity of all other family members. To make commodities out of such attributes of our humanity is inhuman.

A not dissimilar argument applies to our labour power. When labour is commodified, it is the value of human life that comes to be determined by market forces.[42] As a result people are likely to take an increasingly instrumental view of themselves and of each other. In a labour market, as already Thomas Hobbes noted, 'your worth is a matter of your price', and your price is subject to forces far beyond your control.[43] Often a sudden dip in the business cycle or a crash in the stock market can dramatically change your fortune.[44] Without quite understanding what has happened, you find that there suddenly is no demand for your services. In practice, none of us may genuinely accept that market evaluations really represent our true worth, yet it is difficult to completely ignore them since money is the accepted measure of value in our society. In a competitive market-society poor people are regarded as losers, and they are not for a second allowed to forget it.

Much the same applies to the commodification of other factors of production. Obviously a sophisticated capitalist economy could never function without a market in land and capital. It is only once these inputs into the production process are given a price that they can come to be efficiently allocated.[45] And yet to treat land as a commodity is necessarily to take a particular view of it.[46] When land is commodified, nature itself is turned into a 'resource' that is used for economic gain. As a result it is appreciated only for what it yields, and before long it is inevitably over-exploited. Similarly, when capital is commodified, industrial capitalism comes to be replaced by financial capitalism, and instead of making money producing things, money is made through speculation in the money markets. Before long the entire economic system becomes subject to recurring manias, panics and crashes.[47]

The eventual and complete commodification of every aspect of our lives will make us poorer rather than richer. The reason is simply that markets, no matter how deep, never can provide adequately for all of our needs. There are far too many things – indeed the most important things in life – which by their very nature cannot be bought and sold. Above all, markets can never provide us with the kind of recognition we need in order to establish secure identities for ourselves.[48] As human beings we crave appreciation, friendship and love, and we need people around who can recognize us as particular individuals with human qualities that are uniquely our own. None of this the market can provide. Friendship, companionship and emotional support have to be freely given, they cannot be bought and sold. You cannot keep your friends on a pay-roll and prostitution is not a market-based equivalent of love. While rich people certainly have unique ways of gaining recognition for themselves – by sponsoring arts centres, for example, or by buying football teams – the public nature of such efforts only proves the point. Rich people too want to be appreciated for who they are and not for what they have.

If we only thought about it properly, and occasionally we do, we would all acknowledge the truth of these elementary facts. The problem is only that alternative non-market-based standards have become more difficult to defend since by definition they cannot be expressed in monetary terms. Whatever happens outside of the market is for that reason likely to receive less of our time. As a result we pay less attention than we should to the things that really matter to us. The real business of living and loving takes place on the sly, as it were, outside of working hours, in the half-forgotten margins of our lives.

Mechanisms of Convergence

Finally, consider the question of convergence. Capitalism, we pointed out above, is likely to lead to convergence between societies and ways of life as it relentlessly rationalizes, streamlines and demystifies everything we do. The more we think of the world only in terms of economic costs and benefits, the more we will all come to resemble each other; all quirks and idiosyncrasies will be ironed out in the never-ending quest for profits. As Marx pointed out, capitalism 'compels all nations, on pain of extinction, to adopt the bourgeois mode of production; it compels them to introduce what it calls civilization into their midst, i.e. to become bourgeois themselves'.[49] 'The capitalist outlook', to quote Joseph Schumpeter, the Harvard economist and one-time Austrian minister of finance,

> starts upon its conqueror's career subjugating – rationalizing – man's tools and philosophies, his medical practice, his picture of the cosmos, his outlook on life, everything, in fact including his concepts of beauty and justice and his spiritual ambitions.[50]

In addition, capitalism is likely to lead to convergence since successful capitalist development requires the establishment of institutions which are necessarily more or less alike. Well-functioning markets require the same kinds of financial and legal frameworks, monetary systems and mechanisms that assure political predictability. When this institutional paraphernalia is put in place, there will be less scope for variation between societies.[51]

These homogenizing effects become even stronger once we introduce a high degree of competition. As we know from other walks of life, those who compete with each other will quite automatically come to resemble each other. Think of the way the bodies of athletes become increasingly alike as they compete for the same Olympic medals, or the way states in military competition develop the same kinds of nuclear arsenals.[52] The logic here is the one we find in all cases of evolution. Consider, for example, the way the process of evolution has provided aquatic animals with the same kinds of torpedo-shaped bodies.[53] As it turns out, this body-form is simply the most efficient way of getting through water, of catching prey or of getting away from predators. Those who fail to adjust to this standard will never live long enough to reproduce.

The most famous illustration of this evolutionary logic concerns dolphins, or rather the land-dwelling hippopotamus-like creatures who some 10 million years ago were forced back into the oceans.[54] Adjusting to their new environment, they eventually became quite similar to fish – indeed, before the rise of modern biological science, dolphins were usually regarded as species of fish. For a social example of the same evolutionary logic consider two car companies.[55] To the extent that they compete in the same markets the two are forced to become more and more alike in a number of respects. This is even the case for companies located in separate countries as long as they try to appeal to the tastes of the same customers. Most obviously the car models they produce will over time become more or less indistinguishable.

Societies too may feel the same competitive pressures. Consider for example the competition for foreign direct investments.[56] In the quest to woo foreign investors no country can afford to appear an expensive or cumbersome place in which to do business. A state may thus be forced to reduce its tax rates and bring other regulations into line with those of other states. Alternatively, given the high level of mobility afforded by global capitalism, companies can blackmail the governments of the countries in which they operate.[57] By threatening to close down their plants and move their production elsewhere, companies can block legislation that might hurt their interests. For that reason convergence is likely to take place at the level most advantageous to the most mobile corporations.

A similar mechanism operates through the competition taking place in financial markets. In a truly globalized financial system the price of credit will no longer be set by governments but instead by the free interplay of supply and demand. As a result governments will no longer be able to control interest rates; money, just like water, will instead find its own level.[58] This means not only that governments lose this particular tool of policy-making but also that they expose themselves to the verdicts of international investors. Borrowing from the same institutions, debtors around the world are forced to abide by the same conditions. In order to obtain loans on the best possible terms, they all have to abstain from behaviour which in one way or another may be deemed 'irresponsible' or 'reckless'.[59] By imposing financial penalties on behaviour that makes one borrower different from another, conformity is enforced.

Exposed to these mechanisms and to other mechanisms like them, the hands of companies and governments are increasingly tied. Markets are taking control and dictating to politics, and after some initial hesitation everyone is responding in the same uniform manner. In the end only the most rational, the most efficient, model survives and companies and societies are all forced to conform. Although this world may correspond to the economists' fondest dream – imagine seeing the day when all your theories are verified! – it is surely everyone else's nightmare. It is an odourless world, painted in shades of grey, with muted sounds and the same endlessly reiterated décor. Wherever we go we will only encounter copies of the already known; we look into the faces of others and see only ourselves. There is no outside, only insides; everything is intimately known and for that reason simultaneously both comforting and alienating. This is a contradiction, to be sure, but a contradiction familiar to all consumers of globalized brands. While we may appreciate the familiarity of a Benetton sweater, an IKEA table or a cup of Nescafé, none of these products has a clear connection to a time or a place. Their lack of context accounts for their universal appeal, but they do not belong to us rather than to someone else.

This inability to make distinctions has an impact on our ability to form identities. Social philosophers have long foretold the arrival of the day when the fully extended mass market will create a mass society in its own image.[60] Succumbing to the crowd, we will become one with it and think and act only together with others. There is no doubt that this will be hailed as a great liberation by many. Relieved of the burden of our identity we will no longer have to assert ourselves nor take responsibility for our actions. Our only deliberations will concern how best to spend our money and how to have a good time; we will be consumers rather than citizens and human beings. And as consumers we will easily be manipulated by market forces:

> Above this race of men stands an immense and tutelary power, which takes upon itself alone to secure their gratifications and to watch over their fate. That power is absolute, minute, regular, provident, and mild. It would be like the authority of a parent if, like that authority, its object was to prepare men for manhood; but it seeks, on the contrary, to keep them in perpetual childhood; it is well content that the people should rejoice, provided they think of nothing but rejoicing.[61]

2

How Society Protects Itself

Given this long list of negative social consequences – and much more could have been said along the same lines – it is surprising that most people complain as little as they do. Given the high costs imposed by the continuous widening and deepening of markets, one would expect us to go crazy and society to break apart. Yet on the whole we don't and it doesn't. This fact is enough to make us start doubting the validity of the analysis presented above. If capitalism really is this difficult to live with, one may legitimately ask, why do people on the whole seem fairly content? Why, for example, did the revolution which Marx prophesized never happen? Why are many of us on the contrary reasonably comfortable with a system that has such obvious flaws?

The answer as so often lies hidden in the assumptions. Economists, as we pointed out above, usually feel quite ill at ease when discussing the actual world and prefer instead to talk about the world they have created in their theoretical models. This was the premise also of our discussion. The argument concerned the social consequences that *would have* materialized as long as everything else remained equal. Yet in the real world, as economists are constantly reminded, nothing ever remains equal and the effects predicted always interact with other, counter-balancing, effects. The same is true of our analysis. Instead of simply succumbing to capitalism and paying the costs it imposes, people have devised various strategies for protecting themselves. Rather than doing away with capitalism, they have found ways of living with it. This is why things in practice never are as bad as the theoretical considerations would suggest. This is also no doubt why the long-prophesized revolution never happened.

Put slightly differently, economists, whether radical or neo-classical, have always exaggerated the role of markets. Although there is much that capitalism can do, there are also definite limits to its world-transforming powers. Society is not some kind of malleable clay which market forces are free to shape and reshape in any way they require. On the contrary, human beings are often very good at defending themselves. Using a common label these defensive reactions might be referred to as 'protective responses', and the arrangements through which protection is provided might be referred to as 'protective arrangements'.[1] While people happily, even eagerly, acknowledge the benefits that capitalism produces, protective arrangements help to compensate us for its noxious side-effects. The outcome is a model that is quite a bit less efficient than that described by the economists' text-books but that is also something far easier to live with.[2] In the end the market must serve society, and not society the market.

Protective Arrangements

Despite all talk of a 'new economy', capitalism has not rearranged society in its own image and market relations have not come to replace all other kinds of relations. This will not and it could not happen. Humans are social beings by nature, and as such we could never survive in a society reorganized in the form of a gigantic shopping-mall. Although there are relative social losses that can be compensated for by relative economic gains, no one is prepared to go ahead and completely trade the one off for the other.[3] In fact, apart from a basic set of quickly satisfied urges, all our needs are social; what we really want is acceptance, appreciation, friendship and love. While markets certainly may play a role in satisfying these desires – as when we buy a birthday present for someone we love – the satisfaction itself is achieved outside the market, not inside it.

To the extent that the expansion of markets undermines these non-market values, expansion undermines the rationale also of the markets themselves. Intuitively realizing as much, we have come up with various ingenious ways of protecting ourselves. When the market puts pressure on us, we look for ways of muting, dodging and redirecting its power; we step aside, keep our heads down and bide our time. And while such guerilla tactics would seem to require both organization and political dedication, this is far from the case. Quite automatically and usually without ever really planning to, we defend our humanity and the integrity of our lives.

Successful resistance depends on the existence of alternative social spheres governed by rules other than those governing the market. A line must be drawn, in other words, between the market and the non-market sphere. Sometimes this line is physical – as when doors are locked to the seminar room, the school, the church or the union hall – but often the barrier is instead cultural or social.[4] Beyond the barrier, however constructed, social life is organized on a different basis.[5] What matters in the seminar room and the school is the pursuit of knowledge, and what matters in the church or the union hall is, respectively, the pursuit of salvation and the strengthening of working-class solidarity. There are specific rules for attain-ing these goods which are intrinsic to the spheres themselves, and in these respects money is, or should be, powerless. When entering the alternative sphere we are expected to leave our wallets behind, much as medieval knights left their swords at the gates of churches.

Once we have made our escape to the safety of this alternative world we can relax and begin to live proper social and emotional lives. Suddenly we are surrounded by people who know our names and recognize our faces; we are known, liked and loved as particular someones and no longer treated merely as abstract factors of production; we are appreciated not for our efficiency but for our personal qualities, our loyalty, our friendship and our commitment. And we can finally start taking it easy. We hang out with friends, eat with our families, drink too much, watch TV, log on to chat-rooms, daydream, remember, hope and pray. From an economic point of view these are all unproductive – indeed, slothful – uses of our time, and as such they are always roundly condemned by the self-appointed custodians of a market-driven work ethic. 'Lose no time,' as Benjamin Franklin put it in an admonition to himself. 'Be always employ'd in something useful; cut off all unnecessary actions.'[6] Yet we know that more than laziness is involved. It is through these kinds of activities that our identities are estab-lished and maintained. It is only safely away from the market that we have a chance to become who we are.

This is thus how we deal with the deleterious impact of the division of labour. If factory labour is alienating and dehumanizing, we look for ways in which we can restore dignity to our work.[7] If markets make us compete with each other on unbearable terms, we come up with clandestine ways of cooperating. If nothing else, we find ways of regaining our humanity once our shift is over and we go drinking with our mates. In much the same way we insist on the importance of our family and friends. If the expansion of markets breaks up existing social networks, we rely on protective arrange-ments to reaffirm them or to create new networks that can take their place. This, after all, is how runaway serfs dealt with city life in the Middle Ages in Europe, and it is how the 'floating population' of China deals with city life today.

This is also how we have handled the impact of commodification. When the market presents us with the substitutability and transience of all things, including the substitutability and transience of our own lives and the lives of the people we love, we insist on their uniqueness and permanence. Sometimes we may invoke religious sanctions in our support. To call something 'sacred' or 'taboo' is to contrast it with the profane and thus to place it beyond economic evaluations.[8] Sometimes æsthetic judgements serve the same purpose. Although we may happily decide to sell even a priceless work of art, few would suggest that there is a perfect correspondence between price tag and artistic merit. A £1 million Picasso is *not* worth the same as 2 million cans of soft drink at 50 pence each. In addition there are also legal prohibitions. The law may, for example, insist on the 'inalienability' of human rights. To have an inalienable right means to have a right that we cannot sell, even if we wanted to.[9]

Yet we should be careful not to romanticize. Protective arrangements are alternatives to the market but they also have their alternative hierarchies, power-games and discriminatory practices. We are protected from market forces but we are at the same time exposed to other forces which have their separate, and not necessarily benign, effects. Although life in a monastery, to take an example, may offer perfect decommodification, it may warp us in other ways. Besides, not all protective arrangements work equally well and protect us all in the same manner. There may be some arrangements that provide very reliable cradle-to-grave safety-nets whereas others provide only intermittent support. The same arrangements can also function very differently for different people, and some groups may be entirely excluded as a matter of principle.[10] Who is protected, how well and in what way is ultimately a question of politics.

Economists are *qua* economists unlikely to understand any of this. At most they may see protective arrangements as attempts at 'rent-seeking'.[11] A rent is here defined as a benefit that accrues to economic actors who manipulate the market for their private gain. The textbook example is a trade union in which workers collude with each other in order to jack up the price of their labour. By classically trained economists such behaviour is usually condemned in the strongest possible terms. And yet such an economistic interpretation fundamentally misrepresents at least half of what it is that trade unions do. Although unions certainly seek to increase the pay of their members, they also have other and broader aims. Historically, trade unions concerned themselves at least as much with social activities as with salary increases. Trade unions were founded to fight for the dignity of their members and in order to provide a sense of togetherness and camaraderie. Trade unions were protective arrangements and not merely economic cartels.

And yet it would be a great mistake to see protective arrangements as antithetical to the market. If anything, they are complementing the market, adding to it and helping it out in various ways.[12] Protective arrangements perform functions that are crucial for the way in which markets operate but which markets themselves cannot satisfactorily perform. Consider, for example, the way in which young people are brought up and taught how to behave according to the various rules and expectations of the society in which they live. Such basic socialization is surely crucial for the operations of capitalism, yet it is not something that markets themselves could organize. Families can raise children but markets cannot. Hence it makes sense to leave the raising of children to this particular non-market sphere. Much the same applies to a wide range of other educational, emotional and existential services.[13]

Protective arrangements in this way simultaneously play two rather different roles. On the one hand they protect people from market forces, but on the other hand they also prepare them for their encounters with market forces. They train, socialize and equip us to become more successful market participants. By protecting us they reduce the social costs imposed by markets and make it possible for us to make our peace with capitalism. But by preparing and equipping us for our encounters with markets they make sure that capitalism comes to operate more efficiently. Protective arrangements are exactly what the old Leninist left used to warn the working class about – they are reformist compromises.

Limits to Convergence

This argument also has implications for the problem of convergence. As we have said, societies often differ quite considerably in the protective arrangements they construct, and this fact can help to limit the degree to which societies come to converge. Although exposure to market forces and increased competition are likely to make us all more alike in a number of respects, the way we protect ourselves against markets and competition will allow us to retain a measure of uniqueness. Although we may compete in the same fashion, we protect ourselves quite differently, and as a result convergence will never be complete. Hence, paradoxically, the expansion of markets may turn out to entrench differences between societies rather than to abolish them.[14]

In order to make sense of this argument consider why it is that a certain society protects itself in a certain manner. Perhaps we could think of this as a matter of the 'grammar' that organizes social interaction in the society concerned.[15] Just as the words in a language must be organized in some fashion before they make sense, actions and individuals must be put into a context of social meaning. The grammar of a society tells us what our place in society is, what places others occupy, and how different places relate to each other. Depending on the grammatical rules, we will see ourselves as having different obligations to fulfil and different expectations regarding whatever help, trust and cooperation others may provide. In this way a social grammar sets the terms on which people are prepared to work together and it influences the kinds of organizations they are likely to create.

There is no doubt a considerable overlap between the grammatical rules of one society and another, and the vast majority of actions and reactions are decoded in much the same way throughout the world.[16] And yet there are also some considerable variations from one society to the next. People in the United States and Germany, for example, do not think of themselves in completely identical ways, and people cooperate differently, and form different kinds of organizations, in China and Japan. It is ultimately because of grammatical differences such as these that protective arrangements vary between countries. When confronting the unfamiliar we reach for the familiar; when trying to protect ourselves against an alien threat we do so in terms of well-established social principles.

Yet no such application of grammatical rules is ever automatic or necessary. It is not the case that the past simply hands down a protective arrangement that we go on to use. Rather, just like the grammar of a language, a social grammar allows a large number of different things to be expressed. Many of these expressions may diverge from each other and some are outright contradictory. The grammar, that is, determines *how* we say something but not *what* we say; what we say is instead a matter of what we want to say, and this is not given by grammatical rules. Analogously, the form of a protective arrangement may follow the rules of a social grammar and yet its content may vary widely. Which protective arrangements we arrive at in the end is a result of a negotiation between various groups; it is a matter of what some people propose and what other people are prepared to live with. That is, far from being a matter of 'culture' or 'tradition', it is a matter of the exercise of power.

Consider another similarity between a social and a linguistic grammar. In both cases it is striking how ignorant most people usually are of the grammatical rules they so effortlessly employ. A grammar is not something that we purposely sit down to study – instead, we simply start speaking, and whenever we make a mistake we are corrected by our peers. Our knowledge of grammar is in this way intuitively acquired and largely tacit.[17] Much the same can be said of the grammatical rules that govern our interpersonal relationships. By being born and growing up in a certain society we naturally come to adopt a certain way of thinking of ourselves in relation to others. And while we use these rules to make sense of the world, the rules themselves are usually not verbalized.

As tacitly acquired and as a precondition for human interaction, a social grammar is likely to change only slowly. It is for that reason likely to remain in place even as other aspects of society are rapidly being transformed. For this reason, no matter how decisively a new political regime tries to break with the past, chances are that it will be less than completely successful. The new regime will say new things, to be sure, but it will do so in a social grammar that is curiously familiar.[18] For this reason a social grammar is also difficult for outsiders to change. As a part of the taken-for-granted microstructure of everyday life, it is not directly exposed to external pressure. This is why protective arrangements are likely to change more slowly than other aspects of society. Even though globalization and increased competition may make our societies more alike, protective arrangements are relatively shielded from the pressure to converge.

This argument allows us to return to the evolutionary model we briefly discussed above. Evolution, we said, takes place only one step at a time, and like all step-by-step processes it necessarily comes to follow a certain path. Species evolve only given the positions they have attained, and where they are will always depend on where they have been.[19] Adaptation to a particular ecological environment will for that reason never change a species completely but instead change it only in certain respects. The path-dependence of evolutionary change means that later life forms will continue to carry many of the features of their ancestors with them. No matter how far a species has branched out, it will stay connected to the trunk of the same tree.

This argument can be proved with the help of a simple experiment. Since they have adapted themselves to the same aquatic environment for the last

10 million years, dolphins resemble fish – and yet if we cut them open we will immediately notice the differences between the two. In their anatomical structures dolphins are far closer to human beings than they are to fish; their anatomy reveals them to be mammals that must once have lived on land.[20] The reason for these abiding differences is that evolutionary pressure only works on some features of an organism and not on others. There are external features that are exposed to competition and thus forced to adapt, but there are also internal features that are better protected and far less easily altered. In the end the make-up of a species is a combination of these two faces, of the exposed and the protected, of some things that change and other things that stay the same.

This argument explains not only why convergence happens but also what its limits are. Differences between species will remain since the process of evolution has found no reason to abolish them. Because dolphins and fish have chanced upon functionally equivalent solutions to the same problems, there is no reason why either of them should become more like the other. They are both doing well if in different ways. Much the same would apply to human beings if we ever were forced back into the oceans. After the requisite number of years we too would end up looking quite similar to dolphins or fish. Yet this is not to say that we ever would *become* dolphins or fish. We would remain human, if in a distinctly different form.

The same argument applies to the social examples we briefly discussed above. Take the case of the two car companies. Since each company has developed according to its own historical trajectory, crucial differences between them are likely to remain even as they come to compete ever more ferociously in the same global marketplace. Not all features of a company are equally exposed to competitive pressure, after all, and there are many different but functionally equivalent ways of making cars.[21] Just as in the case of dolphins and fish we would expect the 'anatomies' of the two companies to remain more or less distinct. Or, in the terminology introduced above, they will be organized according to different social grammars – they will have different corporate cultures, rely on different operational procedures, relations between staff and executives will be different, and so on.

If this is likely to be the case in the highly competitive field of international car sales, it is even more likely to be the case in relations between societies. Societies, after all, compete with each other in far less a direct fashion and they contain more elaborate and better protected internal codes. And just as for car manufacturers, there are many different but functionally equivalent ways of dealing with the same challenges. In this way increasing convergence can perfectly well coexist with abiding differences – indeed, the differences may become increasingly pronounced the more the competition increases. Or rather, the two processes occur at the same time. Even as societies become more similar to each other in a number of external respects, we would find, if we were to cut them up, that their social anatomies remain quite distinct.

Putting these pieces together, what we get is a more sophisticated understanding of the homogenizing effects of capitalism. Although the push toward convergence is undeniable, the expansion of markets is unlikely to make us all alike. Rather, the forces of convergence operate on pre-existing social structures which are organized according to their own rules. Societies react to the pressures put on them by coming up with various protective arrangements, but because these are organized in terms of a given social grammar, the reactions are likely to vary from one society to the next. In the end convergence will certainly happen, but it will not be complete. Although everyone may feel the same need to be 'competitive', 'efficient' and 'modern', such goals can be achieved in many different but function-ally equivalent ways. What we end up with are dolphins and fish; societies that resemble each other in external respects while remaining quite distinct in terms of their internal organization. Capitalism makes all societies more similar to each other, but our separate ways of protecting ourselves against capitalism allow us to retain our differences.

Families, Associations, the State

A problem with the discussion above is that it is far too general. We need to put more empirical meat on these rather dry conceptual bones. For an illus-tration, consider the protection we are offered by our families, by associations and by the state.[22]

The family is perhaps the most obvious example of a protective arrange-ment. We all have families of one kind or another, and its primary task is to protect its members, in particular the young. It is not too difficult to imagine that these arrangements could be extended to cover us also against the threats posed by the expansion of markets. The greatest advantage of the family is the highly personalized nature of the services it offers. The family home is an intimate and friendly setting where security is combined with care, rest and relaxation. Few people are likely to know you better or care about you more than your family members. On the other hand, families have little or no power over the world outside the home and consequently little power over the market. The family can never change, regulate, or in any way alter the way in which market forces operate. The family is also quite fragile since its character depends on the actions and reactions of its individual members. And family members, as we know, have a tendency to fall out with, and cheat on, each other. This sets limits to the family's role as a protective arrangement.

Although families may be universal, not all families are the same. What families do, apart from the care they provide for their young, is never given. And as any anthropologist or historian will tell us, families vary consider-ably across space and time. In Europe the nuclear family seems to have been firmly established at least since the twelfth century and few important changes have taken place since then. But if we look more closely, we will immediately notice large regional variations in family size, in the nature of the household and in the tasks allotted to different family members. Before long it becomes clear that there is no such thing as a uniquely European type of family, and if we take our analysis to other continents we will discover even more variation. Considering these differences it is hardly surprising that families differ in the protection they provide their members.

But protection can also be found outside of the family – for example, in the various organizations that make up what is sometimes referred to as 'civil society'.[23] Here we find a plethora of associations as diverse as religious and political sects, book, sports, horticultural and gambling clubs, secret, medical, musical and learned societies, trade and insurance unions, as well as businesses corporations and cooperatives of various kinds. Despite the obvious differences between them, what this motley crew has in common is a particular position in social life.[24] They are all located between the individual on the one hand and the market on the other. In relation to the individual, the organization presents itself as a public arena. It is a more exotic and more exciting place than the home and it is populated mainly by strangers. By becoming a member, we escape the narrow horizons of family life and learn to act together with others in the pursuit of common goals. In relation to the market, however, the association is private. Not everyone, after all, has a right to join whichever club he or she chooses – all associations keep non-desirables out and discriminate against non-members.

This intermediary position is what allows associations and clubs to function as protective arrangements. To the extent that they are closed to the market they are shielded from the impact of market forces. The association is ruled not by the impersonal forces of supply and demand but instead by laws that apply only to particular people and in particular ways. What matters are the personal relations between people who know and care about each other; what matters is how loyal you are to the association and what contributions you make to the common cause. By fellow members you are known as a 'comrade', a 'brother', a 'mate' or a 'fellow'. Associations, when they function well, are similar to families; they are homes away from home. Some of them have a certain power over markets, such as trade unions that can compel employers to raise wages and improve working conditions. And since they are organized around formal rules, they are not as obviously subject to the whims of their members.

At the same time there is considerable variation in the way associations operate. Some countries – famously the United States – take great pride in the vibrancy of their civic activism and in the official rhetoric an image is conjured up of an active associative life which empowers individuals who otherwise would have remained isolated and powerless.[25] Other countries – Germany and Sweden come to mind – have very large, centralized, and all-encompassing associations where the members are largely passive. Here membership may do little to alleviate isolation and what is empowered are institutions rather than individuals. Looking at other parts of the world, the associative flora is even more variegated. Take the example of China with its lineage, dialect and surname associations, or Thailand which sometimes is said to have extremely few intermediary organizations of any kind.[26]

Finally, there is the state. Given its unrivalled position in society, it is not surprising that people often have turned to the state for protection. The state is the only force in society which potentially at least is more powerful than the market. The state can regulate markets, mitigate their effects, and change their outcomes at will; the state can redistribute resources and for example take from the rich and give to the poor. The state can even decide to replace the market entirely, as happened in Russia after 1917 and in China after 1949. The state is not only powerful, however, but also highly robust. Governed by institutions and constitutional provisions it is virtually independent of the actions and reactions of the people subject to it. Given this awesome authority, as long as we have the state on our side, it would seem we have nothing much to fear.

In practice of course it never really works that way. Instead, the state has always been forced to make concessions to the market in order to be able to finance its activities. In particular it has been crucial to keep entrepreneurs and financiers happy, or otherwise, investments – and therefore economic growth – are likely to suffer.[27] Trying simultaneously to please both voters and businessmen, the state has had to make concessions to both, and this has inevitably involved it in contradictions.[28] Thus, while the state protects people by addressing the problems that markets create, the protection is not supposed actually to impede the interaction of market forces.

In addition, the state is never as powerful a protector as it may appear. There are always a number of things it is unable to do. A basic weakness is that the state is forced to treat each of its subjects as equals. Although people certainly do want to be treated equally to others, they also want to be treated differently from others, at least some of the time and in certain respects. We want to be recognized as individuals with identities that are uniquely our own. Such recognition of individual differences the state is unable to provide.[29] In the end the state cares more about 'the people' than about the individuals of whom this collective entity is composed. In this respect the state is often as impersonal as ever the market is, and often at least as insensitive.

Comparing states with each other, we once again come across considerable variation. In the academic study of politics there is an entire sub-field – comparative politics – devoted to investigating the many ways in which political systems differ from each other. This is not least the case when it comes to the position the state takes in relation to economic markets.[30] The policies pursued by the Social-Democratic welfare states of northern Europe are explicitly rejected by neo-liberal Anglo-Saxon states, and both differ considerably from the *étatism* traditionally practised in France. This variety is compounded if we study the way states relate to markets in other parts of the world – say, East Asia.

This Book

The chapters that follow are an investigation of the validity of this analytical framework. What we want to know is what people have done in order to survive the negative side-effects of the widening and deepening of markets. We want to understand how they have dealt with the alienation brought on by the division of labour, with the erosion of values caused by commodification, and to what extent societies and lifestyles really have converged. In order to get a grasp on this last issue we need to investigate how people have protected themselves in different societies. A comparative study is also the only way in which we can appreciate the advantages and disadvantages of various protective arrangements. We want to know who is being protected and who is not, and on what terms.

The focus throughout will be on Europe, North America and East Asia, and in the case of East Asia we will be particularly interested in China, Japan and Thailand. It is in these societies that markets have the longest history – in the case of China stretching back over 2,000 years – and it is here that markets recently have been at their most dynamic. Not surprisingly, it is also here that the protective arrangements have been most elaborately developed. Comparing these disparate societies, we are likely to find both similarities and differences.

So much for historical sociology, but the ultimate aim is to better understand the predicament we ourselves are in. The question here is what is likely to happen if capitalism continues expanding and we all one day come to live in a unified and perfectly globalized market which is as wide and as deep as it ever possibly could be. Which protective arrangements are likely to hold up under these circumstances and how will they operate? Who will be protected, on what terms – and will it still be possible to distinguish various social models from each other? Is convergence inevitable, or is there anything we can do to resist it?

There is a sense of urgency about this investigation. As we will discover, many of the arrangements that have traditionally protected us are today in a state of serious decay. They are still around, to be sure; they are still operating – but they are not operating as well as they once did, and often not in the same manner. Moreover, many protective arrangements are today under ferocious attack from the proponents of unfettered capitalism, and even people who should know better have started making concessions. Tempted by a promise of a new and more efficient sort of capitalism, people are bamboozled into accepting the unacceptable. The situation is potentially serious and the consequences far-reaching. Under such circumstances a historical investigation, no matter how scholarly, can never be a matter of idle curiosity.

IN THE BOSOM OF
THE FAMILY

3

The European Idea of the Home

As far as the history of the family in Europe is concerned, it can be told in a number of different ways and there are considerable variations in family patterns across the continent. One dimension concerns the family's size, another dimension what sorts of people and how many generations the family has included. Both dimensions are quantifiable and the changes taking place over time are easily summarized.[1] Over the last 500 years the size of the family has constantly gone down, and there is a particularly sharp dip in the twentieth century. In England, for example, the average family size was 4.75 members between the sixteenth and the nineteenth centuries, but it was 4.49 members in 1901 and only 2.4 in 1996. As far as the kinds of people the family has included, the nuclear family – the parent-and-children group – seems to have been firmly established at least since the twelfth century, and few important changes have taken place since then.

However, an understanding of the family as a protective arrangement requires more than an analysis of numerical data. What matters is not the size and composition of the family as much as its nature. The question is how it is regarded by its members and what relationships obtain between the family and the rest of society. What is important above all is the way in which the family provides individuals with a place they can call 'home'. It is the home rather than just the family that protects individuals against the challenges presented by the widening and deepening of markets.

This is not to say that there ever has been only one type of home in Europe. Far from it. The differences are, if anything, even greater than the differences among family types.[2] The shape and size and nature of the home depends first of all on which social class you belong to, but also on where in Europe you come from, and whether you live in the countryside or the city. And yet it is still possible to talk in general terms about something that could be referred to as 'the European idea of the home'. The idea of the home is not an account of the nature of the building materials or the contents of the rooms, but rather an account of what the home is for, which purposes it serves; it is not a matter of what the home is, but what it does. Although this story too varies between social classes and geographical locations, the variations are fewer and more easily summarized. And as we will see, the idea of the home is intimately connected to the history of the development of capitalism.

At Home in Commercial Society

The social divisions created by the development of a commercial society in the sixteenth century were soon translated into great disparities in living conditions. In the new commercial centres a few wonderfully wealthy merchants built great palaces for themselves while members of the middling classes could only occasionally afford their own houses. Meanwhile the urban poor survived as tenants and lodgers in outhouses and attics.

At the top of this social pyramid the most spectacular homes were those of the merchant aristocrats of northern Italy, southern Germany and the Low Countries.[3] These palaces – of a type often referred to as a *casa grande* – were enormous in size and housed not only people who were biologically related to each other but also a large number of other denizens: servants and retainers and assorted young men and women who had come to the city to receive an education. In addition, all sorts of other people – business partners, public officials, delivery men and washerwomen – paid regular visits, and they came and went more or less as they wanted. Clearly, such a *casa grande* was more of a public institution than a private family dwelling.[4]

The public character of these great houses was obvious both from their exterior and their interior.[5] On the outside the sheer scale of the buildings, their many windows, turrets and balconies, testified to the wealth and status of their occupants. On the inside, expensive works of art, fancy furniture and broad staircases made the same statement. Few architectural concessions were made to the comfort and intimate needs of the family members and few distinctions were drawn between rooms designated for public and private use.[6] There were, for example, no bedrooms. Beds were instead portable and could be set up in whatever room the occasion required, and much the same was true of toilets and even bathtubs. Indeed the French *meubles* and the Italian *mobilia* still record the fact that all furniture was once mobile.[7]

Moreover, the lack of corridors meant that privacy was difficult to protect. The layout of the buildings made it necessary to walk through one room in order to get to another, and as a result people were used to seeing, and being seen by, others. Activities that today we may regard as deeply intimate were for that reason often carried out in public, and apparently with no accompanying sense of embarrassment.[8] Hence the many detailed contemporary testimonies regarding the sexual activities of the upper classes, as observed by family members, servants, lodgers or casual visitors.[9] The point of the architecture, in short, was not to protect individuals from the world outside as much as to expose them to it.[10] Their house was a stage on which the aristocratic family could show off; it was a setting intended for conspicuous consumption and for public entertainments, performances and feasts.

Although they lived in more modest accommodation and engaged in less ostentatious displays, the homes of ordinary craftsmen and shopkeepers also had a public rather than a private character.[11] While these houses provided a nuclear family with a place to live, they also catered to all sorts of other people, including servants and lodgers, people taken in as charity cases and young men working as apprentices to the master of the house.[12] In terms of its architectural layout, these middle-class homes were divided into functions corresponding to the different floors. The ground floor was typically reserved for the family business or designated as a place to keep animals, the next floor up – in France known as *la belle étage* – was where the family lived, and other floors, including hovels in the attic, were reserved for apprentices and other lesser denizens.[13] In this way housing was segregated according to social class – but not horizontally, as in our day, but rather vertically, between the floors.

As far as rural homes were concerned, they varied quite considerably, as one would expect, depending on the climate, the building materials available and the economic status of the peasants concerned.[14] Yet everywhere throughout Europe, work was mixed with family life and space was shared with animals, farmhands and maids. People ate and slept together, often in one windowless and usually, at least in northern Europe, unbearably smoke-filled room.[15] Although most tasks were strictly divided according to gender, the family members worked side-by-side in the fields or in the forest throughout the day, sharing meals and relaxing together during breaks. In many parts of Europe few changes took place in these respects until the nineteenth or even the twentieth century.[16]

Yet the commercialization of society had an impact also in the countryside. When new forms of employment opened up in the towns it became increasingly common for the children of farmers to go off to work as apprentices and domestic servants.[17] In early modern Europe perhaps as much as 40 per cent of all adolescents would spend a few years away from their parents in this fashion. Such *Wanderjahren* brought much-needed cash to rural families and it provided young adults with an opportunity to see a bit of the world. In Europe, even in the early modern era, people were expected to leave their families before they got married and to strike out on their own.

To summarize briefly. Despite considerable differences in housing types and living arrangements, what homes in early modern, commercial, society had in common was their public character.[18] The home was not yet a private, but rather a corporate, institution which housed the family while at the same time remaining perfectly open to the world. The home did not protect its inhabitants by presenting itself as a radical alternative to the market. On the contrary, since the home was an economic unit and a place of work, the presence of market forces was only too tangible. And yet to be associated with a certain house was to have a place to belong to, and this membership conferred a corporate identity on its inhabitants. Indeed the word 'family' referred originally to the *famuli*, the 'servants or retainers' who occupied the same living space.[19] As such, all family members were expected to be loyal to the house, and the head of the household was expected to protect them.

At the same time it is obvious that a new conception of the home was gradually being introduced, in particular in places such as the Dutch Republic where capitalism was at its most dynamic.[20] This change is clearly visible in works of seventeenth-century Dutch painters, the first artists to take an interest in the interiors of houses and the people living there.[21] There is a quiet domesticity about the *Young Woman Standing at a Virginal* or the *Woman with a Pearl Necklace* which reveals a new outlook. In Holland, the houses were smaller, there were fewer inhabitants per house – four to five people, rather than 25 as was common in Paris – doors were closed, and visitors were often kept out. The rooms had dedicated uses – they were far cosier, always immaculately clean and filled with more comfortable furniture. In seventeenth-century Holland far more time was spent at home, together with family members, reading, making music or tending the garden.[22]

The same development is observable in England where houses were gradually privatized and domesticated along Dutch lines.[23] Here for the first time there were bedrooms and privies and corridors that allowed people to pass through the house unseeing and unseen. Floors no longer separated social classes but instead the public from the private. To 'go upstairs' was to leave the company of outsiders and to retreat to the sphere of the family. In the oft-quoted words of the lawyer Edward Coke, in England the home was regarded by every man 'as his castle and fortresse, as well as his defence against injury and violence, as for his repose'.[24] And yet it would take a long time before this new definition spread to all countries and social classes, and even longer before it was fully reflected in architectural practice.

At Home in Industrial Society

As one would expect, the industrial revolution had far-reaching effects on the family and on the nature of the home. In its initial stages the new system of production strengthened the traditional peasant family in various ways.[25] Before the big factories were built, and before people were forced to move to the cities, families in the countryside were often employed by entrepreneurs who provided them with raw materials and tools and then collected the finished products at a set time and for a set price.[26] This *Verlagssystem*, or 'putting-out system', allowed people to remain in their farmsteads and to continue working together, and yet the nature of the home changed fundamentally as a result of this intimate contact with the market.[27] In order to maximize their income all family members were put to work; no one was too young or too old to spin, prune or pluck. Before long every hour of daylight was employed in such restless, market-directed, activities.

Once the large factories were up and running, however, this family too came under severe pressure.[28] For most people this was simply a consequence of the fact that they had been forced to move. Suddenly former farmers and farmhands found themselves in factory towns packed into tenements – usually large barracks-like buildings – in which entire families often had to make due with only one room.[29] Sometimes houses intended for a single family could be occupied by as many as 50 people, and even families who lived in a single room might be forced to take in lodgers. Alternatively, dormitories were constructed in which single workers – usually young women – would sleep in row upon row of beds while some matronly figure supervised their virtue. Clearly, such uninspiring surroundings provided little room for something resembling a home.

In addition, the very toil of the factory system undermined the family.[30] Back on the farm family members had worked, eaten and rested together – but wage labour required each one of them to conclude a separate contract with an employer and therefore to face the market alone. The number of family members engaged in full-time employment varied with the nature of the work. Textile mills hired not only fathers and mothers but also children as young as six or seven; in steel mills, by contrast, only male labour was demanded, and this allowed wives to stay at home and cook and clean.[31] In any case, the protection afforded by the tenements was never more than rudimentary. Above all they provided no space for families to be by themselves.[32] Thin walls and common staircases and outhouses made sure that noise levels were high and no secrets were kept for long. And then there was the ever-present problem of poverty. There was rarely enough money for the family to have fun together, in fact there was often not enough money for food.[33]

As far as the middle-class home was concerned, industrialization continued the process of domestication that had begun in the earlier era. It was only now, from the early nineteenth century onward, that the close identification between the home and the conjugal family came to be firmly established.[34] The home was privatized, as it were; apprentices and minor relatives were asked to leave and no longer were rooms reserved for the family business, for storage or for animals. Instead, as sharp as possible a distinction was drawn between the inside of the home and the world outside it, between the family and the market. Outsiders and guests, to the extent that they were admitted, were shown to the parlour – the 'front room' or the 'best room' – which was meticulously cleaned and always ready to receive them.[35] Other rooms were off-limits to visitors and intended exclusively for the family's own use. Inside the home, rooms were distinguished by their functions. There were proper bedrooms, separate ones for parents and children, and the servants – if the family could afford them – lived in their own quarters.[36]

The home thus understood was no longer a stage and it was decidedly not an economic unit. Instead, the middle-class home became the very antithesis of the market. It was ruled by a radically different logic and guided by entirely different goals. More than anything the home was a place of intimacy, tranquillity and rest.[37] It was here that individuals retired after their engagements with the market, or alternatively where they prepared themselves for their coming engagements with it. The home was the family's world, where they ruled, as opposed to the market where they were ruled by managerial hierarchies or, more abstractly, by the forces of supply and demand.[38] At home family members could relax, and speak frankly and intimately with each other, without pretence or hidden agendas. At home they were safe and free. While the market was dehumanizing, the family rehumanized.

Hence the importance that the middle classes of the nineteenth century attached to love. Love was, or was supposed to be, unconditional and not something a person would have to merit.[39] As such it contrasted sharply with the way in which people were assessed in the marketplace. Family members were loved regardless of their productivity or their contributions to the household economy. Thus love removed the commodity status which the labour market had imposed on them; by making love its guiding principle, the non-market status of the family was reinforced.

The ultimate source of these tender feelings was the wife and the mother.[40] She was the custodian of the home, the supreme nurturer, the embodied antithesis of the market economy. 'That her home shall be made a loving place of rest and joy and comfort for those who are dear to her', as Helen Irving concluded in the *Ladies' Wreath and Parlor Annual*, 1850, 'will be the first wish of every true woman's heart'.[41] Although middle-class women worked long hours at home they naturally never expected any remuneration. 'Our men are sufficiently moneymaking,' as Sara Josepha Hale put it in her *Godey's Lady's Book*, 1832.[42] 'Let us keep our women and children from the contagion as long as possible.' Instead, the main task of a woman was to decorate and beautify the home and to make it into a welcoming nest to which the rest of the family could return once their workday was done. In Britain and the United States such activities were known as 'home-making', and before long home-making became an occupation in itself and the goal to which respectable women were expected to dedicate their lives. Good home-making required æsthetic sensibility, plenty of money and a strong pair of arms. 'A house', according to Hale,

> is not only the home center, the retreat and shelter for all the family, it is also the workshop for the mother. It is not only where she is to live, to love, but where she is to care and labor. Her hours, days, weeks, months, and years are spent within its bounds; until she becomes an enthroned fixture, more indispensable than the house itself.[43]

To help women in this quest for enthronement, a whole series of specialist publications appeared which provided tips on everything from embroidery and the arranging of flowers to the playing of pianos.[44]

As nineteenth-century advice books for women made clear, the division between the home and the market coincided with a distinction between morality and vice.[45] A woman of a good middle-class family who crossed the line would immediately jeopardize her reputation. The love which the mother and wife gave so freely was the very opposite of the love of the prostitute for which men were forced to pay. While the husband was free to come and go between the two worlds as he pleased – including visits to brothels – the woman could leave the home only at her financial peril and at the cost of social disapproval.[46] Women did not, for example, have the right to vote, and in many countries married women did not have the right to own property.[47] The home was a nest for the husband, but often enough a prison for the wife.

One of the most important functions of the family was the bringing up of children. The middle-class home became a place where the young were educated and taught the importance of obedience to rules and to their superiors. And although this always had been the case, education had never been more important than in industrial society. In previous times, when the level of social mobility was low, children would simply inherit their occupations and their social positions from their parents. As a result a formal education was often not required and childhood could instead be a time of leisure and fun.[48] In industrial society, by contrast, many more careers were available and social positions could not as easily be handed down from one generation to the next. Where a person ended up depended instead far more on his or her own achievements. This is why it was important for families to make heavy investments in their children's education from an early age.[49] Before long, childhood became a time of relentless preparation and endless moral exercises. This is how the middle-class home became a disciplinary institution.

Geographically, homes characterized by this curious mixture of love and discipline may first have appeared in England, Holland and the United States sometime in the eighteenth century.[50] Continental visitors to the United States were at any rate very surprised to find that children of only a few years of age seemed so grown-up. Often the visitors bemoaned what they interpreted as a loss of innocence. 'Many of the children in this country', the British author Greville Chester explained in his *Transatlantic Sketches*, 1869, 'appear to be painfully precocious – small stuck-up caricatures of men and women, with but little of the fresh ingenuousness and playfulness of childhood.'[51] Other visitors were rather more impressed. 'In democratic societies,' said Alexis de Tocqueville, 'the father exercises no other power than that which is granted to the affection and the experience of age.'

Though he is not hedged in with ceremonial respect, his sons at least accost him with confidence; they have no settled form of addressing him, but they speak to him constantly and are ready to consult him every day. The master and the constituted ruler have vanished; the father remains. [52]

Regardless of how it was assessed, the economic success of the middle-class home in its North Atlantic version made sure that the model came to be widely copied.[53] Before long, children throughout Europe were both loved and disciplined in the same fashion.

Much the same can be said regarding the diffusion of the idea of the middle-class home to other social classes. While the cramped tenements of the first generations of workers never could have accommodated the new ideals, with rising living standards, the working class too came eventually to be better housed.[54] Their aspirations were often supported by upper-class philanthropists who reacted to the filth, noise and vice of the urban ghettos. In the latter part of the nineteenth century, at least in England, working-class families increasingly moved away from the tenements and into self-contained houses.[55] In this way the ideals of the middle class came to spread and the working-class home too became a refuge from the market. Still, the unequal relationship between workers and their employers meant that privacy was difficult to achieve. Often employers would insist on regulating the morality and the behaviour of their workers outside working hours too.[56] This was particularly the case where employers provided company housing or where a town effectively had only one employer.

Eventually the middle-class ideals reached even the members of the aristocracy.[57] Despite the considerable architectural difficulties involved, stately homes and manor houses were converted into private dwellings, complete with bedrooms and living rooms in which family members could relax and be by themselves. There were far fewer and less ostentatious parties, and the servants were confined to their separate quarters. Rather than constantly being on stand-by, maids and butlers were summoned with the help of bell wires – a nineteenth-century invention – whenever their services were required. Thus, by the early part of the twentieth century, everyone in Europe and North America drew more or less the same distinctions between insides and outsides, between protection from markets and exposure to them.

The best way to understand the importance of the home in industrial society is perhaps to consider the notion of homelessness.[58] There have of course always been people who for one reason or another have been without a home. Yet before the nineteenth century this was above all a practical problem of not having access to a roof and somewhere to lay one's head at night. What was missing too was a corporate affiliation, but in previous eras there were plenty of corporate bodies to which people could attach themselves. If nothing else, a homeless person could often join someone else's household in some lowly capacity and in this way find not only work but also food and a modicum of social support. In industrial society, by contrast, homelessness is above all an existential condition. Without a home we are fully exposed to the market and constantly assessed not in terms of our personal qualities but in terms of our market value. Joining someone else's household is out of the question since homes are private places and trespassers are kept out. As a result, homeless people have no access to that sphere of privacy, intimacy and rest which alone is thought to guarantee our humanity.[59] In industrial society, to be without a home is to be denied access to oneself.

At Home in Consumer Society

Many of the architectural changes that took place as a result of industrialization in the nineteenth century have remained to this day. The physical layout of contemporary European and North American homes still resembles the layout of the homes of the urban middle classes of a hundred years ago. This is the case despite the fact that our lives today are far less focused on production. Thanks to a long series of technological advances we are now working nowhere near as hard as people did three generations ago. Instead of production it is consumption that has become the central activity of our lives.[60] After World War II in particular we have surrounded ourselves with innumerable consumer items: cars, household appliances and technological gadgets of all kinds. To make these things is no longer our primary obligation in life but instead to enjoy them. While production has become easier and easier, consumption requires more and more hard work.

Thus while contemporary homes may resemble the middle-class homes of a hundred years ago, they nevertheless function quite differently. Today the home is more than anything the setting for the rituals of consumption. In fact, domesticity itself has become a consumer item. To be together, to relax, even to love one another, is intimately associated with the buying, the enjoying and the discarding of things. Increasingly it has become difficult to conceive of consumption as taking place in any other setting. Today public consumption is often considered not consumption at all but the mere wasting of taxpayers' money.[61] So while our homes become ever more over-decorated, our streets become ever dirtier and our schools fall into disrepair.

Like all social rituals, consumption can be understood as a means of communication; to consume is to communicate with ourselves and with others.[62] In the process of working out what to buy, we learn about the desires of other family members, how to coordinate our wishes, how to make exemptions and arrive at compromises and common plans. Families who consume together, we like to think, stay together. Much of the communication concerns who we take ourselves to be. By consuming things together with our families we affirm our shared preferences and our collective identity. In relation to the rest of the world, consumption is above all a way of defining our status and our social aspirations.[63] Hence the car in the driveway, the perfection of the front-yard lawn and the meticulously manicured hedge.

Today the primary setting for these communicative rituals is the suburban home. To be at home in consumer society is above all to be at home in suburbia. Although residential areas began to be built in cities like Paris and London already in the seventeenth century, it was only from the 1870s onwards that the expansion of the suburbs really took off, and only after World War II that the massive exodus from the city centres began.[64] This was when London developed a series of 'new towns' and the United States came to be graced with 'Levittowns' on the outskirts of every major conurbation.

The reasons for this expansion are easily identified. By its promoters, life in suburbia was conceived of as the very antithesis of life in the city. The city was cramped, stressful and dirty, but suburbia was thought of as rural and clean.[65] The moral values which accompanied these physical descriptions were just as diametrically opposed. Cities were places of licentiousness and vice, and they contained far too many people of doubtful ethnic and geographical origins, while suburbia was a model of decorum and ethnic certainties. In the city, wrote the landscape architect Frederick Law Olmsted in 1868, there could be 'no feeling of privacy, no security from intrusion'.[66] By contrast, 'the essential qualification of a suburb is domesticity.'

This domesticity was well reflected in the revival of assorted long-forgotten architectural styles. Rejecting the classicism of the eighteenth century as far too rationalistic, the new suburbanites yearned instead for the romantic and the whimsical. What they wanted were authentic-looking houses which provided a sense of rootedness. Hence the Cotswold cottages, the miniaturized Tudor estates and the replica Spanish ranches.[67] Suburban dwellings such as these are easily identified as the castles of which Edward Coke spoke 400 years ago. Clearly set off from other buildings and surrounded by a lawn that outsiders trespass on only at their peril, the sense of privacy and seclusion is now complete. Whatever filth, noise and vice that goes on inside the castle walls remains the family's own well-guarded secret.

Inside the house the quest for privacy continues. Here every family member has his or her own room, an individual space that they can organize and decorate in their own fashion. You can close the door and sleep, read a book or play an instrument without other family members interfering. In this way each person has a location for the development of his or her abilities and interests.[68] But there are also shared spaces where the family members gather for common activities such as meals and TV-viewing, and here they are required to follow quite specific rules. Through this architectural set-up, the freedom of the individual is combined with the social control exercised by the family as a whole.[69] By combining freedom and control each person is encouraged to develop his or her full potential.

And yet there are forces powerful enough to penetrate also these castle walls.[70] Consumption, we should not forget, costs money, and it is often exorbitantly expensive to buy the gadgets we need to protect our social status. As addicts of consumption we have become ever more dependent on a steady income, and this dependence has brought us into ever closer contact with the market. As long as wages increase there is no problem, but when they start to stagnate or decline – as they have in Europe and North America since the early 1970s – the family is forced to react.[71] The choice is either to consume less or to work more, and in almost all cases families have opted for the latter. When the father's salary is no longer sufficient, the mother has to start working too, and if one salary is not enough, parents have had to find second or even third jobs. Children, once they grow up, are also required to take up part-time work as a way to pay for their consumption habits.

In order to save time, and in order to release the mother into the labour market, housework has become increasingly rationalized. In the 1890s electricity made its way into the home for the first time, and since then it has powered an ever larger range of appliances.[72] Freeing up time for gainful employment while at the same time serving as status objects in their own right, dishwashers, microwave ovens and baking machines are the perfect investments. Requiring technical skills for their operation, the position of the wife and the mother was redefined as that of a 'household manager', and in the early part of the twentieth century a large number of books appeared promising to teach the 'technology' of 'household management' to women who had previously been carers and nurturers.[73] Before long, however, because no uniquely feminine qualities were called for in such managers, women could insist that the machines be operated also by men. This allowed for the 'liberation' of women after World War II.[74]

As a result of declining incomes, increasing working hours and the rationalization of housework, the contemporary home can no longer be considered as a world away from the market.[75] The home is not ruled by a wife and mother; instead, the mother is herself working and she too comes home hungry, fed up and in need of love and attention. In equal measure the home has less time for education and discipline. When young, the children are taken care of by outsiders who are paid in return for their services. Since everyone is simply too busy, there is even less time for joint consumption. Today, most of what families do consume together as a unit, they consume during a few hectic weeks, or days, during Christmas or summer vacations.[76] Although the home still functions as a protective arrangement, the protection it offers is haphazard and unpredictable. As a result, we are more exposed as individuals, and more alone in relation to the market, than was previously the case.

4

The Chinese Family

It is instructive to compare European families with families in China. Obviously, many of the same caveats apply. When it comes to its structure and the actual living conditions, there is every bit as much variation between Chinese families as there are between European. And yet in China too there was an idea of the family. In fact, the idea of the family was stronger and more explicitly spelled out here than in Europe. In China the family was the primary source of material, emotional and social support, but it was also a political and even a religious institution. The primacy of the family was manifested in legal practices which turned families rather than individuals into property owners, and which held families legally responsible for the actions of their members. In the eyes of the law as well as its members, it was the family and not the individual that constituted the basic building block of social life.[1]

However, the Chinese family can also be understood as a protective arrangement. Capitalism developed early in China – far earlier, in fact, than in Europe – already by the fifth century BCE there were large and well-functioning markets in a long range of consumer goods.[2] As early as in the Han dynasty – 206 BCE to 221 CE – China produced as much cast iron as Europe would in 1750 CE, and during the Song dynasty – 960 to 1279 – man-ufacturing really took off.[3] The later Ming and Qing dynasties saw a dra-matic increase in commercial activities, a rapid growth of cities and considerable movement both horizontally across space and vertically up and down the social hierarchies. At the centre of all these developments stood the family. The family was the main producer, the main consumer, but also the main means of protecting people from the insecurities and risks brought on by quickly expanding markets.

But the Chinese family played an important role not only in China itself. From the end of the nineteenth century in particular, millions of Chinese migrants left the mainland for what they hoped would be better lives in East Asia, North America and Caribbean. Encountering new versions of capital-ism and new opportunities in their adopted homelands, many of the migrants did well for themselves – and some did very well indeed. The question is to what extent the Chinese family was responsible for this success, and to what extent it played a role as a protective arrangement also in the diaspora.

Meanwhile people in China faced quite different challenges as a result of the Communist takeover of 1949. Now the capitalist system was replaced with a system of state direction and central planning. The new leaders often viewed the traditional family with considerable suspicion, and blamed it for a long range of China's ills. At the height of Maoist exuberance the aim was to replace the family with politically supervised collectives in which meals were to be consumed in canteens, property was shared and children brought up communally. In the end, however, capitalism returned and the family survived. More than that, still ostensibly Communist, China has today turned itself into the latest East Asian 'miracle', relying on world markets to propel itself to economic growth rates reaching and exceeding 10 per cent per year. The question is only to what extent the post-Maoist family still can be relied on to deal with the inevitable social consequences of this marketization.

The Family in Imperial China

The role of the family was extensively discussed by the Confucians – by Confucius himself in the fifth century BCE, and by Mengzi, or Mencius, a hundred years later – and it has been discussed by neo-Confucians ever since.[4] All agreed that the family was above all a moral and a political institution. The centrepiece of Confucian thought was the idea of 'the three bonds': between ruler and minister, between father and son, and between husband and wife.[5] Each relationship was associated with a set of obligations which had to be fulfilled if social peace and stability were to be maintained. As the Confucians argued, the entire network of social life would soon unravel if any of these links began to unravel. For this reason, to disobey a father was as great a sin as to disobey an emperor.

The enormous influence which Confucius came to exert during the subsequent two millennia is not due to the power of his thought, however, but rather to the way it was promoted by the imperial state. From the reign of the emperor Han Wudi in the second century BCE, a Confucian state ideology was propagated which emphasized stability and social discipline.[6] The state was to be run by officials who showed filial piety both towards their fathers and towards the emperor.[7] The Han dynasty was also the time when the father was installed as the head of the family in the eyes of the law, and when ancestor worship came to assume a definite ritual form.[8] To worship one's ancestors made sense in a society where the political ideal was stability rather than change. The experiences of previous generations were taken as directly relevant to the lives of the living.

The social ideal was an extended family which included several generations and many stems – 'five generations under one roof' – perhaps some 50 members in all. In practice, however, people rarely lived long enough for such families to form, and brothers would often fall out with each other.[9] Instead, broken-stem families of a more modest size have been the common pattern for at least the last 800 years.[10] Within the family, genders and ages were separated according to each one's comparative advantages. Sons were the most important since they worked in the fields; daughters were married off early and for that reason did not count as proper family members; wives were under the strict supervision of their mother-in-laws at least until they had given birth to the first male heir. Whatever else it was, marriage was not a romantic union between a man and a woman; 'marriage', as Mengzi tersely put it, 'is a bond between two surnames'.[11]

From classical imperial times the family was also an economic unit. This was perhaps most obvious in the countryside, where its members worked side by side in the rice paddies or the fish ponds, but urban craftsmen and merchants relied heavily on their families as well. This made the family into a social setting in which intimate relations were always mixed with endless, often hard and always badly remunerated, labour. In towns, families lived in shop-houses where domestic and commercial activities were thoroughly intertwined. Usually the family business would be located on the ground floor and the family would live on the floor above, yet a distinction between public and private was never clearly drawn. Customers doing their shopping and clients discussing business deals would inevitably run into children washing themselves, older sisters preparing food for sale and grandmothers getting ready for bed. And inevitably, in a corner was the altar to the ancestors with a joss-stick burning in front of it.

But Chinese families also served as protective arrangements. The traditional Chinese family provided full-time and life-long protection against market forces. As a family member there was no need to look for work, to negotiate over pay or to fear dismissal or retirement. Instead, work was right there in front of you – on the family farm or in the family business, the store, the restaurant or the workshop. Instead of wages there was a common family income, and dismissal and retirement happened only at death. Although the family business as a whole was dependent on the market, each individual was connected to it only indirectly. Between the market and the individual there was a dense web of social ties and reciprocal obligations holding and sustaining each person throughout the course of his or her life.

Family lineages were characterized by a similar duality.[12] In southern China in particular, people of the same lineage would often join together in a common cult. The larger lineages, which sometimes included several thousand members, maintained halls where ancestors were worshipped and genealogical records kept. But in addition, the lineages were often great landowners. The lineage supported its members from these assets, provided needy members with relief, gave loans and awarded scholarships to those who studied for state examinations. To this extent the lineage cushioned people against insecurity and risk – and this could make quite a difference during times of rapid social change. But it is also true that many lineages were dominated by wealthy members who used the assets to enrich themselves at everyone else's expense.[13] In relation to the outside world – including in relation to markets – they would stick together, but internally the lineages were often deeply divided.

To briefly summarize. The family in imperial China was organized according to a distinct social grammar by which relations between members were more important than the members themselves.[14] Dependence was valued more highly than independence, and since there was no expectation that they would go off by themselves, there was no need to prepare individuals for a life alone. As a result, fewer resources were invested in each person and more resources were invested instead in the family unit as a whole. Since family members were supposed never to leave, there was no need for a place to come home to that was radically separated from, and ruled by other laws than, the world outside. There was for example no need for an intimate sphere organized by the love of a wife and a mother.[15] Instead, relationships within the family were strictly hierarchical and often also strikingly impersonal. The family was not quietly domestic and closed off from the outside world, but instead a busy place with the doors wide open to the street. And above all, family life never excluded but always presupposed hard work.

In this way the family became the most prominent feature of a distinctive, Chinese-style, capitalism which operated according to its own characteristic logic.[16] In later imperial times – during the Ming and Qing dynasties – the economy expanded dramatically, and so did both the cities and China's total population. Yet there was little by means of technological progress; the changes were instead quantitative rather than qualitative, and the economy grew mainly since more resources were being squeezed out of a system of production which itself remained more or less unchanged.[17] What happened instead was that the family units worked ever harder, producing more output through a higher input of their time and best efforts. Markets were becoming ever more competitive, more efficient, and the families were becoming ever more self-exploitative.[18]

The Family in the Chinese Diaspora

One indicator of the level of hardship in imperial China is the extent to which people tried to escape it. Emigration took off in the nineteenth century when large groups began leaving south-eastern provinces such as Fujian and Guangzhou for new lives in Southeast Asia, the Caribbean and the west coast of the United States.[19] Although life in exile was at first also excruciatingly hard, the conditions here were quite unprecedented. For one thing, the Chinese were now a minority in countries where they did not speak the language, but in addition the economic and political system functioned entirely differently. The question is how the Chinese family fared in these alien settings.

In Southeast Asia, capitalism was generally far slower to develop than in China itself, and when the Chinese arrived, what they encountered were few and badly functioning commodity markets and markets in land and labour which to a large extent were governed by feudal practices such as corvée labour.[20] Subsistence farming was the general norm among local peasants and the money economy was dominated by Europeans who produced a few key commodities for export. The small groups of local merchants and craftsmen were above all serving the needs of the state and the colonial – or in the case of Thailand, the semi-colonial – elite.

Wherever they went, the Chinese were generally met with suspicion and often outright racism, and after 1949 they were sometimes accused of being Communist spies.[21] The Chinese migrants for their part were often equally apprehensive. In almost all cases they started out as sojourners rather than as settlers.[22] In contrast to settlers, sojourners migrate only in order to find work; sojourners are temporary visitors, even if the visits in some cases stretch out over decades and perhaps last an entire lifetime; they are predominantly male, young and have little education.[23] In the alien environment they work hard, saving up money, waiting for the day when they can finally return home with their savings. In fact, the Chinese generally preferred hard labour since hard labour was likely to be better paid and the money would make it possible for them to return sooner. Hence we find the first generations of Chinese immigrants taking up marginal positions both in the economy and in social life. They were making railroads for the colonial government in Burma, working in sugar or rubber plantations in Malaya, in tin mines in southern Thailand and in tanneries in Calcutta.[24]

For these single men – there were only three Chinese women for every 100 Chinese men in the United States at the end of the nineteenth century – the family played the role above all of a distant emotional anchor.[25] Yet many of them were married, and they often sent for their spouses once their budgets allowed. In some countries such as Thailand, on the other hand, the men tended to marry local girls. Throughout the diaspora, by the first decades of the twentieth century, the sex ratio had become far more evenly balanced, and the viability of the Chinese family model was ready to be tested.[26] And as it turned out, it performed splendidly. The traditional Chinese family was in many ways well prepared to deal with the risky and uncertain conditions prevailing in the diaspora. In situations where markets are incomplete, low on information, badly regulated and policed, and where inefficiencies and market failures are common, families have much to offer.[27] Families look after their members, and kinship networks pool economic resources and provide a wealth of personal contacts that can be exploited for social protection as well as economic gain.

Altogether these conditions strengthened rather than weakened the family and its traditional ways of doing business, and the Chinese families often did much better for themselves than the locals.[28] After one generation most migrants had already left their marginal occupations and moved into commerce and manufacturing, first as employees, then increasingly as owner-operators. Even if the factories and sweatshops were small and the hours exceptionally long, people worked for themselves and together with their families. A small proportion of Chinese entrepreneurs became very wealthy indeed, and after World War II this elite turned every political change – from decolonialization in the 1950s to the Vietnam War in the 1960s and the deregulation of financial markets in the 1990s – into an opportunity to make more money.[29] Throughout Southeast Asia, and despite various affirmative action programmes supporting local ethnic groups, people of Chinese descent still overwhelmingly dominate commerce and manufacturing.[30]

By the same token the family became ever more important as a protective arrangement.[31] Family members stuck together since it made economic, social and political sense to do so. Consequently, Chinese companies throughout the diaspora have to this day remained predominantly family-sized and predominantly family-run. The family business provides its members with work, an identity, and a share in a collective income. Just as in imperial China, the family business protects you from having to negotiate with employers and from the consequences of unemployment, old age, sickness and injury. As a result, in every Southeast Asian city there are still Chinese shop-houses where customers do their business while tripping over children and grandmothers as well as altars dedicated to ancestors who died a long time ago in a distant Chinese homeland.

If anything, the inherent dualism of the Chinese family was accentuated by conditions in the diaspora. Ever more crucial for the protection it provided, the family also became increasingly materialistic. Nothing seemed to matter except economic success. Yet money was not perverting the logic of the home, as would have been the case in Europe, and it did not break up the family into its constituent parts.[32] Monetary relations between family members were instead integral to their emotional relations. There was nothing inappropriate about giving away money as a present, and nothing strange about turning the home into a business and a workshop. Family members were cared for to the same degree as they were used. The 15-hour workdays in front of some piece of machinery, six days a week, or on a rotating basis by which all family members had their shifts, was not exploitation but rather self-exploitation. The abstract forces of the marketplace were personalized and therefore made acceptable.[33]

Taiwanese-style capitalism provides a good illustration of this family-based business logic.[34] Together with Hong Kong and Macao the only part of the Chinese mainland where capitalism survived after 1949, Taiwan allows us to imagine how Chinese-style capitalism might have developed but for the Communist takeover. There is no doubt that the Taiwanese family has been transformed in a number of radical ways since World War II.[35] The multi-generational, multi-stem household has been simplified and nuclearized; women are better educated and marry later; they have higher salaries and fewer children. At the same time it is easy to detect the continuation of a characteristic pattern. More than half of the population still lives in extended households; there is still a preference for sons; and wives still predominantly move into their husbands' families.

Moreover, markets in Taiwan are entirely dominated by family businesses. Somewhere between 80 and 90 per cent of all Taiwanese companies are family-run and around 70 per cent of them have fewer than nine employees.[36] It is to a large extent these companies that are the engines of the country's spectacular economic growth.[37] Families are the sources of the savings which establish the companies in the first place, and profit levels are maintained since family members receive lower wages or no wages at all, although they work far longer hours than other employees.[38] Family members are also more reliable and more loyal, and they stay with the company even when brighter prospects open up elsewhere. As a result it makes sense to train and educate them properly for their tasks. In addition, the patriarchal structure of the company makes it easy to make decisions and to implement them; everyone knows who the boss is, and even if they disagree, most sons prefer simply to bide their time. Eventually the day will come when they will be in charge.

Yet it would not be correct to see this as merely a continuation of an imperial Chinese tradition.[39] On the contrary, looking more closely at the family in Taiwan we find that a large number of things have changed – most conspicuously the roles of husband and wife, but also the hopes and aspirations of children.[40] The question is consequently why some things have changed while others have stayed more or less the same. The answer is that much of the traditional family survives, not as the result of the automatic transition of some ancient cultural patterns, but instead as the result of an active implementation of them. It is the outcome of an exercise of power by which fathers, in particular, have been forced to negotiate with their family members. This is above all the case where the wife works.[41] The loyalty of wives and older children is now conditional rather than absolute, and they are prepared to accept the set-up as long as they are given more autonomy both as family members and as employees. They can live with the arrangements as long as the family still functions adequately as a protective arrangement.

The Family in Post-Mao China

And then from the late 1970s onward, capitalism was gradually reintroduced in mainland China itself. Turning their backs on the Mao-era experiments as an embarrassing interlude, everyone instead began making money for themselves. Once the Communist revolution stopped, the capitalist revolution began. Amazingly, China went from the total absence of capitalist markets to full exposure to global capitalism in the course of only a few years. As a result, the country started changing extremely rapidly, creating new opportunities and new wealth but also new forms of poverty and social dislocation.[42] The question is how people have coped with this transition, and in particular what, if anything, is left of the traditional Chinese family.

One striking consequence of the reintroduction of markets – together with the omnipresence of building sites, the fancy foreign cars and the boom in youth culture – is an unprecedented level of internal migration. In 1997 some 100 million people, or nearly 8 per cent of the country's population, were on the move in the largest migratory movement in world history.[43] Compare this with the situation under Communism, when everyone was forced to register as a resident of a particular location; you were either a countryside person or a city person, and changes in residence status were next to unknown.[44] Although this registration system formally remains in place to this day, the lopsided nature of the post-Maoist boom has made it completely redundant. People leave areas such as the western interior, where growth is sluggish, for the eastern seaboard where growth is extraordinarily rapid. The new migrants enjoy neither welfare benefits nor job security and their wages are significantly lower than those in other industries.[45]

At the same time, the extensive welfare system created during the Communist era – often referred to as the 'iron rice-bowl' – has been seriously undermined.[46] This is particularly the case in the countryside where the social and medical services provided by the collective farms have vanished together with the collective farms themselves. As the new generation of leaders boldly explain, too much social welfare provides people with 'the wrong incentives' and slows down growth.[47] The new demand for profitability has also meant that state-run companies have been privatized and many people fired. In 1998 there were some 17 million redundant former workers looking for new jobs.[48] Although a rudimentary system of unemployment insurance exists, it is not nearly adequate.[49] As a result, the post-Mao reforms have simultaneously left people more exposed to market forces and worse protected from them.

Under these circumstances one could expect that the protective arrangements of traditional Chinese society would begin to reassert themselves – families in particular. The problem is that these are precisely the institutions the Communists tried for so long to abolish.[50] Families and lineages were regarded as vestiges of the feudal past, and as such as obstacles to modernization. Through one revolutionary campaign after another the extended family was broken up, its property taken from it, and family members turned into wage earners and members of production teams. Care of the young, the old and the infirm instead became the responsibility of state-run factories and their work units.[51]

Put slightly differently, modernization – even in its revolutionary Chinese version – was modelled almost exclusively on European examples. It invoked the ideals of the eighteenth-century Enlightenment.[52] After all, European thinkers had also often regarded families as obstacles to progress. The focus, they declared, should be on individuals rather than on the relations between individuals; social relations should be made abstract, homogenous and neutral. Only in this way could the intrinsic equality of all men be realized and vested privileges and injustices abolished. The way to accomplish these task, in Europe as in China, was to break up all particularistic associations, including the family, and instead reunite individuals in and through the agency of the state.[53] As the declared heirs to this tradition, the Chinese Communists pursued a particularly ruthless, Maoist, version of the programme.

Despite the persistent anti-family rhetoric of the Maoist years, the most powerful assault on the traditional Chinese family came only after the Chairman's death. According to the so called 'one-child policy' implemented in 1978, no Chinese couples are allowed more than one child, exceptions being made only for ethnic minorities and for people living in some rural areas.[54] 'One-child certificates', guaranteeing access to a range of different benefits, were issued to couples who promised to limit their childbearing, and for those who broke their promises a range of penalties were imposed, including deductions from pay and the denial of rations.[55] Not surprisingly, the policy has profoundly altered the nature of the Chinese family. Large families were always the social ideal; by contrast, the new policy means that there is only one child to each couple and also only one grandchild to each four grandparents. If the policy is maintained, China will one day become a country completely without aunts, uncles and cousins.

The social consequences of such social engineering are far-reaching.[56] With only one chance to perpetuate the family line, the pressures put on that one child have risen enormously. These 'little emperors' are alternatively pampered, intimidated and subjected to intense academic pressure. A handicapped child or a particularly stupid or ugly one is a serious blow to the family's fortunes, and there is evidence of an increase in infanticides in which girls have been singled out.[57] By the same token it is suddenly more difficult to imagine a full-scale revival of Chinese-style family-based capitalism. The one-child policy means that there are fewer hands helping out in the family business or on the farm, and if the child insists on pursuing a different career, the business is lost.[58] Their far smaller size also means that families have become less effective as protective arrangements. The social network shielding people from the market has been stretched; there is less togetherness and fewer significant others to rely on for material and emotional support. There is, for example, only one person to help each couple in their old age.

Admittedly, people have come up with various ways of subverting this draconian decree. In the countryside many farmers have simply ignored it, removed the contraceptive devices and gone ahead and had at least one more child.[59] This has been particularly common if the first child is a girl. Often local officials have turned their backs on such practices, and with the disappearance of the communes they have had far fewer sticks and carrots with which to enforce the plan.[60] In many places in the countryside the local cadre have given up the policy and instead the focus is on preventing third and fourth children.[61] In the cities others have decided that it is worth paying the penalty for an extra child. With increased prosperity the fine is easier to afford, and with the disappearance of the Chinese welfare state more children are increasingly necessary.[62]

Meanwhile the market reforms have had their independent impact on family life. On the whole many rural families have done reasonably well for themselves. The system of residence registration of the communist era meant that the family units remained surprisingly intact, and since people were not allowed to leave their places of residence the social structure of the countryside, including that of the family, stayed as if frozen in time.[63] When property was finally returned to them in the late 1970s, it was easy for the families to pick up where they had left off in the 1950s. Today, when the official welfare state is all but dismantled in the countryside, the peasant family provides a person's only safety-net.[64] There is thus a return to the traditional pattern. Today, fathers are once again working with their sons in the fields and mothers-in-law are once again chastizing daughters-in-law for being lazy and insubordinate.[65] Family members, are once again both decommodified and exploited.

Economic development, however, is accompanied by problems of its own. A more productive agriculture means that less human input is required, and as a result perhaps as many as 200 million people in the countryside are today unemployed or underemployed.[66] This is the next to bottomless pool from which China's internal migrants are drawn. Many of them are sojourners along the traditional Chinese pattern, with all the traditional social problems that brings. Family life suffers when a father or the only child is away from home for extended periods, and of the once-thriving Chinese family there are now only two persons left on the farm. As far as the migrants themselves are concerned, they are forced to face the often alienating and dehumanizing conditions of city life without the support of an extensive kinship network.

For urban families the story is quite different.[67] In the cities the state-owned housing estates never managed to accommodate traditional multi-stem families, and instead small families in small housing units became the norm. The family was also far easier to break up in the city than in the countryside. From 1952 all non-state-owned businesses were abolished, and within five years all official signs of capitalism were removed. This policy was taken to an extreme during the Cultural Revolution, when even country fairs and urban markets were closed down.[68] The abolition of capitalism more than anything meant the abolition of the Chinese-style family business. Urban families were turned into workers in state-run factories, and as a result after privatization there was no property that easily could be returned to them. The cities are also where the one-child policy has been most stringently implemented. In the last three decades of the twentieth century, the size of an average family in Beijing has next to halved.[69]

There is thus no doubt that the Communist state has managed to significantly undermine the power of families, in particular in the cities. This is not to say, however, that the family has disappeared and that all family ties have been broken. Despite its reduced size, the entrepreneurial spirit reawakened by the market reforms is to a large extent still using the family as its vehicle, and shops, workshops and businesses are once again often family-owned. Moreover, the emotional bonds remain. Even if they no longer live in the same flats, family members still share the burdens of child care and the care of the elderly, and they keep in close contact.[70] Restaurants in every city throughout China are still filled with round tables large enough to accommodate extended families. Families have become more 'networked', but not necessarily less united. There is potential here for a revival, yet a revival can never mean a simple return to a tradition. If nothing else, the sheer pace of change in contemporary China means that filial piety can never again come to mean what it once meant. The experiences of older generations are today completely irrelevant to the lives of the young.[71] Similarly, one-child policy or not, the large families of imperial times are not likely to return. It is the experience of all industrialized countries that the labour of women can be more productively employed in the workplace than in the home, and birth rates are therefore likely to stay low.

AMONG BROTHERS, FRIENDS
AND COLLEAGUES

5

European Sects, Guilds and Trade Unions

Associations, we said above, occupy an intermediary position in social life. Associations are located somewhere between the state and the family, in a world which at the same time is both public and private. This intermediary position is what gives them their unique characteristics. They have far more power over their environment than families, and they are also more robust since they are governed to a larger extent by rules than by the actions and reactions of individuals. By becoming a member of an association we escape the narrow confines of family life and learn to act together with others in the pursuit of common goals. Here were are all 'brothers', 'sisters', 'comrades' and 'mates'. And yet, as we have pointed out, associations have authority structures of their own. Just like the home itself these homes-away-from-home have their own ways of manipulating us. Who is protected and on what terms is ultimately a political matter – that is to say, a matter of power.

Europe has experienced three great waves of association-formation corresponding roughly to three great spurts in the development of markets. The first wave took place when money was reintroduced after the eleventh century and markets first began expanding. The second wave came with the great upsurge in trade after the sixteenth century. The third wave, associated with industrialization and the unleashing of *laissez-faire* economics, happened in the nineteenth century. At each stage the economy grew, new opportunities presented themselves together with new forms of human misery and the traditional fabric of social life was torn apart. Associations represented one of the chief ways of capitalizing on the new opportunities which presented themselves, while at the same time protecting people against these threats. Since many of the earliest associations survived into later periods, Europe by the twentieth century presented an associational flora that was both rich and varied.

For the last couple of hundred years at least the Europeans have had their own distinct ways of associating.[1] The people who join associations become members; membership is voluntary; all members are equal and they join up out of their own free choice. Pre-existing social bonds mean little in this regard. You join an association not because your family and friends already have but becauses it is in your interest to do so. Individuals are the generic building blocks out of which associations are constructed, and from the point of view of the association, any one member is as good as any other. Like pieces of Lego, members can easily be substituted for one another and they can be combined in a great number of ways. This means that associations can take on virtually any form, size or function as long as the members are only provided with the right incentives. However, if the right incentives are not there, collective action will be difficult or even impossible to organize. Unless the association serves the interest of its members, they will not join it in the first place or they will quickly cancel their memberships once they realize that participation brings few benefits.

Religious Sects

The reintroduction of money in Europe after the eleventh century led to a large number of far-reaching changes.[2] Money allowed trade to be conducted more efficiently, and before long a new class of merchants had established itself in towns throughout both the Mediterranean and the Baltic. In these 'free cities' runaway serfs turned themselves into craftsmen or, more commonly, into members of a new proletarian underclass. In towns such as Ypres, Ghent, Bruges, Lyon and Douai there were factories run by merchant capitalists who produced woollen cloth for a Europe-wide market. After the Black Death decimated the population by perhaps as much as one-third in many parts of Europe, the lords realized that they only could keep people on the manors if they began paying them.[3] This was how market relations gradually came to replace feudal relations in the countryside.

As the main source of intellectual and moral authority of the era, the Church was quick to react to these changes, and officially at least it was highly sceptical. It disliked the social divisions that suddenly appeared and it disapproved of the ways that money was being made.[4] As the priests pointed out in their sermons, the obsession with money-making undermined the social order and diverted people's attention away from the contemplation of higher things. Moneylenders were a popular target and usury – the profit derived from moneylending – was condemned in the strongest possible terms. Usurers produced nothing, it was pointed out, instead they let their money work for them, and they lived well off the back-breaking toil of others. Even more scandalously, money kept multiplying even on the Sabbath:

> Every man stops working on holidays, but the oxen of usury work unceasingly and thus offend God and all the saints; and, since usury is an endless sin, it should in like manner be endlessly punished.[5]

Despite these firmly expressed views, it did not take long before the Church became heavily involved in elaborate financial dealings of its own, including both the lending and borrowing of money against interest.[6] In addition, the Church benefited greatly from a buoyant trade in religious services and artefacts. By the fifteenth century, if you only had the money you could buy yourself everything from the absolution of sins to eternal life – or at least a bone off the corpse of a minor saint.[7]

A more convincing critique came from more popular quarters. In the twelfth and thirteenth centuries a number of colourful movements appeared which condemned the new money economy much as the Church had, but without the hypocrisy.[8] The most famous examples were the Franciscans, founded in 1210, and the Dominicans, founded in 1216. Both orders rejected the world that money had created and preached instead a gospel of poverty. In their internal organization these mendicant orders were intended as radical alternatives to the avarice and sin of the outside world.[9] Here the new social hierarchies were replaced by equality; each monk was a *frater*, a 'brother', and as such in principle at least equal to every other monk. Monks could not own property or engage in economic activities on their own behalf – instead, they interacted with markets only as a collective entity; the order was in the market, but at the same time not of it.

Franciscans and Dominicans were not alone. Together with the two mendicant orders a large number of other sects appeared that preached similar messages.[10] The most important of these were the Waldensians, known as 'the Poor of Lyons', and the Albigenses, active in southern France. In contrast to Franciscans and Dominicans, however, Waldensians and Albigenses were never officially recognized by the Church and more often than not they were actively persecuted. But there were many other similar movements, including Beguines, Petrobrusians, Henricians, Bogomils, Paulicians, Flagellants and Adamists. The Flagellants were famous for marching around the streets while beating themselves, and the Adamists seem to have carried out most their activities, including the preaching of the gospel, in the nude.[11]

Theologically, this exotic collection of sects shared an obsession with the sinfulness of man and a strong belief that the end of the world was nigh.[12] Drawing on the Book of Revelation, assorted millenarian myths and snippets of neo-Platonic philosophizing, the preachers urged their congregations to put their hopes in a radical renewal of the world. First the Anti-Christ would come and then the Christ, and when He returned, the reign of money would finally come to an end. Wreaking vengeance on behalf of those who believed in Him, the unjust order would perish and the first would become the last.[13] While waiting for this glorious day, the faithful spent their time organizing their communities according to what they took to be divine spec-ifications. In outlaw settlements beyond the reach of the authorities, or sur-reptitiously established beneath a façade of acceptability, the sects combined the ideals of poverty and equality. Often the members would hold all property in common, and in some cases they would share women.[14]

Significantly, these sects recruited heavily from segments of the population marginalized by the development of markets: the urban poor, journeymen and unskilled workers, peasants without land, beggars and vagabonds, prostitutes and cripples.[15] A particularly susceptible audience were the workers in the textile factories of northern France. All too often the freedom they experienced as newly released serfs was fundamentally undermined by the precariousness of their existence. Yet as sect members they were no longer urban proletarians but instead the children of god; they were the Chosen Ones who would be with Him eternally in heaven.

By comparison the messages of religious reformers such as Martin Luther and Jean Calvin may seem rather bland. Luther and Calvin were neither millenarians nor egalitarians and they did not believe in the pooling of women. More importantly, they were not against the market system as such and they did not advocate shared poverty as an alternative to it. In their time – the sixteenth and seventeenth centuries – monetized markets had long been taken for granted and society was rapidly becoming ever more commercialized. This was when trade with East Asia took off and when a pan-European market was created in goods ranging from Baltic wheat and Spanish wine to cod from the North Atlantic.[16] This commercial revolution, just like the monetary revolution of the eleventh century, presented the usual mix of opportunities and miseries; again waves of migrants left the countryside and settled in commercial hubs, this time predominantly north European cities like Amsterdam and London. The challenge for Luther and Calvin was how to accommodate religion to these changes and to the social order that was emerging.[17]

The received wisdom is that Protestantism was a great boon to the development of capitalism. According to a famous argument first intro-duced by Max Weber, Protestantism instilled a unique entrepreneurial ethos – a 'Protestant ethic' – in at least some of its adherents, and this ethic is what supposedly stimulated economic growth.[18] People worked hard in order to quiet the anxiety they felt about the prospect of their salvation. And yet in theory at least there was never a great deal of difference between the economic outlook of Protestants and Catholics.[19] Protestant preachers too were perfectly ready to condemn usury and avarice, and they were no friends of luxury consumption. Foreign trade, said Martin Luther, which brings useless articles 'from Calcutta and India and such places,' would never be permitted 'if we had proper government and princes'.[20]

Still, the Protestants seemed more ready than the Catholics to strike deals with Mammon.[21] Instead of rejecting commercial society as a sinful perver-sion, Luther and Calvin insisted that salvation could be found within it. It is not true, they argued, that monks are closer to god than ordinary men – and there is no need for priests to intercede with heaven on our behalf. Salvation is instead a DIY job. God has provided us with a calling in life, and as we respond to his call, we all come to serve him in our various ways. Here the division of labour created by the expansion of markets is given a religious significance; for Martin Luther it became nothing less than the means to our salvation:

> A cobbler, a smith, a peasant, each has the world and office of his trade, and yet they are all alike consecrated priests and bishops. Further, everyone must benefit and serve every other by means of his own work or office so that in this way many kinds of work may be done for the bodily and spiritual welfare of the community, just as all the members of the body serve one another.[22]

God and Mammon could thus coexist quite peacefully, and there was no contradiction involved in simultaneously serving both. As a result, poverty and equality ceased to be religious ideals and there was no reason for people to retreat to monasteries in order to live god-fearing lives. In a commercial society, even a saint would have to work for a living.

In addition to the denominations founded by Luther and Calvin, a large number of other sects sprang up across Europe. And much as in the Middle Ages their names were at least as colourful as their teachings. Among many others there were Quakers and Shakers, Pietists and Læstadians, Herrnhutians, Mennonites, Collegiants and Christadelphians, not to mention Baptists, Anabaptists and Methodists. Just like their medieval predecessors these groups recruited heavily from people uprooted and marginalized by the expansion of markets.[23] In the sixteenth and seventeenth centuries Protestant sects established themselves quickly among craftsmen, shopkeepers and professionals in Holland, England and northern France, as they did in the North American colonies.

The great advantage of the sect over the church is that its criteria for membership are far more demanding. Not everyone is admitted to the sect, after all, but only those who manage to live by its exacting standards. In all sects adultery, theft and profane language were banned, but often also things that were merely entertaining – such as dancing and alcohol – or frivolous – such as expensive clothes or even curtains. In addition to a certain self-righteousness, the ability to live by such demanding rules created a strong sense of community among the faithful. Sect members were 'saints', they were 'the elect', and the stricter the moral code, the more the members stood out from the mainstream of society.

The sect was also a far smaller community than the church. The members knew each other better and socialized more closely; they belonged to the same big family and were all 'brothers and sisters in Christ'.[24] Chatting before the Sunday service or after a Wednesday evening prayer meeting, people made friends, and found business partners and future spouses.[25] When striking up these relationships, faith always mattered far more than deeds and religious piety more than economic efficiency. For migrant workers in particular, such contacts were crucial since they helped secure a standing and a reputation in the community; ignored by the market, the new arrivals obtained recognition for their commitment to god and to the congregation. God looked after his flock in the same measure as the flock looked after itself.

Yet the sect never provided more than partial protection from the effects of market forces. The sects were social settings that people could retreat to after their engagements with capitalism or where they could pray for future economic success, but they never replaced the market. Or rather, when they tried to break away from commercial society and organize themselves according to religious principles – as in the utopian communes set up in particular in North America – the sects generally failed.[26] The communal experiments that survived the longest were those which allowed some private property, individual marriages, a family life, and which in other ways made concessions to ordinariness.[27] The communes that survived the longest were those that were the least communal.

In the same manner religious organizations played a role in negotiating the transition from agricultural to industrial society. As such they were always vilified by Karl Marx and the Marxists who dismissed religion as 'the sigh of the oppressed creature, the heart of a heartless world ... the spirit of spiritless conditions'.[28] Religion, they argued, was an opiate that dulled the pain suffered by the working class; it was a false solution to a problem to which a revolution was the only true solution. And it is certainly the case that a sect such as Methodism, which was popular among the English working class in the early stages of the Industrial Revolution, did much to instil a new work-ethic in their members, including sobriety, a new consciousness of time and a general submissiveness.[29] Yet not everything turned out the way the pastors intended, and many activities of the Methodist congregation served other, more subversive or at least ambiguous ends.[30]

In many respects, however, Marx managed to prove himself wrong. A large proportion of the working class was simply not particularly religious.[31] As recent settlers in the city many of them had lost connections with their congregations and their churchgoing habits, and often their dirty and tiring work left them with little time and in no mood to praise the Lord. Industrial capitalism posed the theodicy problem in a new and acute version: 'where was god in a world where work was so hard and demeaning, wages so low, and where children died for lack of medical attention?' The level of irreligion seems to have been particularly high in Germany where working-class areas always had the lowest levels of church attendance and where even funerals were sometimes conducted without the presence of a priest.[32] As Paul Göhre, an Evangelical pastor who in 1891 worked undercover as a manual labourer in a factory in Chemnitz, reported with some considerable horror, the Marxist catechism was everywhere replacing the Christian. 'What Jesus Christ has been in the past,' his fellow-workers had informed him, 'Bebel and Liebknecht will be in the future'.[33]

Miraculously, however, religion has managed to survive to this day, and it seems to be most active in societies with ruthless economic markets and high levels of social mobility – conditions today best exemplified in the United

States.[34] In America, when the advance of science turned belief in god into a superstition, the religious community became ever more real. Americans are still religious to a surprising degree, and, as one would expect, this is particularly the case for people marginalized by market forces: immigrants, women, the poor, members of ethnic minorities and inhabitants of an American heartland increasingly hit by downsizing, outsourcing and other twenty-first-century corporate practices.[35] God blesses America, and America blesses god.

Guilds and Trade Unions

Instead of waiting for god to save us, however, many prefer to take fate into their own hands. One way to do this is to look for ways of manipulating the market to one's own advantage; to somehow extract more from an exchange than one would normally receive. Yet because individuals on their own are completely powerless in relation to market forces, this can only be achieved by means of a concerted effort. Only by joining together with others do people have a reasonable chance of improving their terms of trade. Historically, there are two particularly important examples of such collective actions: guilds and trade unions.

Guilds appeared in Europe in the twelfth century at the time when markets were initially monetized and the first towns emerged.[36] The term 'guild' itself covers a range of associative practices. The so called craft guilds were organizations made up of the masters who practised a particular trade in a particular town, together with the journeymen and apprentices who worked for them. But many guilds were more similar to clubs or societies for mutual support.[37] Regardless of their structures, however, the guilds sought explicitly to undo the logic of the marketplace and to advantage themselves. Although their control of the market was never anything like complete, they sought to regulate working hours, prices and wages, as well as the number of workers and tools that could be employed in each workshop.[38] Many used strikes to attain their goals. Already in 1229 the tailors of the Flemish town of Douai downed their needles, and in 1285 the weavers of Rouen were accused of forming illegitimate alliances.[39]

By later economists the guilds would be accused of a range of crimes – 'monopolistic practices' and 'rent-seeking' most conspicuously among them.[40] Yet this judgement is too hasty. There are on the contrary solid reasons to believe that guilds encouraged rather than impeded economic growth.[41] And in any case, what the economists miss is the extent to which the guilds were social institutions; never mere 'interest groups', they were *fraternitates*, 'brotherhoods', or *corporationes*, 'bodies'.[42] As such their activities were only partly economic. In addition they served various religious functions, dispensed physical and social support – including unemployment insurance – and engaged in a considerable amount of feasting and carousing. The guilds gave their members a political voice and helped them obtain a reputation in the local community without which, in the absence of state regulations and proper financial institutions, it would have been quite impossible to survive.[43]

With the first stirrings of industrial capitalism at the end of the eighteenth century, this merry world of regulated capitalism became the target of a vociferous critique.[44] Detailed guild regulations, Adam Smith argued in *The Wealth of Nations*, 1776, are always presented as a way to protect the general public from shoddy goods and fraudulent practices. In practice, however, it is instead the guilds themselves that are defrauding us. Through their collusion they increase prices while reducing the quality of the goods they produce. But Smith was suspicious also of their social activities. 'People of the same trade seldom meet together,' he observed, 'even for merriment and diversion, but the conversation ends in a conspiracy against the public, or in some contrivance to raise prices.'[45] If only the masters could be kept apart and be deprived of the means of communicating with each other, the general public would benefit greatly.

And that is more or less what happened. With the commercialization of agriculture from the sixteenth century onwards, guild regulations became increasingly difficult to maintain. Producers were scattered over much larger areas and they had far fewer opportunities to socialize with each other and to conspire. By Smith's own time the guilds were all but gone in Britain itself, and new attempts to organize collectively were outlawed by the Combination Acts of 1799 and 1800.[46] In France the guilds were formally abolished in 1776, but because this reform was met with widespread defiance they had to be abolished again after the Revolution in 1789, and yet again in 1791.[47] Additional legislation against *compagnonnages* – informal brotherhoods made up of journeymen – were simultaneously brought in. In Germany the same development took somewhat longer, but even here the guilds had more or less disappeared by the beginning of the nineteenth century.

Among enlightened thinkers and liberal modernizers alike the dissolution of the guilds was regarded as a great step forward. The guilds were seen as remnants of the old feudal order and as limitations on the freedom of individuals to choose their own occupation. Against the privileges – the *privi-legii* or 'private laws' – of the *anciens régimes*, the revolutionaries affirmed the universal applicability of the *droits de l'homme*. 'We have now,' said the *Journal des Décrets de l'Assemblée Nationale* in February 1791, once the guilds once again had been abolished, 'done away with these last vestiges of servitude; all men will have the means to make use of their skills.'[48]

However, simultaneously releasing both individuals and market forces led to a new sense of insecurity. Without the protection offered by the guilds people were forced to face the market alone, and this at a time when the industrial revolution was poised to radically transform all European societies. Yet it did not take long before people found other means of looking after themselves. The 'friendly society' is an example, and friendly societies experienced an explosive growth at the turn of the nineteenth century.[49] In England these associations had some 704,000 participants in 1802 and perhaps 7 million in 1914; in London perhaps as many as 40 per cent of all working people were members. In France, meanwhile, the outlawed *compagnonnages* often reconstituted themselves as friendly societies and went on operating much as before.[50] Such societies were far more than mere insurance companies – the members also spent time on things like religious processions, not to mention drinking and carousing.

A more significant solution, however, was the trade union. In contrast to the guilds, trade unions admitted only workers, and in contrast to the friendly societies, the unions were fighting for what they regarded as their rights rather than merely trying to cope with injustices. The language they employed was entirely different. A union was a 'movement' engaged in 'struggle,' and what the struggle was for was obvious: higher wages, shorter working hours, better working conditions and political rights.[51]

Yet it would take a long time before anything even remotely resembling a proper movement was established. The first unions were limited to individual factories – they had few members, and were constantly harassed by the police. In England the first crafts-based unions appeared in the last decades of the eighteenth century, but it took until the 1860s for a national organization, the Trades Union Congress, to be established.[52] In subsequent decades the rate of unionization increased rapidly, until it reached 40 per cent of male workers, and proportionately many more in industries such as mining, textiles and the railways. By the end of World War I Britain had some 4 million unionized workers.[53] Germany was another success story, despite the fact that industrialization here began much later, really only in the last decades of the nineteenth century.[54] The large size of the German factories facilitated unionization, although the working-class continued to be run through with cleavages separating Catholics from Protestants, northern Germans from southern, and native workers from Polish immigrants.[55] In 1891 the trade union movement was unified as an umbrella organization which by 1914 had some 2.6 million members.[56] From organizing 1 per cent of the labour force in 1882, German trade unions organized 37 per cent in 1925.

In other countries the unions ran into greater difficulties. Take France, for example, where agriculture remained economically dominant well into the twentieth century.[57] Factories here were small and scattered, and a large proportion of the industrial workforce was of immigrant origin. Unionization was also problematical in the United States, and for similar reasons.[58] Despite considerable successes in particular industries, the union movement as a whole suffered from the volatile conditions of the labour market. One factor was the moving, western, frontier, another the lack of solidarity among different groups of workers. Many unions discriminated against newly freed slaves or, in the latter part of the nineteenth century, against immigrants from southern and eastern Europe.

Although they used more militant rhetoric than guilds and friendly societies, and had more obviously political aims, the trade unions were not only interest groups but also social clubs. Strikes and demonstrations may have been their official rationale, but social activities were often the more urgent parts of their work. More often than not the people who ended up in the factory towns had few bonds in common, and sometimes – especially in the case of the United States – they did not even speak each other's languages. Under such circumstances, to organize ways in which people could get to know one another was nothing short of a political act. Hence for example the importance of alcohol. As Karl Kautsky, the leader of the German Social Democrats, pointed out in 1891:

> for the proletarian in Germany giving up alcohol means giving up social life. He doesn't have a salon at his disposal; he can't invite his friends and comrades into a sitting room. If he wants to get together with them, if he wants to discuss the things that concern them, then he has to go to the pub. ... The solitary bulwark of the proletarian's freedom, which can't be taken from him easily, is the public house. ... Without the pub the German worker is deprived not only of social but also of political life.[59]

The employers seem to have understood this well enough, and the police were often called upon not only to break up strikes but also to put an end to the various social events organized by the unions.[60] Their objection was the same as Adam Smith's complaint against the guilds – that the union members were 'conspiring against the public in some contrivance to raise prices'.

But the social activities were also much appreciated ends in themselves. To rank-and-file members the pub and the workingman's club provided opportunities to interact on completely different terms from those that obtained on the factory floor. The atmosphere here was one of camaraderie and solidarity. In the pub or the club – or in France, in the café – everyone was regarded as an equal and as a mate, and no one was in a position to give or to take orders.[61] Getting together over a pint and a joke, the dignity which the dehumanizing factory had taken away was quickly restored; time passed leisurely again, counted in rounds of drinks rather than in seconds, minutes and hours.[62] This was not least the case since pubs, clubs and cafés were spheres of male sociability where men were bonding with other men and away from the home.[63] Here you were suddenly free not only of your boss but also of your wife.

The pubs, workingman's clubs and cafés were the most visible expressions of an associative life that stretched far further. Despite their lack of time and money, or perhaps because of it, workers throughout Europe formed a wide range of associations which together amounted to nothing short of an alternative, non-market-based, sphere of sociability. There were clubs where they could do gymnastics, play chess and stage theatrical productions; there were ramblers' and cyclists' associations, cooperative shops, reading circles, travelling libraries, choral and *Sprechchor* groups, and a variety of youth and children's organizations.[64] In Germany some 2.3

million people belonged to such societies in 1928, but similar alternative working-class societies also existed in countries such as Italy and Sweden.

In retrospect it is easy to identify the first decades of the twentieth century as the golden age of the trade union movement and its affiliated organizations. This was when the injustices were most conspicuous and when the working class faced real enemies. In several countries, however, these enemies eventually gained the upper hand. In Italy after 1922 and in Germany after 1933 there was no longer an independent working-class movement.[65] After World War II the situation looked quite different again. By now much of the acute tension in the labour market had eased. The general post-war consensus on the need for social reforms meant that more attention was paid to workers' demands, and this provided the unions with a new status. In many countries trade union leaders became official partners in national wage negotiations, and they often had a significant influence on the political agenda.

While the trade union leaders in this way became members of the establishment and de facto co-responsible for the smooth operation of the capitalist system, the involvement of ordinary members gradually atrophied. Strikes and demonstrations became ever more ritualistic, and fewer and fewer members showed up for union-sponsored rallies. Even the social activities drew smaller crowds. After World War II the German Social Democrats decided not to recreate the plethora of working-class-based organizations that had existed before 1933 but instead to work within regular, mainstream, associations.[66] From the 1950s onward, with more time and more money in their pockets, working-class people began looking elsewhere for good times and fun. Since they could now increasingly afford to buy their entertainment on the open market, they no longer had to try so hard to entertain themselves.[67]

A Contrasting Case: *Guanxi* Networks

For a different perspective on these European movements, consider briefly the associative logic that has been predominant in China. Above we noted the ways in which Chinese families both exploited and protected their members. Yet not even Chinese families were ever completely self-reliant. Whether they owned a farm or a business, there were bound to be times when they needed an extra pair of hands. In a market society you are expected to hire help in the same way you organize everything else – you are supposed to be guided only by information regarding the relative prices of goods and services. In China, however, the market was relied on in this manner only intermittently. In addition there was a dense web of social relationships which interacted with the market in both complementary and contradictory ways. As a result, Chinese markets were always deeply personalized.

The Chinese for such relationships is *guanxi*, meaning 'connection'.[68] The creation and maintenance of *guanxi* is something Chinese people seem constantly to be engaged in, and although people in Europe and North America certainly also are known to 'network', Chinese people do it far more obsessively.[69] Thus while the family is the basic unit of Chinese society, the *guanxi* network is its basic organizational principle, and traditionally at least, there have been no other ways in which people associate.[70] In China, associations were never formed as if by individual bits of Lego. Organizational effectiveness was not as vulnerable as in Europe since people could go on feeling loyal to particular others even when they had lost faith in the organization as a whole. On the other hand, the emphasis on personal ties meant that organizations could not take on just any form, size or function; there were limits to the kinds of organizations that could easily be established.[71] In particular, there were fewer organizations based on abstract and horizontal relationships like those of gender or social class. As a result, it was not necessarily the case that collective tasks would come to correspond to collective solutions.

Guanxi connections take their origin in a pre-existing affinity of some kind. Perhaps two individuals are distantly related, share the same last name or come from the same region, or perhaps they went to the same school, or perhaps their parents did.[72] Once some such connection has been identified, the next step is to start giving gifts – perhaps a bottle of liquor, moon-cakes or some exotic or hard-to-get-hold-of item. If the gift is reciprocated, the connection is established, and gifts and services of all kinds can begin to move back and forth, not only between the two parties but also between the parties of their parties. Before long the *guanxi* connection has formed long chains of mutual debts and obligations through which liquor and moon-cakes can circulate but also valuable information, introductions to employers and tip-offs of all kinds. In this way a system of gift exchanges comes to overlay the system of market exchanges. In this alternative economy you achieve your aims and gain status not by buying and selling but, on the contrary, by receiving things and by giving them away.

In terms of a market society, it is difficult to explain how such extra-market relationships can exist at all, particularly since it is often very costly, both in time and in money, to establish and maintain one's *guanxi* connections. An economy and a society that are organized around friendly exchanges would seem to be hopelessly inefficient. This at any rate was always the European presumption, for in Europe modernization has often been defined as the process whereby personal relations are replaced with impersonal and contractual ones.[73] Eager to modernize their country, Chinese reformers have followed these alleged imperatives and fallen over themselves to condemn these 'feudal' practices.[74] In Communist China *guanxi*-based networking has been lambasted as a type of corruption and as a particularly insidious form of 'bourgeois selfishness'.

Before such networks are so roundly condemned, however, we need a better account of why they exist. An obvious explanation might be that *guanxi* networks indeed can be taken as rational where markets function badly or not at all.[75] This is most obviously the case where there is no market in some particular goods or services or where the market is rationed or otherwise restricted. Since a desired item cannot be freely bought we need personal contacts in order to get it. But personal contacts are also crucial in situations where information is unevenly distributed or where risks are high and uncertainty is rife.[76] In a situation where you can trust neither strangers nor political authorities, neither the police nor the law, at least you can still trust your friends. In the absence of markets, spending time and money building networks may indeed make a lot of sense.

Chinese history is full of first-rate illustrations of such market failures. The merchant guilds, for example – uniting traders who come from a specific region of China – were created as a result of the rapid expansion of markets during the Song dynasty.[77] They stuck together because they shared affinities and points of reference. This need for bonds of familiarity became increasingly more important during the Ming and Qing dynasties, when the legal and physical infrastructure was no longer as well maintained.[78] In a situation where weights, measures and coins are no longer standardized, it is simply foolish to do business with strangers. Such insecurity was rife also in the Chinese diaspora where markets were far less developed than in China itself.[79] Access to 'back doors' was essential when there were no front doors; knowing someone was often the only way to get hold of a flat or a job, to change one's household registration or even to acquire a ticket to a concert or a movie. This is why the exhortations of the Party bosses never amounted to very much; the 'feudal practices' could not be abolished because in practice central planning required them.

If market imperfections such as these fully explain the existence of *guanxi* networks, we would expect them to become less important as legal and political institutions become more reliable and as information becomes more evenly distributed. Or more concretely, we would expect them to be less important in Singapore than in Shanghai, and less important in Shanghai today than they were some 30 years ago. This may or may not be the case.[80] And yet it is also possible that the networks maintain much of their power even in markets that are functioning perfectly – indeed, even perfectly functioning markets may require them. One reason is that *guanxi* networks in addition to their instrumental roles also play protective ones; *guanxi* connections humanize impersonal and abstract relations and make it possible to recognize others and to be recognized ourselves. They are protective arrangements, in short, which shield us from the full impact of market forces.

Many foreign observers have had problems making sense of this duality. To them it seems cynical to combine a business ethic with a familial ethic, and for that reason they have concluded that the instrumental use of *guanxi* is the 'real' one and that the affective function is superficial.[81] This, however, is an ethnocentric view which misunderstands the nature of the *guanxi* network.[82] More precisely, such an interpretation is premised on a European understanding that protection is available only in social settings that are radically separated from the market and ruled by logics that are alternative to it. This, however, is not the Chinese view. We noted above how the family manages perfectly well to combine instrumental and affective logics, and much the same applies to the *guanxi* network.

With this alternative consideration in mind it is easy to provide quite a different explanation for the persistence of the networking mentality. Networks proliferated during the Song dynasty not only because they provided merchants with a more reliable way of doing business but also because they provided the new 'floating populations' with a means of forging new social ties.[83] This continued to be the case when markets expanded during the Ming and Qing dynasties and when China forcibly was connected to the world market in the nineteenth century. Banding together, the displaced population formed secret societies, like the notorious Triads, which are mainly regarded today as criminal gangs but which originally only resorted to criminality as one of their many activities.[84] Above all, the secret societies were self-help organizations.[85] Like families they provided work, job security and protection from market forces, and as brotherhoods they were explicitly organized on family lines. In secret rites the Triad members would share each other's blood, and in order to symbolize their status as brothers they would all take the same surname.

Or consider the Chinese diaspora where secret societies were common together with all kinds of place-name, surname, dialect and lineage associations. They were particularly important for the first generation of migrants who did not have their families with them. In Singapore, for example, the Triads had some 10,000 members in 1840 out of a Chinese population of perhaps 20,000.[86] As everywhere else, these networks provided a wide range of services for their members, distributing funds and religious, legal and educational support, but also social prestige. And the number of networks does not seem to have declined as markets became better organized. In the Bangkok area, for example, there were 522 Chinese associations in 1993, and 80 per cent of them had been created since 1959.[87] As elsewhere, their dual nature is conspicuous. It is to a large extent the instrumental uses of the *guanxi*-based networks which have allowed the Chinese business elite in Thailand to achieve its prosperity.[88] At the same time the networks have shielded them from the negative social consequences of their own success.

This is why the networks formed during the Communist era continue operating also in the privatized and marketized environment of the new People's Republic. Or rather, the market reforms provide us with a powerful test of this hypothesis. If indeed traditional *guanxi* networks such as lineages and secret societies are revived, and if neo-traditional networks such as those formed around work units and village cooperatives go on flourishing, this would provide evidence that markets which are better regulated and institutionalized also require this form of personalization.[89] Far from disappearing, the need for them would increase.

6

Japanese Business Corporations

At first glance a discussion of business corporations would seem to fit rather badly with the guilds, unions and sects examined in the previous chapter. Companies are run for profit, after all, and as such they have entirely different aims than those of these other, more altruistically-oriented organizations. And although this is undoubtedly true, private businesses are associations of a sort too. Just like guilds, unions and sects, they occupy an intermediary position in social life somewhere between the individual and the market. Companies are private in the sense that they are owned by private individuals, but they are simultaneously public in the sense that they are 'PLCs', companies publicly available on the stock market. Moreover, companies occupy an intermediary position also in the sense that they provide a way for individuals to leave their private spheres and work together with others in the pursuit of common goals. They are places where strangers become colleagues and friends.

The etymology of the word is revealing in this respect. 'Corporation' derives from *corpus*, the Latin for 'body', and in the Middle Ages the body in question consisted of partners who pooled their resources in order to be able to invest in some common project, above all in trade ventures over-seas.[1] By owning a part rather than the whole of a company, merchants were able to reduce their exposure to risk. The corporation was best com-pared to a guild or a brotherhood, and as such the first corporations also had a thriving social life. They too had their patron saints, secret rituals and solemn oaths. Far from being passive shareholders, the owners wined and dined the corporate executives, and each other, on regular occasions throughout the year. Companies were made up of *compagnons*, from the medieval Latin *com-pania*, meaning people 'with whom one shares bread'.[2]

Although this quaint social environment may seem far removed from today's money-orientated no-nonsense business world, it is still true that companies are places where economic and social pursuits are combined. Corporations are still nothing less than guild-like in their ability to provide the people who work for them with opportunities for social interaction.[3] Although the secret oaths are fewer and the feasting has been cut back, con-temporary corporations are still social and not only economic entities. In many cases we spend more time together with workmates and colleagues than with any other people, including our family members. And although some of this interaction is businesslike enough, most of it is plainly not. Much of the time we spend gossiping or bantering with our workmates; we make friends around the water-cooler, chat each other up by the copy-machine and go out for drinks after work.

The basic reason why companies can play such alternative roles is that although they certainly are actors in economic markets, they are not themselves markets.[4] Because of the often vociferous pro-market rhetoric of their executives, it is easy to forget that companies are bureaucratic organizations ruled through hierarchical chains of command and not through the interaction of supply and demand. Employees are bossed around; they are not selling their services on an item-by-item, hour-by-hour, basis. Companies, in short, are social entities governed by social rules rather than simply by the imperatives of profit maximization. Working in a company is not a matter of helping the bosses make money as much as a matter of getting along with others, and of keeping one's nose clean.

This is also why companies can serve as protective arrangements. The company connects us to social networks of friends and colleagues; it provides us with a purpose and an identity, and it gives us a path to pursue. As employees, we are placed on different rungs of corporate ladders that provide us each with a role. As a person moves from one rung to the next, his or her career starts to take shape, and life takes on a linear, easily narrated, structure.[5] We know where we are and where we are going. Slightly pathetic though it may sound, companies help provide meaning to our lives and give us a sense of purpose.

There is no better illustration of this logic than the Japanese corporations of the decades that followed World War II. The company is where most male members of Japanese society spend most of their time, in many cases between 14 and 16 hours a day.[6] Japanese companies are also explicitly thought of as social and not just as economic entities, and they take a full-time and total responsibility for the well-being of their employees. The company is a kind of family writ large. Avoiding the pro-market rhetoric of their American counterparts, many of the practices of Japanese corporations are designed to reduce competition between employees and to cut the link between productivity and pay.

The Japanese Employment System

The many exotic features of the Japanese employment system have been discussed in great detail in Europe and North America, especially during the long decades of the country's economic boom.[7] In these accounts the aim has typically been to show not only how different Japan is but also how vastly superior. If we could only 'learn from Japan', one best-selling author after another used to declare, we too could succeed equally spectacularly.[8] With hindsight it is easy to make fun of such conclusions – but even if we question the superiority of the Japanese employment system, there are fewer doubts about its unique character. And strikingly, many of its most peculiar features are there to protect people from contact with market forces.

Consider lifetime employment. The policy of giving employees a job for life is common in all large Japanese companies, comprising perhaps 20 per cent of the total labour force, and uniquely it pertains not only to white-collar workers but to blue-collar workers as well.[8] From the point of view of the employees, the advantages of life-time tenure are obvious. Although they forfeit the possibility of regularly testing their market values, and thereby increasing their salaries, what they gain is job security and a perfectly dependable income. They always know exactly who they will work for and where they will be, and they can plan their lives accordingly; buy a house, make friends, extend their roots. Once you sign your contract, you are decommodified for life, and you never have to present yourself to the market again. There is therefore virtually no labour market for *sarariimen* except for the hectic but temporary hustle when recent university graduates are allocated to their future employers.[9]

The seniority system decommodifies in a similar manner.[10] Again this is a feature above all of large companies, and it covers roughly the same proportion of workers as lifetime employment. In Japan, once you join a company you belong to a cohort of fellow employees who all joined in the same year. Together with this group you move up through the ranks as you gradually gain seniority and reach higher pay-grades. As a result, although a proportion of the salary may be determined through an assessment of individual achievements, everyone can be assured of getting a regular increase. This makes for cooperative rather than competitive relations between colleagues, and it encourages team-work. It also promotes long-term commitments. It is only by staying with the same employer for the long haul, and by collecting one increment after another, that one's hard work eventually pays off. To switch jobs is regarded not only as disloyal but as foolish since it takes one back to the bottom of the seniority ladder.

Employees are further protected by the way in which workplaces are organized. The building blocks of Japanese corporations are small hierarchical teams made up of leaders, referred to as *oyakata* – literally, he who plays the 'part of the parent' – and subordinates, referred to as *kokata* – he who plays the 'part of the child'.[11] As this terminology indicates, the relationship between superiors and inferiors is not contractual as much as personal. The *oyakata* is expected to show parental care and affection for the *kokata*, and the *kokata* is expected to be unswervingly loyal and to work hard. Rather than the boss bossing his underlings around, the *oyakata*'s task is to make people work with a minimum of explicit policing. Interestingly, whereas people in Europe and North America tend to resent a boss who takes too much interest in their work and complain about 'interference' and 'nosiness', people in Japan are likely to welcome the same interest as a sign of the superior's appreciation of their efforts.

At the same time, since the relationship between *oyakata* and *kokata* is fixed, both parties must be as flexible as possible in dealing with one another. The *oyakata* must be sensitive to the concerns of the people working under him, and the *kokata* must be prepared to carry out whatever tasks the *oyakata* identifies. This is why positions in Japanese companies usually lack explicit job descriptions.[12] Employees are employed not to for any particular duties but instead for whatever assignments the company gives them. For the company this has the obvious advantage that people can be shifted around to posts where their services happen to be required. For the individual the same vagueness provides plenty of opportunities for improvisation and independent initiative, and it makes supervision less intrusive.[13] Working with a variety of tasks also makes it possible to obtain a better understanding of the various stages of the production process. As a result, to work in a Japanese factory is likely to be less alienating.

Japanese employees also seem to be both more trusted and more responsible than their European counterparts. Often they are given the task of guaranteeing the quality of the products they make, and this provides every employee with a personal stake in the manufacturing process. In many highly automated factories every employee has the power to stop the production process if something goes wrong. There are certainly trade unions in Japan too and the vast majority of employees are members, but unions are company-based and for that reason more similar to the 'yellow' unions so intensely hated by workers in Europe and North America. Unions are part of the structure of the corporation; they are a way to make sure that the interests of employees are adequately represented. Unions would therefore never do anything that might actually harm the company. Although strikes and demonstrations might occur, they are usually restricted to, say, the lunch break.[14]

In addition, Japanese companies provide their employees with a rich social environment.[15] In order to build a collective spirit and to make work a pleasant place to be, plenty of time is set aside for social activities both during and after official working hours. Collective callisthenics and the singing of company songs may look like examples of lingering military-style regimentation, but the spirit is collegial rather than disciplinarian. There are also few marks of hierarchy between various categories of workers. Everyone dresses in the same uniform and everyone eats together in the same canteen. After work colleagues often get together to drink, sing in karaoke bars or play *mahjang*.[16] In fact, after-hours drinking sessions are strongly promoted by the *oyakata* since they are thought to build more cohesive teams. A bar-based relationship forged over endless glasses of *o-sake* is seen as more solid than an office-based relationship forged over endless cups of green tea. For each *sarariiman* this emphasis on socializing means that there always are people around who know him and care about his well-being. And thanks to lifetime employment, the time horizon which colleagues share extends far into the future.

To this should be added a number of company-based welfare programmes of a more specific nature.[17] Until state-organized welfare provisions were improved in the 1980s, it was Japanese corporations that provided child allowances, housing subsidies, savings plans and retirement benefits. And companies are still heavily involved in these schemes. There are often also company-owned housing estates on which employees can live, and nurseries and schools to which they can send their children. Vacations are short in Japan – at most two weeks a year, and out of loyalty to the company many prefer not to take them – but when on vacation, a person may often spend time on company trips or in company-owned holiday camps or resorts. Even a person's love-life is considered a corporate concern, and employees are often encouraged to restrict their dating to approved in-house partners. Weddings, blessed by the boss, are celebrated in company-spon-sored ceremonies, just as funerals take place in company-sponsored coffins.

The ultimate aim of all these programmes is to make sure that as much as possible of a person's life is controlled by the company rather than by outside institutions.[18] In this way a strong sense of commitment is fostered among employees. Non-company-based activities soon become insignifi-cant in comparison, not least because work, commuting and socializing take up just about all of the employees' time. In this way people are provided not only with an income, and a social life, but also with a company-based identity. Someone working for Kajima Kensetsu becomes a 'Kajima Kensetsu man', and this identity is constantly reaffirmed through interac-tion with other Kajima Kensetsu men.

An alternative social setting which suffers is the home. The home is a place to which the *sarariiman*-cum-father makes only occasional, and all-brief, visits.[19] From a European or North American perspective this may seem perverse, since the home in these societies is identified as the setting in which a person's most important and most authentic relationships are formed. As a Japanese *sarariiman* might explain, however, there is no reason why meaningful relationships and authenticity cannot be found also in an office. The company is the centre of a *sarariiman*'s life and not just another way to earn a living.[20] This is his true home, as it were, and for him the family dwelling is mainly the logistical arrangement which makes the real-ization of working life possible.

Yet there is plenty of evidence that Japanese employees are unhappy both with this way of life and this way of working, and discontent has been growing in recent decades. Comparisons between Japan and Europe and North America consistently show that Japanese employees are considerably better motivated for their work, but also that they are far more dissatisfied with it.[21] They know only too well that they are exploited by their employ-ers and that they sell their time and their efforts far too cheaply. Yet this is a form of exploitation that resembles more the exploitation that takes place in families than in workplaces, and as such it goes perfectly well together with protection against market forces. Indeed, if a person's identity is sufficiently closely linked to his or her identity as an employee, it can even be portrayed as a form of self-exploitation. The employees themselves may even come to believe that this is the case.

It must also be remembered that protection against market forces is limited to people on full-time employment. This means that virtually all women are excluded, since women are still supposed to work only until the birth of the first child and after that to be content with life as a mother and housewife – and when the children grow bigger perhaps work part-time.[22] It also excludes all who work on temporary contracts, such as students and day-labourers. These categories of workers are hired and fired as the business cycles require; they have few or none of the privileges of regular full-time employees, and their wages are set in relation to changes in the supply and demand of labour. They are the shock absorbers of the Japanese economy.[23]

The *Ie*

The many unique features of the Japanese employment system are often blamed on Japanese culture. The employment system is so peculiar, the argument goes, since Japanese culture is so peculiar. This was the premise of much of the 'learn from Japan' literature that proliferated in the 1980s.[24] What this conclusion ignores, however, is that the Japanese employment system has varied quite considerably over the course of the years. It was not always all that exotic. What also is ignored is the fact that Japanese business leaders learned many of their techniques from their study of European and North American models. In the 1880s there was an all-out attempt to 'become like the West', and this was repeated in the 1950s when Japanese mangers diligently studied foreign business practices.[25] The question remains why the country ended up with the particular system it has.

To begin with, the features that look most distinctly Japanese are probably those we referred to above, notably the respective roles associated with the *oyakata* and the *kokata*. As the terminology indicates, these relationships are explicitly modelled on those of the Japanese family. In pre-Meiji Japan, just as in imperial China, the family was the basic building-block of social life, and the family unit was always far more important than the individuals it comprised.[26] Yet the Japanese family differed from the Chinese in a number of crucial respects. Above all, it was not only made up of kin but included any other person who happened to live under its roof – servants, apprentices and charity cases. The relevant unit was not the *dozoku*, the biological unit, but rather the *ie*, the 'house'.[27]

The *ie* was a corporate rather than a familial term, and although it usually relied on procreation for its propagation, this was not always the case.[28] In situations where there was no son, a daughter might instead take a husband who would then adopt the family's surname. Where a couple had no children at all, the *ie* might even adopt a married couple and change their names in order to assure the continuation of the house. At the same time the *ie* was a profoundly patriarchal institution. The vertical relationship between parent and child mattered far more than the horizontal relationships between parents or between children. What was required of a child was above all obedience and loyalty, and for his part the father was supposed to show benevolence to the people subject to him. This was not an oppressive relationship – as often had been the case in China – but in theory at least a nurturing and caring one. Japanese paternalism, one could say, was strikingly maternal.[29] Moreover, the father was subject to the collective authority of the house; property, for example, was not owned individually by him, but collectively by the whole *ie*.

With the commercialization of society in the course of the eighteenth century this traditional set-up began to change.[30] A new entrepreneurial ethos emerged in cities like Edo and Osaka, and as people moved in order to capitalize on the new opportunities, Japan became increasingly urbanized. The custom of primogeniture meant that whatever property a family owned was inherited by the oldest son, and for that reason it was usually only the younger siblings – the surplus population, as it were – who left for the city, leaving the number of rural households intact. Once they arrived in the city these migrants typically associated themselves with social settings which strongly resembled the ones they had left behind. In the city too there were plenty of *ie*-like organizations – sometimes known as *iemoto* groups – headed by patriarchal figures who expected loyalty from their members in return for benevolence and paternal care.[31]

The system was particularly useful for merchants who in this way could expand their family businesses even when they did not have enough children of their own.[32] This was also how craftsmen organized their workshops. Young apprentices would be taken in, asked to prove their dedication to the master, and made fully-fledged members of the household. Much the same can be said of troupes of *kabuki* actors or *o-sumo* wrestlers.[33] In all cases the master was referred to as *oyakata* and the subordinates referred to as *kokata*.[34]

In this way it might seem that the social organization of the *ie* was simply transferred onto the modern business corporation. This, however, was not the case. On the contrary, once industrialization was under way in the Meiji period, these traditional protective arrangements came under severe strain.[35] As one of the employers' organizations, Daisankai Noshoko Koto Kaigi, asked rhetorically, 'Can one talk of a family relationship between employer and employee when they don't even know each other by sight?'[36] From the 1890s onward, the country erupted in wildcat strikes and acts of sabotage, and many workers simply downed tools and ran away.[37] Employers did not hesitate to crack down on such activities with the help of the police or by hiring their own thugs. Far from a picture of harmony and cooperation, the Japanese labour market at the turn of the twentieth century was in a state of constant turmoil.[38] The question was what to do.

As government officials suggested, the kind of benevolent paternalism that English factory owners displayed towards their workers did not come naturally to the Japanese.[39] Such attitudes would instead have to be imported from abroad together with the new technology.

This was when the social organization of the *ie* was updated to suit the contemporary needs of the employers. The solution was basically to stop thinking of a company as consisting of thousands of employees, and instead to break it down into much smaller teams of workers which themselves could be organized according to *ie*-like principles.[40] The leader of such small company teams was the de facto employer as far as the ordinary workers were concerned; he was the *oyakata* while his team of workers were the *kokata*.[41] Once broken down to a more manageable size, factory labour became less intimidating and impersonal. A worker took pride in belonging to the circle of a respected *oyakata*, and the *oyakata* looked out for the *kokata* and made sure that they got preferential treatment, better tasks to perform and higher pay.

This solution worked in the sense that it helped reduced the number of strikes. Yet it was not a traditional solution handed down to the present from an immemorial past. It was not traditional but neo-traditional, not paternalistic but neo-paternalistic, and it came to be recognized as 'the Japanese employment system' only as a result of the active propaganda put out by the employers' organizations. Employers had to be convinced that it was a feasible way to go.[42] More than anything this points to the powerlessness of Japanese workers. Only after the fact could the system be presented as inevitable and as inextricably Japanese. It is indeed a perfectly Japanese solution, but also a profoundly political one.

A Contrasting Case: American Corporations

For a different perspective on the Japanese employment system, briefly consider the way corporations have been organized in the United States. Today, American companies take themselves to be very good friends of market forces, and this is often a source of considerable pride. There is a self-congratulatory machismo to this pro-market rhetoric where Americans compare themselves favourably above all with their European, and allegedly far more effeminate, counterparts.[43] The current ideal is a corporation that has very few core competencies. Most services are instead contracted for as they are required; people are hired and fired in synch with fluctuations of the market. Corporations are supposed to be small, with few administrative overheads, few bosses and employees. Or differently put, corporations provide no job security, no benefits, no job-training and no social life.[44] Corporations such as these could never serve as a protective arrangement.

This understanding of the nature of American capitalism is reinforced through an analysis of the first corporations that appeared in the latter half of the nineteenth century. They too embraced the same *laissez-faire* rhetoric and sported the same lean and mean structures.[45] Even companies that were later to become very large indeed were at the time skeletal structures organized around the vision of individual venture capitalists. The core task was to arrange financing of the business ventures, and most other tasks were farmed out to subcontractors. The advantages of this set-up for the company were obvious. There was for example no need to build, own and service any expensive machinery, and there was no need to take on the responsibility for, or to train, a large and possibly unruly labour force. The precursor of General Motors is a good example of this logic.[46] The Durant-Dort Carriage Company was strictly a marketing outfit which slapped its own labels on carriages produced by a wide range of local constructors.

Gradually, however, as the factory system came to be more thoroughly established, Americans companies moved away from this market-based model. The company founded by Henry Ford is the classic example. Conspicuously different from the precursor of GM, it moved all its activities in-house. In Ford's plant in Highland Park, various pieces of metal and cowhide went in through one door and brand new automobiles rolled out through the other. And Fordism, as the system came to be known, became the model for others to follow.[47] The new ideal was the vast multi-divisional corporation in which an enormous staff engaged in a large number of diverse activities.[48] Characteristically, ordinary Americans were often intensely proud of these corporate behemoths too. The way they constantly grew in size and power made them into the perfect symbols of the potency of US-style capitalism. The fact that each corporation in its internal operations was more like a centrally planned economy than a market was not something anyone worried much about.

Yet centrally planned economies can under certain conditions be more efficient than markets. This is above all the case where markets are costly and cumbersome to organize.[49] And this was very much the case in early twentieth-century America. The reason for the spectacular growth of US corporations was that they required more control over the inputs into the production process, and especially more control over labour.[50] Just as in Japan the supply of labour was far too erratic, especially at times of low unemployment. Besides, people were not used to working in factories, and given the rapid transformation of American society they often had many, and more attractive, alternatives open to them. High turnover rates of labour produced bottlenecks, and poorly motivated workers produced shoddy goods. It was in order to get around such difficulties that more and more of the manufacturing process was moved in-house.

Instead of being lean and mean, American businesses grew not only flabby but also increasingly generous. The decades from the early 1930s into the 1960s and 1970s was the era of the 'good corporation' – the corporation understood as a friend of the people who worked for it and of the communities in which it operated. In the good corporation a psychological contract was concluded between employers and employees.[51] The company committed itself to the well-being of its workers and the workers committed themselves to the well-being of the company. Here jobs were secure and employees were to a large extent protected from market pressure.[52] Pay, for example, depended more on a person's job-title than on his or her individual performance; positions were filled through internal labour markets and promotions happened largely on the basis of seniority. In this way risks were minimized and predictability assured. Employees could take out mortgages and plan the education of their children based on a clear understanding of what the future would hold.[53] The company became the guarantor of the stability of the social world of its employees, and it engaged in a large number of community-building and charitable activities.

The outcome was an American corporation which in several respects resembled the Japanese. To work at Ford, General Electric or Goodyear in the 1960s was not all that different from working at Toyota, Matsushita Denki or Bridgestone, at least if you were a white-collar worker. In the United States too, metaphors describing the company as a 'family' and 'a home' were constantly invoked by management and there was a real sense in which employees felt protected by their employers. In fact, at the time prominent sociologists worried about these trends.[54] American workers were perceived as 'organization men', people with a complete dedication to their jobs but with little sense of personal initiative. From being a nation of independent-minded entrepreneurs, Americans had somehow transformed themselves into a nation of collectivistic bureaucrats.[55]

What a comparison with the United States tells us is consequently how many features of the Japanese employment system that can be, and have been, replicated elsewhere. Instead of being the innate effect of purely cultural variables, corporations organize themselves and their relations to their workforce as a rational response to imperfections in the market. The gigantic everything-under-one-roof corporation solved problems which the market itself could not solve, and like all extra-market institutions it soon came to provide protection against market forces.

And yet it is clear that a considerable cultural residual remains. Although Japanese and American corporations reacted to the same imperatives, the reactions were formulated in quite distinct ways. There is, for example, hardly any doubt that the prominent sociologists were exaggerating. American workers, particularly blue-collar workers, were never as passive and collective-minded as was suggested, and few of them actually believed the talk of the company as a family or a home. To most US employees, even in the 1950s, work was just a contractual relationship.[56] Most employees, for example, went promptly home at five to spend time with adoring children and devoted wives.

And there is cultural residual also in the case of Japan. Although market imperfections may have constituted the initial impetus for the construction of the Japanese employment system, it still displayed many distinctive traits. This is true *inter alia* of the relationship between *oyakata* and *kokata*, the social censure of those who change jobs, the obvious loyalty which employees feel to their workplaces, and the 'maternal paternalism' of the employers, not to mention the discrimination against female and part-time workers. These features, and others like them, were present also in agrarian Japan, although they originally were attached to quite different entities.[57]

7

Personal Thais, and How They Survived the Boom

Between 1984 and 1994 Thailand was the country with the highest economic growth rate in the world – around 10 per cent annually.[1] These were the years of the boom when Thailand was industrializing, urbanizing and modernizing at an astonishing speed. Asphalt was poured over rice paddies and concrete over tropical beaches; foreign companies located their assembly plants here, and international banks and hoteliers built skyscrapers. Pollution increased, occupational safety standards slipped, and new disparities in wealth made Thailand one of the most inegalitarian countries in the world.[2]

The old pre-boom Thailand had been a far more quiet and more predictable place.[3] It was a country of peasants run by a series of authoritarian, if never actually repressive, military regimes in cahoots with a small class of Chinese businessmen and a large class of hidebound civil servants. With close to 90 per cent of the population living in the countryside, farming completely dominated economic and social life. Agriculture was commercialized late, and in remote parts of the country such as the north-eastern region of Isaan subsistence farming lasted well into the 1960s. In the pre-boom years there was little in the way of manufacturing industry and no working-class. In fact, apart from the capital, there were not even any genuine cities.

Changes which in other countries took centuries to accomplish were thus in the case of Thailand dramatically compressed. In the span of a few short decades former subsistence farmers were exposed to the full force of global capitalism. The question is what happens to a society that is forced to change this quickly and this irrevocably. How can people maintain a sense of who they are, and how can the fabric of social life be preserved? The answer in the case of Thailand, as in the case of all societies, is necessarily complex. In the end individuals and groups employ all kinds of different strategies. What made a great difference in the case of Thailand, however, is the structure of the traditional agricultural village and the personal networks which people had formed there.[4] These networks constituted the social grammar which the villagers brought with them as they migrated to the rapidly expanding cities.

The Thai Village

Before the 1960s Thailand was predominantly rural, Thais were predominantly peasants, and many of them had little or nothing to do with the money economy.[5] Until 1905, instead of paying their taxes in ready cash, people worked as corvée labourers for up to half the year on the land of the feudal lords.[6] Since labour could be extracted by force, there was little need for a labour market. Neither was there a market in land, but the reason was primarily that land was so extraordinarily plentiful.[7] Before agriculture was thoroughly commercialized in the 1960s, there was far more land than anyone ever needed, and for that reason it had no proper price. There was always more virgin forest to be cut down and fields to be cleared further north and further east.

However, traditional village life was quite different from romantic European notions of the 'Asian village'. It was not best described as a tightly-knit community in which everyone was helping everyone else out in times of need.[8] In many cases this was above all because the village was a rather badly defined unit. Often it was simply impossible to tell where one village ended and another village began, and who should be included as a member. Under such circumstances a strong sense of community was difficult to forge. In fact, it has often been argued that there were few social organizations of any kind in traditional Thai society, apart from the family and the monkhood. And even the family and the monkhood were in many ways surprisingly impermanent. Monastic vows were, for example, easily rescinded, and although a large proportion of young males spent time in a monastery, it was a rite of passage which only lasted a few months. Similarly, because land was plentiful, many young couples preferred to leave their parents and settle in a house of their own once they were married. Rural Thailand was matrilocal rather than patrilocal – couples moved in with the wife's family rather than the groom's – but often enough it was simply neolocal, meaning that the couple ended up living somewhere altogether new.[9]

The first American anthropologists who arrived in the country after World War II were quick to identify this as the 'loose' structure of Thai society.[10] As they concluded, the over-abundance of land and the constantly moving internal frontier had created – just as in their own country in the nineteenth century – a unique 'frontier spirit'. The Thais were constantly on the move, always breaking up and starting again somewhere else. As a result they never paid much attention to rights or duties, and they cared little for social discipline and regimentation.[11] Just like the rugged occupants of one of the most enduring of American myths, Thai farmers were perceived as committed individualists.

But if this is individualism, it is an individualism that allows surprisingly little space for individuals. In contrast to the situation in Europe and North America, individual members of Thai society were not expected to make it on their own. The traditional Thai conception of the person was relational rather than atomistic; people defined themselves in relation to others rather than as independent units sufficient unto themselves.[12] Hence the importance of gifts and gift-giving, the obsession with saving or losing 'face', and the acute sense of hierarchy that characterizes most social interactions.[13] Consider too the extraordinarily detailed vocabulary which the Thai language provides for describing relations of kinship.[14] In a society where unique labels are given to maternal and paternal cousins, or to a father's oldest and youngest brothers, families can surely not be completely unimportant.

The puzzle is how to combine the 'looseness' of the social structure with this obvious attention to social relationships. A solution can be found by looking at the way in which Thai farmers dealt with problems of collective action. Since rice farming is highly labour-intensive at particular times during the year, farmers always need additional help. And yet, in the case of Thailand, the exit options created by the moving frontier meant that it was difficult to coerce or cajole people into helping each other out. Since membership of the village was fluid, commitments were not credible. A similar logic applied within families, although parents tried their best to instil cooperative values in their children.[15] Daughters, in particular, were expected to be on hand and support their parents. As a way to elicit their cooperation, the youngest, stay-at-home, daughter would typically get to inherit the family farm. And yet the availability of land meant that young couples could often afford to ignore their obligations.

This is not to say that people were left entirely to their own devices. Although few formal labour-sharing schemes existed, farmers relied heavily on informal ones.[16] The best example was a person's network of friends. His personal friends were the people a farmer knew he could depend on, and making and holding on to friends thus became a matter of utmost importance. This explains the great value attached to friendships in agrarian Thai society and the constant socializing that characterizes all interpersonal interaction.[17] It explains the importance of late-night drinking sessions, of music and recurring feasts, as well as the particular Thai obsession with everything that is *sanuk*, or 'fun'.

Expressed more schematically, Thai society was not so much atomistic and individualized as organized in informal relationships formed by social dyads, or pairs of individuals.[18] Everywhere in Thai society there are such pairs, and they are usually hierarchically ordered. In traditional Thailand there were *phrai*, 'freemen', and *nai*, 'masters', and in contemporary society there are patrons surrounding themselves by numerous clients.[19] Families too divide into pairs since the vertical relationships between fathers and sons, or mothers and daughters, are considered more important than the horizontal relationships between spouses or siblings. Much the same is true of friends who, despite their bonds of affection, are rarely completely equal. Such hierarchical pairs – and not individuals taken by themselves – are the true building blocks of Thai society. Individuals mean little, in short, before they are paired-up.

Redefined in this manner, traditional Thai society can be seen at the same time as fluid and as profoundly relational. Although individuals always belong to a social pairing, the pairs never form a single social structure but instead many mini-structures with unclear relationships between them. Instead of forming horizontal organizations with large numbers of individual members as in Europe, the dyads form vertical, but at the same time rather poorly integrated, networks. Social hierarchies are informal, temporary, and perceived in different ways by different people.[20]

However, it is clear that there always have been considerable regional variations in this grammar. What has been said thus far pertains above all to villages in the Chao Phraya river basin in central Thailand. It was here that the problems of collective action were the most acute.[21] In northern and northeastern parts of the country, different rules often applied. Here villages were better defined, but also more isolated and more exposed to the vagaries of nature – and people for that reason were far more dependent on each other. One particularly strong bond was religion, but not the official Buddhism of the Thai state as much as traditional and semi-animist folk beliefs.[22] In Isaan each village had its own guardian spirit, and as a member of the village each person had to make sure that the spirit was kept in a benevolent mood. In this way a spiritual community was created which brought people closer together in other ways too – through communal feasting and merrymaking but also in common enterprises and labour-sharing schemes.[23]

These were consequently the traditional patterns of social interaction as they existed at the time when farming was commercialized. And as for commercialization, a first thing to notice is how uneven the process was. In Thailand domestic markets were always limited in scope. Although there had been trade between Europe and Siam as early as in the seventeenth century, it involved only a few select luxury items.[24] When trade expanded following the conclusion of the Bowring Treaty of 1866, it still concerned only a few key commodities produced mainly in central and southern Thailand.[25] Only in the 1960s did farmers throughout the country really begin producing for the market rather than for themselves. The impetus here was not purely economic. At the time of the Vietnam War, the United States constructed military bases in the jungles of eastern Thailand, and with the bases came roads which opened up the hinterland to commercial opportunities.[26]

This reorientation had a number of far-reaching consequences. First and most fundamentally it meant that land was transformed from an abundant into a scarce resource. When the peasants began producing for the market rather than for themselves, more land was always needed, and before long they started cutting down the jungle in order to enlarge their fields.[27] In this way agricultural land expanded dramatically until the 1980s when there was suddenly no more forest to fell. In 1988 logging, and with it the clearing of new fields, was finally banned by the government.[28] Greeted as a victory for the rainforest by environmental activists around the world, the decision also put an end to a traditional way of life. The social exit option was now closed. There was suddenly nowhere new for people – for newly-weds or others – to go.

At the same time as a market was created in land, a market was created in labour.[29] The people who worked the new fields were increasingly agricultural labourers, hired to carry out a specified job and paid in ready cash. The majority of them were without, or with far too little, land of their own, or they were heavily in debt. In this way the commercialization of agriculture led to a polarization of social conditions in the villages. People with access to land and credit could make good money for themselves, while people without such access were forced to sell their labour in an uncertain labour market. The result was an emiseration and social degradation of the new agricultural working class. Not surprisingly, many of them were highly susceptible to the propaganda of the Thai Communist Party.[30] At the height of its power the Communist guerrillas had up to 5,000 men under arms, and they were active in 34 of Thailand's 72 provinces.

The new commercial environment also put pressure on the traditional labour-sharing schemes.[31] Since work was now undertaken for profit rather than for subsistence, time could be measured in terms of money and not even good friends could be expected to volunteer their labour for free. In central parts of the country this led to a further dissolution of the already loose communal bonds.[32] In northern and north-eastern parts, however, commercialization seems to have had the opposite effect, and cooperative labour exchanges became more, rather than less, common. What made the difference here was the type of village community that preceded commercialization. From the 1960s onward, traditional labour-sharing schemes were put on a more commercial footing. Villagers increasingly established savings and funeral cooperatives as well as rice banks from which members could borrow in times of need.[33] The guardian spirit of the village who had previously protected the people from wild animals and diseases now protected them from the onslaught of commercialization.

For similar reasons the family unit was often strengthened rather than weakened.[34] Once land became scarce and expensive, newlyweds had fewer opportunities to start life together in a new location. The incentive was rather to stay with the parents and the in-laws and to help out on the family farm. It was only in this way that young couples could hope one day to inherit and thereby to make themselves independent. This provided a particular incentive for daughters, since the prospect of inheriting the family farm allowed them access to assets that now had a genuine market value for the first time.

The Years of the Boom

Another coping strategy for the rural poor was to go off and look for new opportunities in the cities. Indeed, from the 1980s onward the new opportunities that were appearing in urban areas seemed roughly proportionate to the old opportunities that were disappearing in the countryside. More than anywhere else it was to Bangkok that everyone wanted to go – and when everyone suddenly did, the city started growing at a phenomenal pace.[35] From 1 million people in 1947, the capital expanded to more than 6.3 million 50 years later, with an additional 3 million people in the greater metropolitan area. Before long the capital had become a sprawling, chaotic megalopolis famous above all for its traffic jams, its glistening high-rise buildings and its colourful slums.[36] 'Bangkok is not place to live,' as its governor Bhichit Rattakul put it in 1997. 'There are fumes, disasters, accidents, uncollected garbage, uncontrolled goods in the supermarkets.... This is a jungle, an unorganized place.'[37]

As the predominant centre of commerce and industry, not to mention consumption and entertainment, Bangkok is the generally recognized symbol of modernity and of a *thamsamai*, 'up-to-date', lifestyle.[38] Although Bangkokians have always been better off, the relative advantage of the capital increased markedly during the years of the boom. The difference between the capital and the provinces in the north and the north-east, from which a majority of the migrants come, is particularly striking. Pushed by unemployment and pulled by expectations of high wages and modernity, former rice farmers soon queued up to do any number of odd jobs. Today, some work in factories and on construction sites; others have become maids and nannies; many young men drive taxis and tuk-tuks and many young women are go-go dancers and masseuses in the capital's rapidly proliferating red-light districts.[39]

As a matter of logistics, the question is how all these millions of bodies could be moved from the countryside and slotted into the rudimentary social infrastructure of the metropolis. As a personal problem, the question is who a recent arrival in the city might rely on for emotional and material support. The answer to both questions is basically that the vast majority of migrants rely on their traditional social networks of neighbours, relatives and friends. Although the migrants may leave their villages alone, they nearly always go to someone in the city they know beforehand.[40] This contact is the person who sets them up, lends them money, and finds them a job and a place to stay. In this way, instead of simply breaking social ties, migration often ends up reaffirming them.

The move to the city has also been facilitated by the fact that the migrants have brought such a lot of their rural lives with them. By the middle of the 1980s the culture of the countryside had established a visible presence everywhere throughout the capital. Street-hawkers were selling the hot food of Isaan – *som tam*, papaya salad, and *khao niaow*, sticky rice – and radio stations on the prestigious FM band were playing *phlaeng luk thung*, Thai-style country-and-western music.[41] Additional protection was provided by the small shrines, known as *sampapoom* or 'spirit houses', that occupy every empty plot of land throughout the city, and to which even busy office workers bring flowers, food and incense during their lunch breaks.[42] The guardian spirits and are now looking after the villagers while they seek their fortune far away from home.

It is striking how even born-and-bred Bangkokians seem to enjoy the new rural fads, although a majority of them strictly speaking are of Chinese rather than Thai descent.[43] Eating the food and listening to the music, everyone is able to reconnect with their real or their imaginary roots. The fact that the rural culture is commercially available only makes it more appealing; it is a commodified lifestyle which urbanites can consume without actually having to give up any of their modern conveniences. The need for rural roots seems to have been particularly pressing in the aftermath of the financial crisis of 1997, when nostalgia for the simple life suddenly overcame a large proportion of the urban population.[44] For example, Thai newspapers were inundated with stories of elephants, a wise and friendly animal and a powerful symbol of the traditional way of life.

But there were many other ways of coping. A belief in the protective powers of amulets has always been a part of popular Buddhism, and prominent monks have often been active participants in the vigorous commerce that surrounds them.[45] During the boom years, as well as in the subsequent bust, this trade gathered unprecedented momentum. When the economy was growing, everyone sought to assure themselves of success, and when the economy was contracting, everyone sought protection against disaster. New 'prosperity religions', based on Daoist beliefs common among families of Chinese descent, benefited from the same anxieties, as did various charismatic Buddhist movements which flourished in particular among members of the middle class.[46] In addition, a new cult emerged centred on King Rama V, king Chulalongkorn, who modernized the country in the nineteenth century and preserved its independence in the face of European imperialism.[47] In 1990 people began gathering around the king's equestrian statue in the centre of Bangkok making offerings of flowers, candles and the Scotch whisky he is said to have favoured. By the middle of the decade these meetings were held two evenings a week.

The true secret of survival in Bangkok, however, is that most of the migrants never plan to stay all that long. At least in their own minds they are not settlers but sojourners.[48] Just like the workers who migrated from China in the nineteenth century, they have been forced to leave their homes in search of work. In the city the sojourners are outsiders and spectators and they have only a physical and not a social presence. But more often than not, this is precisely as they want it to be. They take whatever work they can find, and if the job is risky and dirty, all the better, as long as the pay is correspondingly higher. The more money they can make, the sooner they can return to where their real lives are – back home in the village.

In Thailand the most obvious sojourners of this kind are the hundreds of thousands of people who synchronize their migration to coincide with the seasons of the agricultural calendar.[49] Rice farming is a labour-intensive occupation during the planting and harvesting seasons, but at other times many peasants are free to go off to the city to work for a cash wage. In the boom years such temporary migration increased dramatically. It seems clear – although exact figures are difficult to establish – that most migrants are young and single, and a majority are female.[50] Many such seasonal workers become cab-drivers or construction workers, and many women end up as domestic servants or in the sex industry.

This is consequently how the Thais survived capitalism. By moving back and forth between two separate worlds organized according to two different logics, they are able to reap the benefits of both. The migrants are able to cope with the city since they only have to stay there for a couple of months at a time.[51] In the city they are commodified, but taking on the temporary role of sojourner, they accept this fact. They do not pretend to belong to Bangkok and they do not look for recognition from the people who live there. Hence commodification results in no loss of prestige or standing. On the contrary, prestige and standing accumulate at the same rate as their savings, and the day is constantly coming closer when they can go back home and cash in. At the same time, migration is not only a way to make money but also a way of preserving social relationships – people are separated, but by means of seasonal migration they are reunited again. When the dyadic partner arrives in Bangkok, the pair once more live and work together. In this way the social units remain intact despite the social turmoil that takes place around them.

If this is how the Thais survived the years of the economic boom, it is also how they survived the subsequent bust.[52] After the financial crisis of 1997, while the true Bangkokians were harking back to their imaginary memories of rural life, the cab-drivers and nannies just went home to the rice fields. Back on the farm there would always be something for them to do and something for them to eat. That is why there was little unemployment as a result of the crisis, and seemingly little social dislocation.[53] In this way, however, the problems produced in the city were simply transferred back to the countryside.[54] More migrants were returning and fewer migrants were leaving, so there were more mouths to feed and fewer remittances to collect. In the end it was the Thai peasants who absorbed the shocks caused by the global financial market.

Commidified Labour

The most striking example of the commodification of labour is surely the many girls from rural backgrounds who find work in the flourishing sex industry. The exact number of prostitutes is difficult to estimate due to the nature of their work, but the most commonly cited numbers are between 80,000 and 150,000.[55] Among them a majority are recent arrivals in the city – many are temporary migrants, and they are almost exclusively from the north and the north-east.[56] It is poverty that compels the girls to go to

Bangkok, although a small percentage are forced into prostitution or even sold to pimps and brothels by their parents. Work in the sex industry is far better remunerated than any other job a country girl might hope to get, and many prostitutes make far more money than their clients. In a high-class massage parlour a woman can take home as much as 35,000 baht per month, whereas in a factory she would make only about 1500 baht. A reasonably well-paid prostitute makes as much money as a newly graduated university lecturer.[57]

Reports on the sex industry – full of moral outrage yet at the same time quite deliberately titillating – probably represent the most common images of Thailand to be found in foreign media.[58] The standard explanation given in the voice-overs is that the girls in the pictures are the innocent victims of a domestic culture that is chauvinistic and exploitative, together with an international culture of tourism that promotes the commodification of sex. Many urban Thais for their part are more inclined to view prostitution as a nefarious consequence of modernization and as a sign of decadent foreign influences. In traditional Thai society, they like to believe, Thai women were chaste and incorruptible.

Some of these views are simply inaccurate. It is not true, for example, that prostitution is a problem brought on by foreigners.[59] The part of the sex industry most visible to foreign media – the go-go bars in the red-light districts of Bangkok and the major beach resorts – may be a foreign import, initially created to service American visitors from the Vietnam War. Yet Thai men have long sought the services of 'consort women' and 'second wives', and today perhaps as much as 95 per cent of the prostitution is Thai-on-Thai rather than Thai-on-foreigner.[60] At the same time it is clear that the process of modernization has changed the nature of this traditional trade. The pattern of seasonal migration has created a vast new demand for sexual services, and the emiseration of many families in the countryside has meant that they lack alternative sources of income.[61] Previously, prostitution was mainly an urban phenomenon, but with the rapid growth of the cities the trade has grown in equal proportion. It used above all to feature girls of Chinese descent, often smuggled into the country, but now although foreign girls are involved – still commonly Chinese, but also Burmese and Laotian – the far larger proportion are rural Thais.[62]

Yet there are also quite different ways to understand Thai prostitution. One is to see the women as entrepreneurs and as agents of their own fate rather than as passive victims of outside forces.[63] They might not like what they do, this argument goes, but given the options available to them, their choices are nevertheless rational. They make good money in an industry that is more glamorous than factory work and more *thamsamai* than a rice field. And they learn to deal with the degradation through the same strategies available to all sojourners. The girls go off to work in the big city, but not to settle there or to assimilate. They are indeed commodified, but they survive socially and emotionally since they appear in the marketplace only as bodies. Although they are treated as objects by their customers, their real lives happen elsewhere.[64] When they go back home, their value as human beings is restored and they can walk through the village with their heads held high. In the villages there is little moral censure of prostitution even though it accords spectacularly badly with traditional sexual mores.[65] The women have made money, and this fact alone will stop the tongues from wagging.

Another reason why it is possible to cope is that prostitution serves to affirm traditional family values. In peasant society, we said, daughters were given a particular responsibility for supporting their parents, and in next to all cases this is what prostitutes do. As many as three quarters of all sex-workers reported that they regularly send money home – often half or more of their income.[66] Studies show that families with daughters in the sex industry are poorer than other families, but that they have more electric appliances and better clothes. In addition, the daughter's remittances often help cover family debts or pay for a sibling's education, a new house, additional paddy fields or the parents' medical bills. Being able to help out in these ways is a source of considerable pride to the women concerned.[67] Instead of undermining the traditional social code, therefore, their city jobs help strengthen it.

Just as in the case of male migrants, but even more starkly so, prostitutes move between worlds ruled by opposing logics – a commodified life in the city and a decommodified life back home. And just like their brothers and fathers, they help preserve traditional social ties through their migratory movements. It is rarely a coincidence, after all, in which particular brothel or go-go bar a woman ends up working.[68] In the vast majority of cases it is a friend or a family member who has introduced her to the job. Some 63 per cent of girls aged under sixteen are brought to the brothel by their parents, and in perhaps half of the cases a close relative – a sister or a cousin – is already working for the same employer.[69] From some villages in northern Thailand up to 70 per cent of all young girls end up in the sex industry, often working in the same establishments.[70]

None of this reduces the degree of commodification which the sex industry imposes, yet it goes a long way towards explaining how the girls cope with it. Once restored, the social bonds with family and villagers provide much-needed protection from the dehumanizing environment in which they work. Sisters and friends look out for each other and support each other in the face of aggression from customers, pimps and the police. They have moved out of the village, their line of business has changed, but they are still together, working alongside each other much as they would have done planting rice back in the village.

THE STATE

THE SLATE

8

Versions of the European State

The state is potentially our best ally when it comes to dealing with the problems that capitalism causes. The state is, at least in theory, tremendously powerful; nothing and no one can match the width and depth of its reach. According to a well-worn theory first enunciated in the Renaissance, the state is 'sovereign,' meaning that there is no authority above it – no emperors or popes – and no authority below it – no feudal lords or independent peasant communities – that can challenge its position. The state is, in Max Weber's famous definition, 'a human community that successfully claims the monopoly of the legitimate use of physical force within a given territory'.[1] The state can imprison people, expropriate their assets, send them to war to kill or to die, and it can do so legitimately. The question is whether there is a way to use this formidable entity to protect us against the impact of markets.

The state, in the European tradition, is not only tremendously powerful but also highly robust. It is made up not of individuals but of institutions, standardized procedures and regulatory frameworks. As such it always outlasts the people who happen to occupy its positions, and it is also highly resistant to attempts at reform. The state is somehow too large and too complex for anyone to properly control or manipulate. Moreover, the European state is sometime given what perhaps best is described as a transcendental status.[2] In addition to its concrete manifestations the state is thought to embody ideas and values which are nothing short of eternal. This is *la France éternelle*, the 'land of the free' of the United States' national anthem, or the Hegelian *Staat* guided by the cunning logic of the *Weltgeist*. And while we may reject the more grandiose among such claims, we all continue to see the state as the repository of inalienable values: 'democracy', 'liberty', 'justice', or some combination of similar notions, equally worthy and vague.

The question is who controls this awesome entity, and the answer during the last 200 years is that sovereignty is vested in the people. We are all citizens; all citizens are equal, and all citizens have the same right to have a say on, and influence over, state policy. It follows that the state must be impartial in its dealings with the people subject to it. The state is universal – it grants rights to everyone and treats everyone in the same manner. However, such evenhandedness is both a source of strength and a source of

weakness. It is by treating its subjects fairly that the state comes to be seen
as legitimate. But at the same time fairness is not always enough – we want
also to be treated differently from others, at least some of the time, and in
certain respects. We want to be recognized as individuals with identities
that are uniquely our own.[3] In the end the state cares more about 'the
people' than about the individual human beings of whom this collective
entity is composed.

Yet the reality was of course always quite different. No matter how often
the ideals of popular sovereignty, universality and fairness are invoked, the
state has always been made use of by particular people for particular ends.[4]
More than anything the state has been forced to make concessions to the
market in order to be able to finance its activities. Above all it has been
crucial to keep entrepreneurs and financiers happy, or investments – and
thereby economic growth – would suffer.[5] This fact has set very clear limits
to the ability of the state to function as a protective arrangement. Although the
state protects people by addressing the problems that markets create, the protection is not supposed to actually impede the interaction of market forces.

The *Rechtsstaat*

Since the seventeenth century at least, European states have presented themselves as founded on law. European states are *Rechtsstaaten*, constitutional
states.[6] In a constitutional state, authority is considered legitimate not
because it is blessed by god or by tradition but because it is exercised in
accordance with the requirements of law. The constitution stipulates how the
state machinery is to function, and what rights and obligations that belong to
the people subject to it.

The first constitutional documents appeared in Germanic parts of Europe
in the middle of the seventeenth century. The Swedish Regeringsform of
1634 is sometimes considered the first example, but similar texts were
simultaneously drawn up in various principalities around Germany and
elsewhere on the Continent.[7] Yet the rationale behind these texts had little
to do with liberal politics or with the 'rights of man', and instead everything
to do with the requirements of statecraft. According to the new science of
Cameralism or *Polizeiwissenschaft*, as taught in German universities, the goal
of politics was to assure that the army was strong, the subjects well fed, and
the state as well organized as possible.[8] The ideal was the efficient machine
or the smoothly running clockwork. In the words of Johann Heinrich
Gottlieb von Justi, Professor of Cameralist Studies at the Universities of
Vienna and Göttingen, writing in the 1760s:

> A well-constituted state must resemble a machine where all wheels
> and gears fit each other with the utmost precision; and the ruler
> must be the engineer, the first driving spring or the soul, ... that sets
> everything in motion.[9]

In order to make their societies run as smoothly as clockworks, rulers began issuing Polizei- or Landesordnungen, administrative ordinances, which stipulated in great detail how society should be organized and how people should live.[10] An important part of these edicts concerned economic activities – they regulated competition between towns and the countryside and sought to make sure that peasants remained on the land; they set prices and qualities of goods and determined wages for apprentices and yeomen; they made sure that inns, postal relays and roads were well maintained, that midwives were properly trained, that sewers were cleaned, and that chimneys were not only regularly swept but also of sufficient height.[11]

The state, in short, meddled in anything and everything. The imperatives were political and moral rather than economic, and before long all of society was overlaid with a dense web of regulation. As the Cameralists insisted, market forces must be controlled if society is to be well governed. This is the idea of the *Polizeistaat*, understood in its etymologically correct sense.[12] Before the nineteenth century the policing functions of society were always closely related to policy-making, and state administrators were understood to be both policemen and social workers. Indeed, through the ancient Greek *polis*, meaning 'political community', 'police' and 'policy' reveal themselves to have a common root. A *Polizeistaat*, in other words, is a state which cares deeply about the well-being of its subjects while at the same time controlling them for their own good. The state is 'like a well-intentioned genius', as the German politician and writer Günther Heinrich von Berg put it, who

> cleans the air that they breathe; secures the villages and holdings in which they dwell, and the streets along which they walk; protects the fields that they cultivate, secures their homes against fire and flood, and they themselves against illness, poverty, ignorance, superstition and immorality ... Its watchful eye is ubiquitous; its helping hand is ever-ready, and we are invisibly surrounded by its unceasing care.[13]

Von Berg's seven-volume work was compiled in 1802, and at the time Cameralism was still taught at major European universities. A few decades later, however, this understanding of the relationship between regulation and the market had been almost completely replaced by the new Anglo-Saxon science of economics.[14] Here regulation played an entirely different role. Instead of trying to control the outcomes markets produce, Adam Smith and his followers insisted that regulation should provide the institutional framework that markets need in order to regulate themselves. Above all, the state should make sure that people are in a position to pursue whatever activities they themselves choose – the constitution should safeguard the rights of individuals, and in particular their property rights.[15] By Smith's own time property rights were already well established, enshrined in the constitutional settlement of the Glorious Revolution of 1688. Since the greatest threat to property rights were said to come from the state – from its tendency to default on loans, to expropriate property and to raise taxes – the primary task of the constitution was to limit the state's power.[16]

This tradition was invoked in the next wave of constitution-making which took place in the latter half of the eighteenth century. The most celebrated texts here were the Constitution of the United States, 1787, and the French Déclaration des droits de l'homme et du citoyen, 1789.[17] Phrased in the vocabulary of the Enlightenment, the protection afforded to individuals was here expanded into virtual catalogues of rights. As these documents made clear, individuals have the right to the freedom of expression and assembly, the right to vote and the right to participate in the political and social lives of their communities. These rights belong to human beings by nature; they are inalienable and to be granted equally to everyone. Since everyone enjoys the same rights, everyone can make the same claims to human dignity; man, as Robespierre put it, 'should be made happy and free by means of laws'.[18]

In relation to markets these documents enshrined the obligation of each citizen to fend for him or herself. The system of privileges and guilds was abolished – we discussed this above – and with it the entire network of protective arrangements of the *ancien régime*. Yet this does not mean that the French revolutionaries were unconcerned about the social consequences of capitalism. Far from it. In 1797 they established a system of communal Bureaux de bienfaisance which was to provide food, charcoal and cash grants for the poor, and there was even talk of a universal right to public assistance.[19] However, the French state could never raise enough revenue to help more than a fraction of the needy, and before long the revolutionary wars devoured all extra resources. As for the constitutional documents, they were silent on the topic of poverty.[20] Although there were plenty of references to the intrusive character of the state, there were no references to the intrusive character of capitalism. In this narrow sense the constitutional documents provided no protection whatsoever against market forces.

Yet in a more general sense the constitutions were crucial. By recognizing every individual as a subject vested with rights, people were given a status that the state promised to uphold.[21] In this way the constitutional provisions, even while they remained above and beyond economics, set definite limits to what capitalism could legitimately do to a person. Whereas the market may treat us as commodities and as less than fully human, the constitution recognizes our humanity and defends it on our behalf. Once individuals were recognized in this manner, the case for protection against market forces was easily constructed. As subjects vested with rights, people were protected against degrading working conditions and unfair wages, and before long they demanded that the state intervene to help them. And while most governments, citing *laissez-faire* sensibilities, were initially more than reluctant to render such assistance, the logic of the demands was difficult to ignore. This was especially the case once the members of the working class had gained the right to vote.

In a series of legislative acts from the middle of the nineteenth century onwards, the status which the constitution had granted individuals was gradually extended to the sphere of work.[22] One set of legislation concerned the employment of vulnerable groups, like women and children, whose working hours were restricted and who were banned from particular kinds of work such as coal mining. Other legislation applied equally to all categories of workers and concerned a 10-hour working day, and later an 8-hour working day; the right to form trade unions was also gradually recognized. Further, if less momentous, legislation was enacted throughout the twentieth century, including the improvement of occupational safety standards, protection against unfair dismissals and the regulation of working hours and vacations. Obviously, such legal benevolence applies only to people in work; the unemployed and unemployable, housewives and old people, are not covered, nor are farmers and the self-employed.

The reaction on the part of the employers to this barrage of legislation was initially almost entirely negative. For them stricter laws translated into higher costs and lower profits. French industry, its representatives declared, was too diverse to be 'imprisoned in the vice of uniform, immutable legislative texts'.[23] And yet the new legislation was never actually anti-market. The question was always how markets should be regulated, not how they should be replaced by something else. And the protection provided by the constitutional state was in practice always fairly limited. Individuals were still required to go out and work in markets where outcomes were determined by the interplay of supply and demand. If anything, such regulation of working conditions helped make capitalism more acceptable, and as a result strengthened rather than weakened it. The more enlightened among the employers understood this point.

As the representatives of the working class saw it, there was a great discrepancy between the way people were treated by the law and the way they were treated by the market.[24] The question they asked was why the constitutional state never bothered to do more. In a way it seemed unable to make up its mind. While abstractly proclaiming that all individuals were equal, it refused to do anything about the very real inequalities that capitalism created. As both Liberals and Social Democrats concluded, constitutional protection may be a necessary first step, but it is surely not enough.[25]

The Nation-State

From the point of view of people displaced by the development of markets, the constitutional state was always a thoroughly abstract entity. The kinds of individuals the law recognizes us as has next to nothing to do with the kinds of persons we take ourselves to be. Our legal *persona* is a kind of ghost, an abstract caricature of who we really are. For this reason it is not surprising that the sense of community provided by the constitutional state was always far too weak. In a community based only on rights, the bond between people is primarily a negative one; we are united above all by our mutual desire to be left alone. Obviously, however, this is not the kind of entity that can command our allegiance.[26] The constitutional state, to paraphrase the German eighteenth-century philosopher Johann Gottfried Herder, is 'a hut for no-one'.[27]

In the course of the eighteenth century people increasingly came to insist on a richer notion of a community.[28] Or perhaps better put, politicians who promised to deliver a richer notion of a community found that people were ready to rally behind them. The American and the French revolutionaries were the first ones to be successful in this respect. In the French Revolution the machinery of the state was taken over by the representatives of the 'nation', and from this time onward France became a 'nation-state'.[29] That is, a state run not by the king and the aristocracy but instead by all citizens, meaning everyone prepared to regard themselves as an equal and as a brother of everyone else. In this way a radical distinction came to be drawn between citizens and non-citizens; the royalists and the 'counter-revolutionaries' were outsiders, non-nationals, and thereby legitimate targets of the terror meted out by *la nation française*.[30]

When combined with the nation in this way, the formal machinery of the state was given a new lease on life. As a young and ambitious generation of nationalist scholars and activists came to discover, the nation-state had a surprisingly long history and a rich culture, complete with national heroes, songs, customs, cuisines, music, a national language and a *Nationalökonomie*.[31] The state presented itself as custodian and curator of this heritage and derived a new sense of legitimacy from these roles. In order to publicize the glories of the nation, a slew of institutions were established – national museums and opera houses, academies, ethnographic and archaeological societies. The fact that much of this cultural paraphernalia was invented rather than inherited from a time-honoured past did not seem to matter.[32] The important thing was that the inventions were accepted, and overwhelmingly they were. Throughout the nineteenth century, in places where nations had not previously existed, they were quickly created.[33]

At the same time there is no doubt that the success of the nation-state owed much to the development of industrial capitalism.[34] The new nationwide markets that were created in the course of the nineteenth century required that people develop new skills. As the employers increasingly insisted, potential employees had to be able to speak, read and write in a common language, and they had to be able to understand the cultural references that other market participants shared.[35] A national market required a national culture. Yet people with such easily transferable skills were initially in exceedingly short supply. As late as in the 1870s French was a foreign language to half the citizens of France, and at the time of Italy's unification in 1861 only 2.5 per cent of Italians regularly spoke proper Italian.[36]

The people who did not exist, the state took it upon itself to create. 'We have made Italy,' as Massimo d'Azeglio put it at the opening of the first all-Italian parliament, 'now we have to make Italians.'[37] And as rural communities were connected to capital cities by means of railroads and highways, new cultural influences were brought to previously remote regions. The state conscripted people into armies and the compulsory military service – generally established throughout Europe in the 1860s and 1870s – was often the first time that young men came in contact with co-nationals from regions other than their own. Above all, however, the state established national educational systems through which a common curriculum was taught, comprising lessons on the history, culture and language of the nation.[38] The new schools were universal and free, but also compulsory for all children; in the end, no one had a choice but to belong. And eventually, as parents discovered the advantages it brought their offspring, the guttural patois were abandoned for the *lingua franca* of the national tongue.

The community created in this way was far more appealing than the legal construction of the *Rechtsstaat*. The nation-state had a particular rather than a universal reach, and it purposely did not treat all people in the same fashion.[39] The nation drew boundaries between people, created insides and outsides, friends and enemies. As insiders and friends, people were supposed to know and care about each other far more than about strangers, and this despite the fact that they never had met more than a fraction of their co-nationals.[40] The nation was an imagined community, an intimate entity of people of like minds and like spirits. Thus defined, the nation-state could make demands on people's allegiance in a way the constitutional state never could.[41] The nation became something for which people were prepared both to die and to kill.

Once reconceptualized in this manner, the nation-state had much to offer people displaced by the process of industrialization. Although the nation-state provided little by way of practical assistance, and no new legislation, what it did do was to give people a new sense of who they were.[42] Whatever a person's background or economic and social position, he or she was now a member of the same national community. In this way displaced farmers, farmhands and milkmaids were united into new national wholes; the uprooted were replanted in the soil of the nation and protected by means of its icons and incantations. All they had to do in return was to promise to leave their old identities behind. In the new nation there were no ethnic minorities, no economic classes or even any social divisions properly speaking. Nationalist appeals along these lines were particularly important in the case of the United States, where everyone was a foreigner and everyone hailed from a different background.[43] The nation was one under god, united and indivisible.

In a European context this emphasis on consensus and homogeneity identified the nation as a project of the political right. Although at the time of the French Revolution nationalism had been associated with a liberal agenda, one hundred years later it was all about respecting the king, saluting the flag and obeying one's superiors.[44] Not surprisingly, the nationalist rhetoric appealed strongly to political elites and to employers. For members of the working class, however – or at least for its official representatives – nationalist symbols were anathema. Nationalism was a bourgeois ideology, Marx and Engels explained, and as much an opium of the people as ever religion. As for working men, they 'have no country'.[45]

Yet the founding fathers of Communism clearly exaggerated the cosmopolitanism of the rank-and-file members of the working class. As Paul Göhre reported from the shop-floors of Chemnitz in 1891, his fellow workers often manifested 'a surprising affection for the German fatherland, the Emperor and the army', and they always fondly remembered their time in the military service.[46] Much the same seems to have been the case in France, where colonial expansion became a way for the Third Republic to reassert the country's reputation after the *débâcle* of 1871.[47] Jules Ferry, the liberal politician responsible for establishing the public education system, was also a fervent believer in his country's *mission civilisatrice* and in 'the right which the higher races have over the lower races'.[48] Colonialism was a matter of economics, he explained, of access to overseas markets and the protection of French jobs – and all in all, French workers agreed.[49]

At the same time nationalist rhetoric appeared to be highly critical of capitalism. Accusations were made against bankers and profiteers, and people of Jewish descent were often singled out – not just in Germany but throughout Europe and in the United States – as the very symbols of greedy cosmopolitanism.[50] The contrast constantly extolled by the nationalists were the virtues of the countryside.[51] As industrialization was hitting Europe in the course of the nineteenth century, peasant culture became the touchstone of authenticity and the rural roots of the nation-state became proof of its legitimacy. Yet although such references might have been reassuring to people who had themselves recently arrived in the city, they were starkly contradicted by contemporary developments. In the name of economic progress the traditions of the countryside were rapidly being destroyed, and the state was both a principal instigator in this destruction and one of its main beneficiaries.[52] The image of the morally upstanding peasant was invented only to be defeated, and the culture of the countryside was glorified only at the moment of its disappearance.

In the end there was of course never a question of actually restricting the scope of markets in the name of nationalist ideals. The nation-state gave a new sense of identity to people displaced by capitalist development, but it never sought to question or restrict that development. The nation provided only partial and temporary refuge – during national holidays, when singing the national anthem in school, or when including the king in Sunday prayers or celebratory toasts. Once people had redefined themselves as co-nationals and mastered the national rituals, they were still forced to confront markets alone. The nation-state could not be anti-market since it was far too dependent on economic growth. This was particularly the case for countries that saw themselves as lagging behind the leading nations.[53]

This was never more true than in the case of the fascist regimes that came to power in Italy and Germany in the 1920s and 1930s.[54] Here the official rhetoric emphasized the organic nature of the nation and the mystical bonds – the *Blut und Boden* – which united people with each other. The anti-capitalist rhetoric was blended with anti-Semitism, and it was here that the cult of rural traditions reached its apotheosis. Yet apart from a bit of social legislation and a few quasi-Keynesian projects, the anti-capitalism of the fascist regimes never amounted to much.[55] 'As regards economic questions,' as Adolf Hitler boasted in 1936, 'our theory is very simple. We have no theory at all.'[56] What he did have, of course, was a political theory, and before long socialist parties were outlawed and trade unions recreated as corporatist organizations controlled by the state. Social peace was necessary for national aggrandizement, and the large German business conglomerates benefited from both.[57] In the end, the fascist regimes were completely dependent on the health of the capitalist system. Only capitalism, after all, could satisfy their ravenous appetite for military hardware.

To this day nationalist rhetoric has continued to harbour the same contradictions. Nationalism is the language of the defeated and the disgruntled; it is the bitter resentment of people displaced by urbanization, humiliated by industrialization and bewildered by the trashy trinkets constantly thrown up by consumer society.[58] This explains the strength of nationalist feelings in eastern Europe in the nineteenth century, and it explains nationalist feelings in the United States today where jobs are disappearing abroad or given to immigrants who are prepared to work for a pittance.[59] Yet as before, the politicians who benefit from the no-confidence votes of the nationalists never do anything that might actually impede the logic of the marketplace. On the contrary, they have their own, usually ferociously pro-market, agendas. Just like politicians a hundred years ago, they gain legitimacy for themselves by constantly invoking the alleged moral values of the countryside.

The Welfare State

To the representatives of the working class it was always obvious that neither the constitutional state nor the nation-state did enough. The constitutional state was too abstract and the nation-state was too politically tainted. What the workers needed was more by means of practical, hands-on assistance – higher incomes, better housing, healthcare and proper schooling for their children. As the activists saw it, such assistance could come only from the state. The eventual result was a state which took comprehensive responsibility for the welfare of its citizens and provided minimum standards of income, nutrition, health, housing and education as a matter of right rather than official magnanimity.[60]

The English Poor Laws of 1834 constituted a first attempt to deal with the poverty that the Industrial Revolution had created.[61] Inspired by the new science of economics, the problem was here redefined exclusively as a question of the relationship between the supply and demand of labour. If people were poor, economists like Nassau Senior, Thomas Malthus and David Ricardo concluded, it was because they demanded too high wages or because they were too lazy to work.[62] But if that was the case, there was nothing the state could do for them. As economic theory had demonstrated, society as a whole would be better off if the state refrained from intervening in the market. The only exceptions were people who were evidently unable to take care of themselves, and they were to be confined to workhouses. Conditions there had to be so bad that they in no way constituted an alternative to gainful employment. Or as the Poor Law Commission of 1834 made clear, '[e]very penny bestowed, that tends to render the condition of the pauper more eligible than that of the independent labourer, is a bounty on indolence and vice.'[63]

But as the poor themselves saw it, the market was the problem rather than the solution.[64] There were simply too many desperate workers, and as the laws of economics neatly explained, this would mean that labour was always available at the lowest possible price and that working conditions would remain appalling. The system was inhuman, and the conditions were particularly insufferable in Victorian workhouses. 'They slunk about, like dispirited wolves or hyenas,' Charles Dickens reported from the workhouse he visited in 1850, 'and made a pounce at their food when it was served out, much as those animals do.'[65] There was

a sullen or lethargic indifference to what was asked, a blunted sensibility to everything but warmth and food, a moody absence of complaint as being of no use, a dogged silence and resentful desire to be left alone ...

In the end the poor put more trust in politics than in markets. From the middle of the nineteenth century workers began organizing themselves politically, and before long every European country had at least one working-class party. The Sozialdemokratische Partei Deutschlands was founded in 1863; the Workingmen's Party of America in 1876; Sveriges socialdemokratiska arbetareparti in 1889; the French Parti socialiste in 1893; and the British Labour Party in 1898. Where the right to vote was not yet universal, these parties constituted a strong voice in favour of universal suffrage, and where suffrage was universal they were soon making electoral advances. When the German SDP attracted half a million votes in 1877 and gained 12 seats in the Reichstag, elites throughout Europe were seriously worried.[66]

Germany was also where a policy was first devised to try to counter these challenges. In contrast to British politicians, the German ruling classes had never committed themselves to the tenets of economic liberalism and for that reason they were more inclined to disobey the imperatives of *laissez-faire*. The architect of German unification, Otto von Bismarck, is an example. An arch-conservative, he combined a policy of repression of trade unions and socialist parties with considerable concessions to their demands. Only in this way, he thought, could the threat of revolution be effectively countered. From 1883 Germany enacted what is commonly regarded as Europe's first social legislation.[67] Its centrepiece was a set of insurance schemes that protected workers from the effects of accidents, sickness and infirmity, together with an additional programme that provided for pensions in old age. The reforms were successful in Bismarck's terms, but also in the workers' in that they really improved the standard of life.

The German reforms were imitated in all European countries where conservative elites shared a similar fear of the working classes or where liberals felt guilty at the thought of their plight. In Britain a Royal Commission reported in 1905 on the operations of the Poor Laws, and concluded that an overhaul was long overdue.[68] Poverty and unemployment, the Commission argued, should not be regarded as evidence of personal failings, to be treated with repression and moralizing, but as evidence of social ills instead to be treated with political reforms. Following the Commission's recommendations, a series of insurance schemes were put in place which compensated workers in case of accidents and injuries and provided support for the unemployed, the sick and the old. In France too the establishment eventually became sufficiently scared and sufficiently soft-hearted. Reformist groups, inspired by the new science of sociology, began demanding that more attention be paid to *la solidarité sociale* – society, they concluded, was responsible for the good or the bad conditions into which people were born.[69] Yet in France the welfare programmes that emerged remained badly coordinated, and they were underfunded compared to the ones in Germany and Britain.[70]

It was really only after World War II that the welfare state came into its own. By now a new consensus had emerged throughout Europe.[71] Capitalism is basically a good idea, everyone seemed to agree, but it cannot do without the assistance of the state. As the Great Depression had demonstrated, only the state can protect people against unemployment and hard times; the state can help out by running budget deficits and stimulating demand and thereby economic growth.[72] People had to be guaranteed a job and a decent income or they could not be expected to support the system. This was not least the case, nervous representatives of the US administration admitted, as long as the Soviet Union – the self-proclaimed working-class state – continued to pose a military threat to western Europe.

Compared to the constitutional state and the nation-state, the welfare state always had a far more ambitious agenda. Politics, its proponents declared, is not so much a matter of rights as a matter of what the state can achieve on people's behalf. Authority is legitimate not because it is exercised in conformity with the law, but because it is exercised in conformity with the will of the people; the role of the state is to help people satisfy their needs. Once the search was on for needs rather than for rights, a long and comprehensive list was quickly compiled. There were so many things that people needed, and thus so many things for the state to do. Many of the programmes aimed at decommodification. Beginning with the most obvious cases, the state protected those who could not compete with others – the very young, the very old, the handicapped and the mentally ill. But the state also protected those who competed less successfully than others. It provided unemployment benefits for the unemployed, housing benefits for the unhoused, income subsidies for those without an income, and child subsidies for those with children.

The welfare state also made it easier for people to deal with the consequences of the division of labour. It helped people find new jobs, helped them move to places where new jobs were located, or helped them set up businesses of their own. The welfare state retrained and reskilled people to fit better with the ever-changing demands of the labour market. Those who were sick were made healthy in state-run hospitals and clinics, and those who were ignorant were educated in state-run educational facilities. Since many of these services had previously been undertaken by wives and mothers, women were for the first time able to join the labour force on terms equivalent to those of men. The welfare state supported the 'liberation' of women, at least to the extent that liberation was defined as a woman's right to sell her labour at a market price.[73]

Yet the level of generosity varies considerably from one welfare state to the next.[74] The most stingy set-up is perhaps that of the United States. Here the state plays only a limited role in decommodifying people and preparing them for markets, and only those who are most obviously unable to take care of themselves are protected. In the tradition of the English Poor Laws of 1834, welfare provisions are never supposed to be a viable alternative to market provisions. Welfare benefits are popularly referred to as 'hand-outs', and to receive hand-outs is associated with considerable social stigma.

The most generous provisions are probably those of a north-European country such as Sweden. Here welfare is not just for poor people but for everyone; all inhabitants are covered by the same universal and state-sponsored insurance schemes. There is a safety net which protects people from the cradle to the grave. There are next to no private educational or medical facilities in Sweden – all schools and hospitals are instead run by the state and paid for through taxes. Day-care is universal and heavily subsidized; parents can take time off from work when a child is ill; benefits given to the unemployed or sick amount to 85 per cent of the regular salary; everyone receives a state pension, and medical treatment for the elderly, as for everyone else, is free.

This is 'the Swedish model', or in the catch-phrase coined by the ruling Social Democrats in the 1930s, the *folkhem*, the 'home of the people'.[75] This metaphor provided a Swedish and very different version of the 'national socialism' simultaneously imposed on Germany.[76] It provided a model of a state that was also a national community; a state that derived legitimacy from its ability to protect people from the ravages of capitalism. Or differently put, the Swedish state was a *Polizeistaat* in its etymologically correct sense. It was a state which regulated the present and planned for the future; it cared about its people while at the same time controlling them. The paternalism implied by the metaphor corresponded well with the paternalism of the model; like the head of a household, the Swedish state always knew what was best for the people subject to it. Surprisingly often, the state was actually right in this presumption, which meant that anti-state protests necessarily had to be undertaken against the best interests of the protesters concerned.[77]

And yet a Social-Democratic welfare state like the Swedish one has always been in favour of capitalism. In fact, the more generous the provisions, the more dependent the state became on the market since someone in the end had to pay for all the goods the state was handing out. To their credit, the Swedish Social Democrats always realized as much, and regardless of their rhetoric they never missed an opportunity to ensure that private enterprises were thriving.[78] There was a symbiosis, in other words, between the welfare state and capitalism, and this was true not only in Sweden but in every other European country. While capitalism provided the welfare state with sufficient resources to discharge its functions, the welfare state provided the social infrastructure that made capitalism acceptable. The welfare state emasculated capitalism and made it safe for society. In the process the welfare state assured capitalism's success.

9

The State in China and Japan

Let us next turn to states in East Asia, or to be more precise, to the states of China and Japan. Just as in Europe, there is no doubting the formidable power of these entities. Indeed, the power of East Asian rulers was one of the things that most impressed the Europeans who visited this part of the world in the sixteenth century. The emperors of China and Japan, Jesuit missionaries and Dutch sea-captains reported, ruled like tyrants and everyone was forced to obey their commands.[1] For the Europeans the *kowtow* – the practice of prostrating oneself flat on the ground before the ruler – became the symbol of what in the nineteenth century was known as 'Oriental despotism'.[2] In the twentieth century this image of East Asia as governed by omnipotent rulers was only strengthened as Japan subjected its citizens to fascism and much of the rest of Asia to imperialist rule, and as China was taken over by a dictatorship with totalitarian ambitions.[3]

And yet these impressions were quite mistaken. For one thing, authority in the East Asian context was typically understood in personalized rather than in institutionalized terms.[4] In both China and Japan people were seen as connected with each other through long chains of hierarchical relationships stretching from the bottom of society to the very top. These relationships were organized according to particularistic rather than universal rules. In China the emperor governed by virtue of a 'mandate of heaven', but this did not give him a general right to interfere in people's lives. Instead, it was incumbent on all Chinese, the emperors included, first and foremost to fulfil their obligations to their families and friends.[5] If everybody only maintained the order of their respective parts of the great network that was society, the country would be at peace and everybody would prosper. Much the same was true in Japan, where the feudal structure was held together by ties that connected vassals to their lords. Instead of relying on legal abstractions, the Japanese state was governed by personal obligations and codes of honour. As a consequence of such personalizations, East Asian states were never actually as powerful or as robust as the Europeans imagined.

In relation to economic markets, East Asian states were at least as active as their European counterparts. During the Tang dynasty the Chinese state periodically redistributed land in order to make sure that no permanent social inequalities arose, and during the Song dynasty it spent a lot of money and effort constructing a physical and institutional infrastructure. In Japan the various feudal lords ran their own economic policies, welfare programmes and industrial projects. In both countries the state was far more independent of economic interests than was the case in Europe. Both in theory and in practice China was run by its bureaucracy, and Japan by the descendants of its military class. As a result, economic activities were always strictly subordinated to social and political requirements. Although capitalism flourished in both places, economic pursuits were emphatically not what social or political life was about.

The Imperial Chinese State

The precocious development of capitalism in China meant that already the first imperial dynasties had to find ways of dealing with its unsettling effects. In the early centuries BCE the emergence of markets in land allowed a new class of landowners to increase its holdings, at the same rate as a new class of landless peasants was created.[6] Before long the Chinese state felt compelled to react to this incipient class structure. By affirming the position of the state, the position of the new economic elite was undermined and the poor were given a measure of protection. As early as in the second century BCE, the emperor Han Wudi made sure that taxes were paid to the state rather than to the nobles, that politically suspect families were killed off, and that state bureaucrats were chosen from families of lower social status. In addition, the state established monopolies in salt, iron and wine in order both to improve its revenue and to deprive the merchants of these lucrative sources of income.[7] Merchants were also forbidden to wear silk garments, to ride horses and carry arms.[8]

Political control increased still further in the fifth century CE, when all large private landholdings were converted into fiefdoms that were awarded as sinecures to state officials for the duration of their tenure.[9] Other land was distributed equitably to all commoners and to slaves, according to a fixed formula, and the majority of it was to be redistributed after the death of its current holder. The sale of land was made illegal. 'We want to ensure that no land lies neglected,' as the statesman Li An-shi put it:

> that none of our people are vagrants, that powerful families do not monopolize the fertile fields, and that humble persons also have their share of the acreage. These are the means by which we may show pity for poverty, repress greed, equalize wealth and want, and ensure that all the commoners are enrolled in the population registers.[10]

During the Song dynasty this system largely broke down and the landowners reasserted their position.[11] By this time, however, the imperial state took a more relaxed view of the interplay of supply and demand, although land continued to be given as sinecures and the state procured many goods and services at fixed prices.[12] The imperial state was also heavily involved in organizing and regulating markets that would otherwise have operated badly or not at all. Among many other activities the state built roads and canals, set up vast irrigation projects, issued currency, regulated weights and measures, founded schools and published manuals on agriculture, sericulture and metallurgy.[13]

The result of these projects was an unprecedented economic boom and a process of urbanization which swelled the population of Chinese cities and turned them into the sites of wonder marvelled at by European visitors. The southern Song capital of Hangzhou, Marco Polo reported in the thirteenth century, 'is beyond dispute the finest and the noblest in the world'.[14] Its women are 'splendidly attired and abundantly perfumed', and the city has no fewer than 12,000 stone bridges. Its commerce was no less thriving. There were ten principal markets, each frequented by some 50,000 people, filled with every kind of meat and game, wondrous vegetables, fragrant pears and 'fish of sundry kinds, changing with the season'. The city's daily pepper consumption alone amounted to some 43 cartloads.[15]

Yet as Polo makes clear, Hangzhou like all other Chinese cities was not controlled by merchants but by the imperial state. In contrast to Europe, even though some merchants grew fabulously wealthy, they never exercised collective power.[16] As a result, the imperial state was always far less susceptible to outside pressure than its European counterparts. Before the middle of the nineteenth century its finances were usually in excellent shape, and the emperors would lend money to their subjects rather than borrow from them.[17] While this removed a major source of insecurity as far as the property rights of individuals were concerned, it also meant that merchants had little leverage on the state.[18] The examination system contributed to the same end. From the Song dynasty until it was abolished in 1905 – or at least until it became seriously corrupt at the end of the Qing – the state was staffed through entrance examinations which assured that merit prevailed over financial clout.[19] Socially, a state official was 'the thing to be', and the status aspired to by even the richest of merchants.

In addition there was the body of Confucian thought which from the second century BCE served as an official state ideology, and also provided the material on which aspiring bureaucrats were tested in the exams. Confucian thought was always highly dismissive of commercial activities.[20] What mattered were instead the humanist ideals embodied by the *junzi*, the Confucian gentleman; what mattered was a knowledge of morality, of history and the arts. And while money was a precondition for a person's ability to pursue such studies, only fools pursued money for its own sake. Trade, said the Han historian Ban Gu, is a 'licentiously corrupt occupation'.[21] Instead the Confucians extolled the toil of the peasantry, and officially at least, merchants and artisans were regarded as thoroughly unproductive classes. Merchants added nothing to the work of the farmers, they explained, and artisans wasted their time producing nothing but the most frivolous of objects.[22]

Yet the Confucians were never anti-capitalists as such. They understood perfectly well that people had to be fed, and they knew that a regime of low taxation which allowed a free interplay of supply and demand was the best way to accomplish this goal.[23] The 'mandate of heaven', which asserted the emperor's claim to rule, might all too quickly be revoked through the actions of hungry and rebellious mobs. The policy that the state pursued can instead best be described as a uniquely Chinese version of *laissez-faire*.[24] As philosophers of all different schools agreed, if people only were obedient and the social and legal infrastructure was securely in place, there was no need for the state to interfere with the comings and goings of the common man. 'To rule a large state is like cooking small fish,' as the Daoists were fond of saying, 'stir as little as possible.'[25] The premise, however, was the absolute supremacy of the imperial state; economic activities were free only as long as they did not threaten the political order.

In practice, however, any such policy of *laissez-faire* is bound to require a lot of activity on the part of the bureaucrats. For the state to be secure, people had to be controlled but also cared for in a combination reminiscent of the European *Polizeistaat*. Care was exercised by an imperial welfare state which made sure that people were fed, that they had opportunities for schooling, that merchants did not reap monopoly profits, and that justice was maintained.[26] People who were unable to work, a surprised Marco Polo discovered, were taken by watch-patrols 'to one of the hospitals, of which there are many, founded by the ancient kings and endowed with great revenues'.[27] Yet the patrols also doubled as policemen – they arrested criminals, illegal market vendors and people who left fires burning at night; they also kept registers of all inhabitants, carefully recording births and deaths, and they made sure that hostels reported the names of all people staying in them. In addition, the emperors maintained an extensive network of spies who gathered information on the mood of society and on the conduct of state officials.[28]

The imperial *Polizeistaat* remained remarkably unchanged until the middle of the nineteenth century when military and commercial pressure from the Europeans forced changes to take place. Reluctantly at first, but from the 1890s onward increasingly enthusiastically, China also began industrializing.[29] Often it was foreign industrialists who were in charge. They built ship-repair yards, mills for refining sugar, plants for processing hides and wool, and textile factories where cotton was spun and woven. But there were Chinese manufacturers as well, and domestic industry boomed as a result of the demand created in Europe and North America during World War I.[30] As might be expected, conditions in the factories were perfectly Dickensian, including the same pallid and undernourished mothers labouring away with their infants by their sides, the same 10-year-old boys working 12-hour shifts and the same squalid and pest-ridden tenements.[31]

Compared with states in Europe, however, the imperial Chinese state had only limited means with which to respond to these challenges. Consider for example the issue of rights.[32] In China there was never a tradition of negotiating with the subjects and of making legally binding concessions to them; there was no constitution, and a person's dignity was in no way dependent on recognition granted by the state. Consequently, workers' rights were slow to develop. Limited reform proposals in the 1920s – banning factory labour for children and similar modest suggestions – were not enacted into law.[33]

For the same reason, a nation-state never developed in imperial China. Although all people of Chinese descent shared a Confucian heritage and a range of rituals and folk customs, there was no tradition of including commoners in the running of state affairs. This alienation from the regime was particularly strongly felt during the Qing dynasty whose rulers were of Manchu origin rather than Han Chinese.[34] All nationalist appeals were for that reason anti- rather than pro-imperial, and when the nationalists eventually gained power in 1911, the emperor was quickly dethroned. With the imperial bureaucracy disappeared the one legacy that might actually have contributed to the general welfare in a period of industrialization and social upheaval – the Confucian *Polizeistaat* tradition. As a result, from 1911 onward people were neither particularly well controlled nor particularly well cared for. Such protection as was given came instead came from other sources – the Chinese family, above all, and the entrenched *guanxi* networks.

The Imperial State in Corporate Japan

The Japanese state fared better. Before the Meiji Restoration of 1868, Japan had been made up of an assembly of political entities only loosely integrated under the rule of a military leader, the shogun.[35] Outside the feudal elite there was little national unity and few people had a sense of belonging to such a collective entity as 'Japan'.[36] Confucian thought had had a profound impact also on Japanese political culture, and many of the small statelets were ruled in accordance with its precepts, although power always belonged to the class of samurai rather than to the literati.[37] In Japan there were, for example, no entrance examinations to the bureaucracy.

Just as in China, Confucianism provided the shoguns and the many local lords with a rationale for keeping a close eye on society and on the economy. From the seventeenth century onward, Japan experienced something of a commercial revolution, and as always the expansion of markets brought new opportunities for social mobility as well as new social tensions.[38] In 1730 Kyoto had no fewer than 10,000 people working in textile production, Osaka had 2,000 ship's carpenters, and Edo had a total population of over one million. Conservative in their instincts, the shoguns began regulating guilds and money-lenders and granting monopolies for the sale of everything from brass, sulphur and camphor to cinnabar, ginseng and lamp oil.[39] At the same time they made sure to improve their own financial positions. As the eighteenth century progressed, the shogunate took increasing control over the national rice market in Osaka, which all feudal lords relied on in order to convert the taxes they received in kind into readily available cash.

When the foreigners arrived in the middle of the nineteenth century – Commodore Matthew Perry's Black Ships suddenly appeared in Edo Bay in the summer of 1853 – the Japanese leaders began undertaking a series of reforms aimed at 'strengthening the army' and 'expelling the barbarians'.[40] Yet just as in China, the regime did not act quickly and decisively enough to deal with the threat, and it was soon overthrown. In contrast to China, however, this coup was formally a 'restoration' rather than a 'revolution' since it was officially undertaken in the name of the empire and traditional values. Soon enough the emperor, whose ancestors had languished in their palace in Kyoto for centuries, was reinstated as a figurehead of the new regime. In many respects it was only after the Meiji Restoration that Japan became both a proper empire and a proper nation.

The tradition of detailed policy-making survived together with the old institutions. The new Meiji leaders were provincial samurai deeply steeped in the interventionist and regulatory practices of the Confucian administrator, and they naturally regarded industrialization and modernization as tasks to be undertaken by the state.[41] Foreign experts were invited and research missions were dispatched abroad; new technologies were introduced and model factories were set up in which the basics of the factory system were taught both to potential employers and to potential employees.[42] A range of foreign institutions was also adopted – an English central bank, a French-style judicial system, a Prussian army, and American universities. In addition, domestic trade barriers were abolished and the country opened up to foreign commerce, reluctantly at first but soon increasingly confidently. The result was a vast expansion of markets and an economic boom produced by the entrepreneurial initiative of countless private individuals, but at the same time brought on, supervised and regulated, by the state.[43]

Meanwhile the state was becoming ever more nationalistic. As Japanese scholars soon discovered, the country did not only have a long and glorious history but also a number of national traditions, a national language, heroes, art forms, foods and sports which the state took it as its obligation to revive and sustain.[44] The supreme guardian of all things Japanese was the emperor. In the Rescript on Education of 1890, all imperial subjects were encouraged to be 'filial', 'affectionate', 'harmonious' and 'true', and in the event of any emergency to 'offer yourself courageously to the State'.[45] And everywhere references were made to the slightly hazy notion of *wa*, or 'harmony'. 'What is *wa*?' asked the writer Ono Seiichiro in 1938:

> It is not merely peace achieved on the surface. It is inner and spiritual harmony and peace. This ideal brings about a unity of communal spirit

by maintaining not only hierarchical distinctions but also the essential equality of an ethical order. It should be the ethic that will bring forth continuity, integration, and unity in the state.[46]

And yet Japanese workers were clearly far less consensus-orientated than the elites had assumed. As we noted above, the early twentieth century was a time of often violent industrial action and much social strife. Naturally the factory-owners were worried by these trends, and just as in Europe they faced particular problems with the recruitment and retention of a dependable workforce.[47] While individual employers were loath to make concessions to the workers' demands, the government took a more pragmatic approach. As was becoming increasingly clear, something had to be done or the 'social question' would soon overwhelm them all. Or as Soeda Juichi, an official in the Ministry of Finance, noted in 1896:

> If we leave things the way they are today, we will see a process producing extreme social illness much like the one that befell England at the beginning of this century. ... We will have unavoidable problems ending in social evils such as strikes. ... My fervent hope is that we can solve this problem before it develops and save ourselves from the disease of the advanced countries of Europe.[48]

Moreover, labour militancy and high abstention rates created problems for the state itself.[49] If the workers constantly were on strike, production in the arms industry suffered. Clearly, it was possible to 'stregthen the army' only if people were prepared to work diligently in munitions industries, steel plants, shipyards and the like. Furthermore, men who fell ill or were maimed at work did not make particularly good soldiers, just as the quality of future soldiers suffered from having mothers who worked endless shifts, at night, and in dirty and unsanitary conditions.

In response to such military imperatives, just as much as to humanitarian concerns, a series of laws were enacted that provided workers with a modicum of social protection.[50] Already in the 1880s the Ministry of Agriculture and Commerce began preparing a Factory Law, although due to strong opposition from industrialists – from textile manufacturers in particular – it was not until 1911 that it finally came into force. From this time onwards, however, the minimum working age was set at twelve, night work for women was banned, and working hours were limited to twelve hours a day – and these regulations applied to all companies with more than ten employees. Additional laws were passed in the 1920s: a Health Insurance Law in 1922, a revised Factory Law in 1923 and a Labour Disputes Conciliation Law in 1926.[51] In the 1920s trade unions were given an officially recognized status, although despite this only about 6 per cent of the workforce was unionized by 1937.[52]

Just as in Europe there were limits to how much that could be accomplished through legislation alone. The law provided much-needed minimal standards which regulated conditions in the labour market, but the position of many employees was still insecure. Realizing how dependent it had become on its workforce, the Japanese government began from the 1910s onward to take a more long-term view of the workers' needs.[53] With the intention of making them more loyal, the state offered improved conditions and longer-term contracts to people who worked in the armaments industry. The state also encouraged the large industrial conglomerates, the *zaibatsu*, to implement similar policies in the companies they controlled.[54]

In order to produce the best possible soldiers, and in order to conform to the official rhetoric of inclusion, the labour market reforms were intensified as the power of Japan-style fascism grew in the course of the 1930s.[55] Job security was improved, wages were increasingly linked to seniority, and cooperative rather than adversarial relations were encouraged between employers and employees.[56] Under the National Mobilization Law of 1938, state officials were given the power to control most aspect of working conditions in essential industries, and in 1942 a new law, the Ordinance on Labour Management in Essential Industries, was used by the Ministry of Welfare in order to take control of labour relations also in private companies.[57] From this time onward it was the state that organized hirings and firings, working hours, and matters of hygiene and safety at work, as well as welfare facilities, bonuses and wages.

There is no doubt that people in general benefited from such state guidance, and many evidently also came to believe the nationalistic rhetoric that accompanied the reforms. Many Japanese were proud no longer to live in isolated villages but in a powerful nation-state that was sweeping everything before it. Many also sincerely believed that the emperor recognized and appreciated their efforts. As the war wore on, however, ever greater sacrifices were demanded, in particular after the battle of Iojima of March 1945 when the American forces began approaching Japan itself. In the end, the nationalistic rhetoric could not conceal the fact that people were being exploited not by the forces of the market as much as by the state itself.

Post-War States in Japan and China

World War II left China and Japan in ruins, and in both countries radical changes ensued. Japan was occupied by the Americans for some seven years, and the occupiers imposed a new constitution on the country and undertook a number of fundamental reforms. Many of these – such as the right to go on strike and to form trade unions – benefited employees, and this was significant in a post-war setting in which markets were not only reviving but also expanding fast.[58] In China, meanwhile, capitalism was abolished and replaced by a system of central planning.

Let us start with Japan where the US authorities wasted little time in imposing their vision of the country's future. According to General MacArthur and his advisers, Japanese society still displayed far too many feudal – that is to say, anti-capitalist – traits.[59] There was too much collectivism, too much blind obedience, and not enough respect for the principles of a free market economy. The *zaibatsu* were objects of particular concern, but so was the paternalism of the employment system. Yet in the immediate post-war era the Japanese themselves seemed more than happy to abandon these remnants of their past.[60] At the time American management theory became wildly popular among Japanese businessmen, and as one corporation after another began experimenting with 'enterprise training' and 'personnel management', the old paternalism seemed increasingly obsolete.

The viability of these newfangled ideas was soon put to the test. As far as the labour market was concerned, the early post-war years were, like the first decade of the twentieth century, a particularly turbulent time.[61] Although unemployment was high, there was an acute lack of skilled workers in many key industries, and this improved the bargaining power of these sought-after groups. Large strikes took place at the Toshiba plants, in the power industry, at coal mines, in steelworks, the post office and at Yomiuri Shimbun, one of the country's leading newspapers. In the years 1945 to 1947, the number of working hours lost to strikes was comparable to the figures in the United States and Europe.

For conservative members of the bureaucracy who had survived the war with their jobs intact, this upsurge in labour militancy was a source of considerable worry, and by the early 1950s the Americans too had begun to be concerned.[62] In the minds of US policy-makers, once Mao had seized power in Beijing and the Korean War had begun, the threat of Communism had come to replace the threat of renewed Japanese nationalism. The last thing MacArthur and his new conservative allies wanted was an unruly labour market and an increasingly powerful, pro-Communist, left.

This was the political situation in which the state-sponsored employment system of the 1930s was revived.[63] In MITI, the Ministry for International Trade and Industry, an Industrial Rationalization Council was set up in 1949 which produced standards for wages and promotions, for the organization of work sites and for employee training programmes. The Council also provided advice for employers on how to avoid strikes. Soon the employers' own organizations issued similar guidelines to their members. The new policies were adopted since they worked – they made it far easier to recruit skilled labour, and labour militancy declined.

The eventual result was what we have described as 'the Japanese employment system' – a job for life, promotion and pay by seniority, company-based trade unions and an extensive menu of corporate welfare provisions. Large Japanese companies thus became far more 'feudal' in the 1950s than they had ever previously been, and they were to retain these characteristics throughout the subsequent decades of high economic growth. This is ironic not least since the last vestiges of the pre-modern era were wiped out at exactly this time – the *ie* structures, the traditional villages, and the picturesque inner-city neighbourhoods.[64] Feudalism remained in only one social setting – the Japanese business corporation.

As far as the state was concerned, it never tried to recreate the fascist welfare programmes of the inter-war era. On the contrary, after the war it took only a cursory interest in the lives of most people subject to it. Whereas the pre-war state had been boastful and extravagant, the post-war state was self-consciously dull; it was above all a bureaucratic entity that pursued its policies with few references to the wishes of the general public.[65] And as it turns out, the general public cared just as little about the state. In post-war Japan, politics was a matter for politicians – or rather, a matter for bureaucrats.

As a result, comparatively little happened by way of pro-labour legislation, not least since the bureaucrats preferred to rule through 'administrative guidance' rather than through statutory legislation since this gave them far more discretion.[66] Similarly, the Japanese state was no longer dabbling in nationalism – at least, not officially. Any action that might be interpreted as a concession to the small nationalistic right has quickly been condemned by the anti-war lobby both at home and abroad.[67] When it comes to welfare programmes, rather more happened.[68] This was particularly the case in the late 1950s when the government decided that a properly modern country needed a comprehensive welfare system. Yet by the 1970s the emphasis was once again on a 'Japanese-style' system, meaning an emphasis on corporations and on unpaid female labour in the home. Although the pace of welfare reform picked up again in subsequent decades, there is still a long way to go before Japan becomes a welfare state on the European model.

Largely ignoring its individual subjects, the Japanese state has instead turned rights, nationalism and welfare into an agenda aimed at business corporations. Post-war Japan was more than anything a *kigyo shakai*, a 'company-centred society'.[69] It is corporations rather than individuals that the Japanese state has protected from market forces. The only form of nationalism acceptable in the post-war era is a neo-mercantilist policy designed to enrich the country through exports.[70] Similarly, corporations have become the objects of both administrative guidance and welfare provisions.[71] The 'managed competition' encouraged by the state meant that a few 'national champions' were granted unique favours.[72] These elite companies enjoyed financing on favourable terms, help with research and development, and the official blessing of MITI when it came to the acquisition of foreign patents and the allocation of scarce foreign exchange. Individual human beings fit into this system of favours and counter-favours only indirectly. Whereas the companies were to be protected by the state, individuals were to be protected by their companies.

Turning to China, the outright rejection of capitalism which took place after 1949 is a puzzle in need of an explanation. Thriving markets had existed here for at least some 2,500 years and over time Chinese society had, as we have seen, developed very sophisticated ways of protecting itself. Families, *guanxi* networks and the care and control exercised by the state combined to provide people with at least as much protection as any-where else. Just as in Europe, however, urbanization and the spread of the factory system put acute pressure on these arrangements, and once the empire crumbled the state could never effectively rise to the challenge. Yet the anti-capitalist agenda can still not explain the success of the Communist Party. There were never enough members of the working-class in China, and besides, what the vast majority of peasants wanted was not the aboli-tion of markets but simply access to more land.[73] What boosted support for the Communists was instead the nationalistic hope that they were the force that could unify the country and expel the foreigners, together with a presumption that Communism finally would make China modern.

Strange as it may seem to us today, Communism was at the time considered a more rational system than capitalism since it promised to replace the 'chaos' of the marketplace with central planning. The rationalism of this project was seen as more modern, and it was thought to lead to quicker economic results.[74] Choosing the Communist route, China would thus eventually overtake her foreign adversaries. Moreover, although Communism was a foreign ideology, it was an ideology that could be used for anti-foreign ends. It provided a political programme around which the workers of the world could unite and defeat the European imperialists. It was this struggle that Mao and his comrades joined rather than the struggle against the forces of capitalism as such.

Once in power, the Communists embarked on a range of modern, rationalistic and ultimately self-defeating reforms. But although the new leaders ostensibly invoked the programme of scientific materialism, they borrowed heavily from imperial traditions. As we have seen, the imperial state had taken comprehensive responsibility for the well-being of its sub-jects; in imperial China too there had been a tradition of state allocation of land and other resources, and the imperial state had divided people into collective groups in order better to control them.[75] This was an indigenous tradition rather than an imported. Imperial and Communist China were both *Polizeistaaten* in which care was combined with control – although the empire exercised less control and dispensed less welfare, and far fewer people died as a result of its mistakes.[76]

But not everything was continuity. There is hardly any doubt that the Communists managed to do a lot of damage to the grammar of traditional social life. There is an atomizing logic to totalitarian power which Thomas Hobbes and Jean-Jacques Rousseau may have been the first to discover in the case of Europe, but which Chairman Mao also appreciated.[77] By sub-jecting everybody to the authority of the state rather than to the authority of intermediary institutions such as families and *guanxi* networks, feudalism was finally to be destroyed. As a result, Chinese society today is far more atomized than it would have been but for the Communist interlude. This is Marx turned on his head – Communism serving as a precursor to capitalism rather than the other way around.

And then markets were once again introduced. Holding on to their nationalistic agenda and their modernizing ambitions, the leaders simply shelved their Communist ideals. All in all, the aspirations of the post-Communist Chinese state seem rather similar to those of the traditional imperial state – to let people prosper by going about their own business, while at the same time making sure that political dissent is repressed. Yet millions of Chinese have been made to pay the cost of these transformations, first from capitalism to Communism and then back again. Today a hundred million people are on the move, tens of millions are unemployed, and hundreds of thousands of workers are on strike, demonstrating and even engaging in armed skirmishes with the authorities.[78] Although never completely unresponsive to such pressures, the regime has not hesitated to use its coercive apparatus to repress discontent. Independent trade unions are, for example, prohibited. Strong unions would no doubt make China a far less profitable place for foreign direct investments.

The current situation in China is thus ambiguous. Much of the social grammar of traditional society is broken, if not completely destroyed; other parts survive but are expressed in different ways. The regime controls the manner in which people can organize, and it does not hesitate to use repression to enforce its will. Meanwhile the economic miracle continues, combining new prosperity with new hardship. The state has exposed people to the global market while at the same time denying them access both to traditional protective arrangements and to foreign arrangements such as trade unions. This is surely a strange fate for a still ostensibly Communist regime.

CONCLUSIONS

10

How We Survived Capitalism

So this is how we did it – how we survived capitalism while retaining our humanity more or less intact. Capitalism is inevitable, to be sure, and it is unsurpassed in its ability to bring economic prosperity to individuals and societies, and economic prosperity in turn is associated with a long range of highly attractive social goods. Yet as the previous chapters have demonstrated, the expansion of markets also has a number of profoundly unsettling effects. We discussed two in particular – the alienation brought on by the division of labour and the erosion of values brought on by commodification. We are consequently faced with a conflict of imperatives. Since markets are beneficial, we want to extend them ever further, yet because they are also destructive, we want to restrict them. The question is not how capitalism can be replaced by some other kind of system – the question is how we can work out a solution to this dilemma.

As our overview has made clear, there are a large number of solutions here and they vary considerably from one society to the next. The problem is how to summarize this diversity, but also how to explain the pattern that emerges. The obvious answer – indeed, the one that seems to be implied by much of our discussion – is that protective arrangements are the products of the 'traditions' or the 'culture' of each society concerned. People in Japan, that is, protect themselves in a typically Japanese fashion, while people in the United States do so in a typically American way. This is, after all, why the expansion of markets is unlikely to lead to complete convergence between societies and ways of life. Yet such an explanation, even if true, is also embarrassingly simplistic. Cultures and traditions are not just acting on us through some mysterious inertial force emanating from the remote past. Instead, cultures and traditions can play a role only to the extent that they are recreated in the present. They must be mobilized, as it were, and made relevant. The subject of this chapter is how such mobilizations takes place.

Nests, Colonies and Shells

Consider the notion of a social grammar. As we argued above, a grammar is a structure through which meaning is distributed across a system such as a language. A social grammar tells us what our place in society is, what places others occupy, and how different places relate to one another. Differently put, a social grammar designates what we take as essential to social life and what we consider its basic building blocks to be. Depending on what grammar we rely on, quite different protective arrangements can be put together. In all cases, however, what each society most wants to protect are what it regards as its most fundamental units.

Broadly speaking, there are two main options here – either we protect individuals or we protect the relationships through which individuals are connected to each other. What is to be protected, that is, are either the social networks or their nodes. If we take the individual as fundamental, everything else becomes relative; if individuals are given, their environment must be rearranged to accommodate their wishes and needs. This means that protective arrangements must be organized in such a way that protection can be combined with 'freedom', with the right to act in the way one sees fit and to seize opportunities as they come along. Individuals must, for example, be allowed to benefit from their own market transactions and from their entrepreneurial skills. As a result the protective arrangements must be unobtrusive; they must be there, but at the same time not be in the way; they are background assumptions, parts of the institutional furniture of social life.[1]

The question is what kind of protective arrangements these could possibly be. In general terms, they would seem to be something akin to a bird's nest – after all, a bird's nest is also a protective arrangement. Most obviously, a nest is a place where eggs are hatched and chicks protected against attacks by predators, but it is also a place where adult birds can rest after their hunting and foraging expeditions. At the same time, the nest is a temporary structure and it has a very simple division of labour. Once the young are old enough to make it on their own, the nest is abandoned and the family members go off in their separate directions. The point of the nest is above all to provide individuals with sufficient resources so that they one day can make it on their own.

A protective arrangement modelled on a nest would provide us with temporary rather than full-time support. Like a bird's nest it would be a place where individuals can prepare themselves for their engagements with markets, but also where they can rest and recuperate once these engagements are over. In order to simultaneously serve both these ends, the protective arrangement must be separated as radically as possible from the economic environment that surrounds it. The trick to survival, in other words, is to move from the nest to the outside world, and then back again, in the course of one's lifetime or during the course of one day. In this way people are exposed to the market, but only for some of the time and under particular conditions. Their business concluded, they fly home to the nest again in triumph or in desperation.

The alternative is to care less about the individuals themselves and instead more about the integrity of the relationships that bind them together. Here it is the networks and not their nodes that are considered the basic units of society. This is the survival strategy of social animals such as termites, bees or ants.[2] These species all protect themselves by building permanent structures – colonies, hives or hills – where individuals live in close proximity to each other. This is where they are born and where they live for the duration of their lives. The colony is first and foremost a place of incessant labour, yet it is the colony as a whole, rather than its members, that faces the outside world. The biological individuals are protected by a carefully elaborated system of division of labour; intelligence and capabilities are shared and belong to the network as a whole rather than to its constituent parts. As members of the colony the biological individuals are vastly more powerful than any of them would have been alone. They survive together or not at all.

In a social arrangement modelled on a colony, it is the network that is to be protected, and individuals are protected only indirectly as members of the network. Since the network is fixed, individuals have to be infinitely flexible and constantly prepared to make adjustments; there is consequently little talk of 'freedom' and more talk instead of social expectations. Each person has a place where he or she belongs, and this is where he or she is expected to stay. The job each person performs is designated by the protective arrangement rather than by the market; there are no wages or only a weak sense of monetary remuneration. Awards are instead social and predominantly collective in nature. As a result, there is no radical separation of spheres and the protective arrangement is dominated by work; people are exploiting themselves on behalf of networks that they come to regard as second selves.

Grossly simplifying, we could say that protective arrangements modelled on nests are more common in contemporary Europe and North America, whereas protective arrangements modelled on colonies were more common in medieval and early modern Europe and in contemporary China and Japan.[3] The bourgeois home of the nineteenth century was a nest, but so are Protestant sects, trade unions, nation-states and welfare states. They are all alternative worlds that provide occasional support; they are places of temporary refuge, but they are not permanent arrangements. It is by moving back and forth between the nest and the outside world that Europeans and North Americans make a life for themselves. By contrast, many people in China and Japan never have anywhere much to go. They are born into their family businesses or hired by companies at an early age, and work is right there before them until the end of their days. Chinese family members and Japanese *sarariimen* are decommodified, to be sure – and the colony is itself a well organized, friendly and non-competitive place – and yet completely dominated by backbreaking labour.

If we accept some such distinction between Europe and East Asia, the question is why this difference should exist. The case of Europe is particularly interesting in this regard since a clear shift has taken place here, from colony-like arrangements to nest-like ones. It is easy, and no doubt correct, to associate this transformation with the introduction of a new conception of the person sometime during the Enlightenment.[4] During the last 250 years or so, Europeans have increasingly come to think of themselves as self-sufficient, self-directing and self-legislating. A person is considered as an identifiable someone even if he or she completely withdraws from interaction with others.[5] If anything, to withdraw from interaction with others is a way to become more, rather than less, true to oneself since it is only away from the stifling conventions of social life that we can fully express our individuality.[6] For that reason, freedom is understood above all as a matter of being left to one's own devices.

When Europe proceeded to industrialize from the late eighteenth century onwards, it was this conception of the person that provided the basis for the protective arrangements that came to be created. Given who the Europeans perceived themselves to be, colony-like arrangements were regarded as too oppressive and not sufficiently accommodating toward the unique personalities the industrialists and modernizers took themselves to have.[7] In Japan and China, by contrast, industrialization took place while individuals were still firmly embedded in their pre-existing social contexts and before human beings had been redefined in a similarly atomistic fashion. The East Asian industrialists and modernizers were *patres familiæ* and benevolent *oyakata*, with no pretensions to being neither autonomous nor self-sufficient.

This fact was long regarded as a terrible obstacle to economic development. It was why in Japan in the 1880s the Meiji elite tried their utmost to purge the country of its past and embrace European habits. Similarly in the case of China, foreign observers and domestic reformers alike concluded that the country's 'feudal structure' would have to be destroyed before modernization could proceed.[8] Hence the relentless anti-family propaganda of all Chinese modernizers, including the Communist Party leaders. As it turned out, however, these assumptions were quite mistaken. There was no reason to break up existing society in order to create a new one. On the contrary, the old social grammar worked perfectly well with the imported social institutions.[9] This was a discovery first made in Japan and later in the Chinese diaspora and in Taiwan.[10] The 'feudal' arrangements boosted economic development by providing all the extra-market services which capitalism never could provide for itself. Above all, the feudal arrangements protected people from the consequences of the expansion of markets. Since the social grammar was not destroyed, change happened quickly and without too much social strife. In China, by contrast, where the modernizers were hell-bent on rewriting the basic structures of social life, upheavals were endemic and economic development erratic at best.[11]

The difference between protective arrangements could thus ultimately be traced to a difference in the conception of the person. Once upon a time this topic was discussed as a matter of the distinction between 'individualism', on the one hand, and 'collectivism' or 'groupism', on the other.[12] Obviously, it was the Europeans who were the individualists and the East Asians who were the collectivists, and the superiority of the European conception was never in doubt. Collectivism characterized an earlier stage of human development; it implied conformism, an inability to think critically and to act decisively. Such a herd mentality had imposed a 'despotism of custom' on the Chinese, and put an end to social progress.[13]

Yet even a cursory glance at the two parts of the world should make clear how profoundly mistaken this distinction is. European and North American societies are not, after all, filled with self-sufficient individuals but instead with collective agents of all kinds – parties, sects, movements and associations. Far from making it on their own, Europeans and North Americans constantly invoke the help of others.[14] Similarly, in the case of East Asia the most conspicuous feature is not collectivism at all but rather the relative absence of European-style membership associations. Besides, as any knowledge of Chinese or Japanese history reveals, each country has more than its fair share of independent and strong-minded individuals. A lack of decisive action is clearly not the problem.

The basic reason why the Europeans understood China and Japan so badly was that they understood themselves so badly. There were never two kinds of persons – one European, the other Oriental – there was only one kind of person – an individual profoundly dependent on social interaction with others.[15] There are only relational selves, after all, and the notion that a person may be intellectually, emotionally and morally self-sufficient corresponds to no known facts about human life. Officially denying this, the Europeans persistently misunderstood themselves; constantly affirming it, people in China and Japan always knew themselves far better.[16]

The same mistake is still being made today, and it is still a source of confusion. In Europe and North America our autonomy and quest for freedom are taken as self-evident background assumptions of social life. Although we all secretly know that they are myths, this is the way we are supposed to think of ourselves, and obediently we conform. Yet the discrepancy between what we are and what we are told to be forces us constantly to struggle with irreconcilable imperatives. We want to forge meaningful relationships with others, but at the same time we also insist that we should be free of all lasting commitments; we crave security, but when we find it we run away from the obligations it implies; while independence alienates us, we are stifled by dependence. Not surprisingly, relations with family, friends and lovers are easily broken, constantly renegotiated, but never essential.

The question is why the Europeans – including their leading scholars and thinkers – were able to forget these basic truths. The reason, let us hypothesize, was that their protective arrangements always were quite different from those of East Asia. The Europeans were able to regard themselves as self-sufficient and free only since they were supported by families, associations and states that allowed them to think of themselves that way. Ignoring the basic services provided by these social settings, they focused only on those brief moments when they were temporarily away from their nests. At these times they could indeed be described as independent, self-sufficient and free. Yet these definitions were themselves always and necessarily dependent on the support provided at all other times by their nest-like protective arrangements.

In fact, the only protective arrangement that suits a truly atomistic individual is not a nest at all but a shell. Shells are the way snails or mollusc-like oysters and mussels deal with the vagaries of nature. They build hard structures which they can open to let in nutrition, but also quickly retreat into or close if dangers suddenly appear. Molluscs reproduce by squirting eggs or sperm into the surrounding water, but apart from this they have no proper interaction with fellow members of their species. The water brings the nutrition and the oxygen they need. Safe within their adamantine structures they are next to completely self-sufficient.

Understood metaphorically, life inside a shell has two radically different interpretations.[17] On the one hand it is the very image of isolation. People with 'hard shells' are difficult to get to, difficult to understand and hopeless in social situations. What goes on inside their shells we will never know, but chances are we also do not particularly care. On the other hand, the shell represents an ideal of imperviousness and therefore of complete security. Since we never have to interact with others, we cannot be hurt; we are safe within our dreams or within our madness. The shell is a womb or a coffin.

Protective arrangements are unlikely to be organized like shells for the simple reason that human beings are social animals by nature.[18] A shell is unable to provide the love, friendship and appreciation we all crave, and everything else being equal, we would much prefer to live together with others than to live alone. In addition, there is no doubt that we want to have experience – we want to do things and go places – and not just passively be bombarded with sensations.[19] As a desperate form of self-protection, shells are a logical possibility, to be sure, but a society made up entirely of shells would not be identifiably human.

The Politics of Social Grammars

It would thus seem that societies have the protective arrangements they do as a result of their respective social grammars and the historical legacies these grammars have produced. The Japanese employment system thus seems to be little more than an update of the *ie* of Tokugawa Japan; Chinese family businesses to be the contemporary manifestations of Confucian filial piety; the European nation-state to be the heir to an immortal nation, and the welfare-state the incarnation of the heritage of the *Polizeistaat*.

Striking as these parallels may be, they are not particularly enlightening as long as we know little about the mechanisms through which they are maintained. Protective arrangements may be expressions of a social grammar and yet social grammars always allow for a range of different, often contradictory, expressions to be made. Even if we share the same grammar, there is no reason why we should end up saying the same things. Whatever expression is chosen in the end is likely to be contested – that is, it will depend on the conflicting interests of social groups. Although the grammar is a cultural entity, its expression is necessarily political, and for this reason a cultural or historical explanation can never suffice. The task must be to try to retrace the way in which power was exercised when a particular protective arrangement came into being.[20]

Take the Japanese employment system. Given the high levels of labour militancy in the early twentieth century, and again after World War II, it is clear that harmony and consensus are far from inherent traits of the Japanese.[21] It was instead the conditions provided by the government, granted primarily for political and military reasons, that convinced the workers to remain in the factories and to refrain from going on strikes. And it was only when large private employers, pushed by the government, agreed to similar arrangements that the later famous 'Japanese employment system' came into being. This is not to say that the system was a complete invention. Rather, it was an adaptation of an existing social grammar to a new situation, but there was never anything inevitable about this particular interpretation. Things could very well have turned out differently, especially if Japanese workers had been in a more powerful position.

A similar argument can be made about Chinese family businesses.[22] Their paternalism is incontestable, and since paternalism is traditional in China it is easy to see the family-run business simply as a continuation of that same venerable Confucianism. At the same time, paternalism has always been actively perpetuated by the government and by the fathers of the families themselves. In this way, the seemingly traditional is continuously recreated in the present and thus more than anything a product of present-day concerns. Or compare hospitals in Taiwan, where bedpans and bed-linen are changed not by nurses but by family members.[23] Although this may be taken as another example of the same old family spirit, it is also a reflection of the government's chronic underfunding of hospitals.[24] Requiring next-of-kin to help out is a political decision and not a cultural inevitability.

Much the same argument can be made regarding the European nation-state, which nationalists always have presented as a primordial community founded in an immemorial past.[25] Yet we know that the nation is a modern invention roughly contemporaneous with the industrial revolution. Far from being passively inherited, it has actively been recreated in each successive generation and usually for blatantly political reasons.[26] Or consider the welfare state with its obvious parallels in the seventeenth century *Polizeistaat*. There is certainly a connection here, yet as the twentieth century decisively demonstrated, care and control can be exercised in many different ways, and not all of them are equally benign.[27] In the 1930s the Swedes, to take an obvious example, were a lot better off than the Germans or the Russians whose governments in their various ways could lay claims to the same *Polizeistaat* tradition.[28] But this outcome had little to do with culture and instead everything to do with politics, and perhaps good fortune. The cultural forms mattered, but only as politics operated through them.

And power continues to be exercised to this day. Protective arrangements may be presented as friendly social settings run according to generous rules – and of course they sometimes are – yet they have power structures and oppressive practices of their own. They have their specific ways of building you up and putting you down, and while they may protect you against one set of negative consequences, they are likely to expose you to another. For some people this means that they are not necessarily any better off than they would be if unprotected.

Consider the implications for many women. The family, whether in its Confucian or nineteenth-century European middle-class version, was inherently patriarchal and oppressive, but so are many religious sects, business corporations, the union-run sphere of working-class sociability, and also in some ways the welfare state.[29] Given this fact, it is not surprising that exposure to the labour market often has been interpreted as a form of 'liberation'. Hurt by the rock, many women have preferred the hard place. But inevitably, making a life for oneself by moving from the one setting to the other is not a satisfactory long-term solution. Often it is only during the time spent in transition from the one sphere to the other – on the bus to work, for example – that a mother with a career gets a moment's respite and a chance to breathe.

Yet any attempt to change the way the protective arrangements work, and to make them more egalitarian or more inclusive, must begin by acknowledging that there is no escape from politics and that there is no sphere of unadulterated freedom. Every social setting constitutes the locus of a power struggle, although it sometimes takes decades and even centuries between the times when the clashes of competing groups reveal themselves in the open. This is emphatically not to say that all social settings are the same, or that they all are equally oppressive. Everything else being equal, we all need to have somewhere to come home to, and most people stand to benefit even from inadequate forms of protection. Protective arrangements are also far easier to change than is the logic of capitalist markets.[30] We actually have some degree of power over our families, associations and states, although rarely as much power as we are usually told, or as much as we would like to believe.

Good Enough?

Picking up on this last point, the question is not only how the various arrangements should be explained but also whether they provide anything resembling adequate protection. Indeed, from the point of view of the people subject to them, this is surely the more urgent concern. What 'adequate' means here is, of course, far from obvious. Adequacy is a normative matter and norms necessarily vary. Protective arrangements, as we noted above, can be powerful or weak, robust or fragile, intimate or formal, particular or universal, and each dimension will have its own set of normative implications.

Intimacy is surely a value most of us would agree on. Intimacy guarantees that we are regarded as particular someones, with names and qualities that are uniquely our own. The family is the pre-eminent setting for this kind of personalized attention, and no one is likely to understand our needs better, and to love us more, than the members of our own families. Yet the family alone is unlikely to suffice. It has very little power over its environment and no power whatsoever over the market. Families are also fragile since they are only as viable as the behaviour and emotional reactions of their members permit. In addition, and as we have discussed, families have their own distinct ways of oppressing us.

The state provides the opposite combination of advantages and drawbacks. The state is without comparison the most powerful protective arrangement, and it is potentially also the most robust since it is backed up by stipulations based in law and by the full machinery of a state bureaucracy. The state treats all people equally, at least in theory, and if for some reason you are not properly provided for, there are established procedures for making complaints. On the other hand, the protection offered here is exceedingly abstract. The policies of the state apply equally to everyone and will for that reason never address anyone in particular. The state recognizes the humanity of its subjects but not their individuality – and as we know, state power can also be highly intrusive. State protection alone is for that reason never going to be enough.

Associations occupy an intermediary position somewhere between the family and the state, and they combine the advantages and disadvantages of both arrangements. The recognition granted here is more particular than that granted by the state but more universal than that granted by the family. Although fellow members are likely to recognize each other's faces, they are unlikely to recognize each other's innermost feelings. Associations are also more powerful than families and have more influence over the social and economic environments in which they operate. By combining many people's efforts they can mobilize the kind of power a family never could match. Associations are also less fragile than families and more predictable in their operations. They are not governed by emotions, but rather by rules that all members promise to uphold. However, this is not to say that associations provide the perfect combination of arrangements; rather it seems they never are quite intimate, powerful, robust or universal enough.

What is required may instead be a judicious combination of all three arrangements. This would be our normative ideal, in other words. In this way, hopefully, the advantages of each might be added together and the disadvantages compensated for. Protection would be layered, as it were; arranged in boxes within boxes. In this way we would also spread our bets more evenly and have more alternatives to fall back on in case one arrangement begins to falter. And quite clearly, a lack of alternatives has been an issue for example in China, where people have relied very heavily on their families. As long as the family was thriving there was no problem, but once it began to be socially experimented on by the political leaders, and once markets were reintroduced, people were left exposed and with few means of recourse. The Japanese would have a similar problem if the employment system for some reason was radically altered – as would Americans if their civil society associations failed, or the Europeans if there was a collapse of the welfare state.

A related issue concerns how many people actually are covered and what happens to those who are not. All protective arrangements draw some kind of boundaries between members and non-members, and as a result there are always those who end up on the outside.[31] Protection only works if there are people who are not protected. Thus cripples and paupers were not welcome in the medieval guilds, immigrant workers have been kept out of many trade unions, non-believers are not accepted in religious sects, foreigners are a problem for the welfare state, and ethnic minorities cannot find a place in the nation.[32] And, as we discussed above, women are often denied access to proper protection, or are given access only on inferior terms.

Another limitation – obvious when you think about it, but nevertheless easily missed – is that many arrangements cover only those who are in full-time work. This is true of the protection provided by business corporations and trade unions, but also in those cases where the benefits provided by the welfare state are tied to full-time employment.[33] Yet it is not even certain that all workers are protected. In Japan, for example, even at its most dominant, perhaps no more than one fifth of the workforce was covered by life-time guarantees, mainly people working for the largest corporations.[34] Although other welfare programmes and the paternalistic ethos of employers extended far further, there have always been large groups of Japanese workers who have been excluded from most benefits. The glaring example is once again women, who have occupied the most marginal of positions in all corporations.[35]

Which combination of protective arrangements is the best is clearly impossible to determine, and it is difficult to make inter-societal comparisons and to say whether we would be better off in a Chinese or in an American family, or working for a German or a Japanese company.[36] On the other hand, the criteria discussed in this chapter can perhaps help us decide which protective arrangements are the *least* satisfactory. A good candidate is surely contemporary China. Here an East Asian version of Dickensian capitalism is today propagated by a Communist regime in cahoots with multinational companies – and state repression works in tandem with the coercion exercised by market forces. Meanwhile the safety net put together by the Communist authorities is rapidly falling apart, while traditional forms of protection such as families and *guanxi* networks are actively repressed.

Another candidate is Thailand. Here migrants to the capital are often living in very poor conditions, and the only reason they put up with the situation is that they are periodically able to return home to their villages. If the villages are threatened for some reason – as happened after the financial crisis of 1997 – Thai capitalism quickly turns ruthless.[37] A third candidate is the contemporary United States, where welfare benefits are being cut at the same time as the pressure is cranked up on members of the new under-class. The dream of social mobility is what keeps people going, together with a hope of religious salvation and a nationalistic identification with the government and its leaders.[38] This is an unhealthy mix of illusions that can be maintained only by means of ever more intense propaganda.

11

The Coming Crisis

But perhaps everything we have said up to this point is of little but historical interest. Today, developments are afoot which have the potential of radically recasting the entire analysis we have presented. Today, old-fashioned *laissez-faire*, in the guise of a 'new economy', is once again turning things upside-down and melting that which is solid into air. The globalization of markets is intensifying competition and putting pressure on social models to conform to a standardized norm. As a result, many of the arrangements we have previously relied on for protection have come under severe pressure. It is possible to exaggerate these changes, to be sure, but it is also possible to extrapolate from current trends. Doing this, the results are nothing short of alarming. Today, families, associations and states are all changing, weakening and eroding. But if such trends persist, what is going to happen to us? Who or what will protect us in the future?

A first task is to assess the damage done, and a second task is to figure out what, if anything, we can do about the situation. Even if the damage is substantial, there would be no emergency as long as substitutes are readily available. The question is what these substitutes would look like and whether they are likely to do their job. Who knows, maybe we will even be better off in the future than we were in the past? Yet even if we are, this outcome will only serve once again to raise the question of convergence. If the ways in which we have traditionally protected ourselves are being redefined, will we really be able to maintain the traditional differences between social models? To a large extent this will depend on the economic consequences of the various arrangements. In a global market, we are constantly told, where competition is ferocious, only economically viable set-ups are likely to survive. The only question is what is meant by 'economic viability'.

The Extent of the Damage

Consider first the state of the state. Beginning with its capacity as a *Rechtsstaat*, it is obvious that the state has lost much as its former power.[1] As markets have continued to expand, eventually becoming larger than the territory of any one state, state-wide legislation is no longer sufficient. Although formal sovereignty remains, real sovereignty has dissipated. If some measure of political control is to be maintained, sovereignty must be pooled and markets regulated on a supra-state level. In Europe this has meant legislation by the European Union.[2] Corporate law, competition law, consumer law, immigration law and human rights law are today decided, or at least coordinated, by the EU rather than by individual member countries. Although there is considerably resistance to any further expansion of this legal competence – in particular in peripheral places like Sweden, Denmark and Britain – one can easily imagine the day when most regulation with an impact on markets is decided in Brussels. Although other parts of the world have no direct equivalents of the EU, the process of regionalization applies in a similar way.[3]

But the nation-state has been undermined too. Since states today are far more culturally and ethnically diverse than ever previously, nations have become more difficult to define. It is simply impossible to say what a nation might be, apart from the hopelessly outdated images inherited from the nineteenth century.[4] And while neo-nationalists on the political right desperately cling on to precisely these images, the predominant trend goes against them. Although nationalist parties have recently enjoyed considerable electoral success in parts of Europe, they rarely reach more than the 20 per cent of the electorate who seem innately predisposed to accept their propaganda.[5] Meanwhile the remaining 80 or so per cent are becoming less, rather than more, nationalistic. Surveys persistently show that Europeans are taking less pride in their nations, are less willing to die for their sake, and have less faith in their country's military capability.[6] As a result, the nation is less of a home than ever before. The obvious exception is the Unites States, where nationalistic references still manage to stir people's hearts.[7] It is surely not a coincidence that the resurgence of American militarism takes place in the uncertain environment created by today's new and globalizing economy.

As for the welfare state, its demise has been foretold for years now, yet its basic infrastructure remains surprisingly intact.[8] People in Europe are still overwhelmingly in favour of state-run tax-and-spend programmes. In fact, the bigger the economic challenges they face, the more they want the state to do for them.[9] And yet there are obvious limits to any traditional welfare policies. In many countries the state has hit a tax ceiling – the highest rate of taxation it can reasonably impose – and the days of welfare expansion are for that reason surely over.[10] Since continuous expansion was a crucial part of the ethos of the welfare state, stagnation has led to a lack of self-confidence. And even though a majority of the social programmes have remained in place, the level of payments has gone down and the rules have been tightened up. The United States is where this is most obviously the case, and the cut-backs have been particularly severe in places where there are many poor people claiming benefits.[11]

The Japanese state also has been dramatically transformed. There is these days little or no confidence in the idea of an industrial policy, and corporate welfare and neo-mercantilist programmes are no longer actively pursued.[12] Even MITI itself has been reorganized and is today officially charged not with economic planning, but instead with the very different tasks of deregulation and the reformation of corporate law.[13] And China is of course the country where the transformation has been the most dramatic. Here the Communist state has turned itself into a general agent working on behalf of global capitalism. Although the leaders periodically express a will to do something about the country's social problems, the results so far have been less than impressive.[14]

Turning to associations, they may be the protective arrangement that has suffered the most damage in recent years.[15] For one reason or another people no longer seem to participate in common activities in the way they once did. Trade unions are a good example.[16] Union membership has universally declined. It is only in the Scandinavian countries that more than one third of the workforce is unionized, and here largely because unemployment benefits are tied to union membership. In the United States only some 14 per cent of workers are members, down from 32 per cent in 1950.[17] Membership in political parties is down as well, as is the willingness of people to help out in electoral campaigns or to run for public office.[18] Moreover, membership is exercised in more passive ways, mainly through the writing of cheques. Religious groups are suffering from the same trends, except for certain Evangelical sects in parts of the United States.[19] People are not even going to the pub any more. In both Germany and Britain the number of pub licences has declined steadily since the nineteenth century.[20]

As far as business corporations are concerned, they would at first glance seem to be in far better shape. There are plenty of companies around, after all, and they employ plenty of people. And yet corporations are no longer committing themselves to protecting their employees in the way they once did.[21] The whole point of the new economy after all is to downsize, to outsource, and to rely on market forces whenever possible. Companies today offer far less by means of job security and no predictable career paths. Today, nearly 30 per cent of the American workforce has some form of 'contingent' or 'non-standard' employment.[22] In Europe part-time jobs have also become far more common, for men but in particular for women, the young and the under-educated.[23] Instead of having a steady job, you have a CV which you continually embellish and send around.

Even those who are lucky enough to have a permanent job are experiencing a number of unsettling changes. There are, for example, numerous new ways of monitoring the workforce. In the United States some two thirds of employers record the voice-mail, e-mails or phone calls of their employees.[24] While this may make for a more productive business, it also allows employees far fewer opportunities to socialize and to waste time together.[25] New technology has also made it possible to separate people from one another both physically and socially. Today, less information is communicated face-to-face around water-coolers and copy-machines and more instead communicated via computers. As a result you can come in to your office less often, keep different hours, or perhaps not come in at all. People are more flexible, more free, but they spend far less time together.

As for *guanxi* networks, their future is, as we have seen, a topic of intense debate among China specialists. Although we might wish for a different outcome, there are good reasons to believe that these networks may be losing their hold. With better laws in China and more transparency, people can put their trust in institutions rather than in personal contacts. As for Thailand, however, the changes may indeed be fewer. Here there was never an elaborate system of protective arrangements, and what did exist is still largely in place. At the same time it is easy to identify the challenges that one day may undermine the Thai system of protection. With salaried work requiring more extensive commitments, there will be less time for socializing and for *sanuk*; once the sojourners are permanently settled, the ties to a particular village will be cut and all that remains will be a general nostalgia for rural life.

As for Japanese companies, they have of course been badly hit by the country's prolonged economic slump.[26] Ever since stagnation began in the early 1990s, increasingly vocal demands have been raised for radical reforms, and one obvious target is the employment system.[27] According to Japanese market fundamentalists, lifetime employment must be scrapped and a proper labour market created; pay must be more closely related to individual achievements; and no one should be socially censured for occasionally changing jobs.[28] Despite such demands, however, much of the Japanese employment system remains in place. Relatively few companies make, or plan to make, dismissals or force employees to take early retirement. The system of seniority pay is still there, as is lifetime employment, and there is still no proper job market for white-collar professionals.[29] It is instead the people outside of the protective arrangements that have borne the main costs of the recession – people working in smaller companies, women, older and part-time workers.[30] There is still a great difference compared with the United States. In the booming American economy of the 1990s companies were eagerly firing employees; in Japan during a severe recession employees are being stubbornly retained.

This leaves only the family – but here too there are problems, and they are as well-documented as they are well-known. Today, fewer and fewer people get married, and those who do marry later and have fewer children. The change is really quite dramatic. In Europe the average woman had 2.39 children in 1970 but only 1.43 children in 1995; a quarter of all children are born out of wedlock, except in Sweden and Denmark where the number is close to half.[31] Divorce rates have gone up too, from 15 divorces per 100 marriages in 1970 to 40 today.[32] It is revealing that some 28 per cent of all households in Europe consist of only one person, and in many cities this figure approaches 50 per cent. Perhaps most damagingly of all, families on average spend only half as much time together as they did 30 years ago.[33]

And even when they stay together, families are more atomized.[34] Today, instead of consuming things together, individual family members increasingly consume things on their own. Instead of having one common TV, family members have their own individual sets; instead of eating dinner together, family members microwave their separate meals and eat alone; instead of driving to a common destination in a family car, family members drive to their separate destinations in their separate cars. Everybody gets what they want in the end, utilities are maximized, but the family comes to exist in name only.[35]

This destructive process may be operating also on Chinese families, but here it is combined with the destructive policies pursued by the Chinese state. And as we discussed above, the effects are far from uniform. On the whole, families in the countryside have been doing better than families in the city. Throughout China families still matter, and the fully atomized household is rare, yet families are not nearly as important as they once were. It is only in Taiwan and in the diaspora throughout Southeast Asia that something of the former glory of the Chinese family remains.

Taken together these trends point to a serious challenge to all protective arrangements. Extrapolating from current trends, it is easy to foresee the day – perhaps as soon as in a few decades' time – when many of the arrangements we have relied on for protection against market forces have fundamentally changed or even disappeared altogether. The question is what will happen to us as individuals and as communities when that day comes. Will we find a way to revive our families, associations and states, or can we come up with new alternatives that can replace them? If so, what alternatives are these, and how will they operate?

The Question of Economic Viability

The answer to many of these questions is surely that those protective arrangements will survive which can be considered economically viable. The problem is plainly that often they are not. Many protective arrangements blatantly slow down the operations of market forces, distort prices or even block exchanges altogether. The result, as the market fundamentalists are eager to point out, is a misallocation of resources, inefficiencies, shortages and waste.

Yet it is also possible to question this negative conclusion. Briefly, it is not certain that the most efficient markets are the ones most conducive to long-term economic growth.[36] The reason is that the efficient allocation of resources will tell us next to nothing about the social, economic and technological potential of society. Or expressed slightly differently, there are efficiencies of different kinds.[37] It is one thing to allocate existing resources as efficiently as possible within a given economy, but something quite different to develop resources that do not yet exist. Yet this is what long-term economic growth requires. What should be efficiently allocated, in other words, are not the actual resources of an economy but instead the potential resources.[38] To achieve this, a far more comprehensive view of economic activities is required. 'Improvement must', as John Stuart Mill put it in *Principles of Political Economy*, 1848:

> be understood in a wide sense, including not only new industrial inventions, or an extended use of those already known, but improvements in institutions, education, opinions, and human affairs generally, provided they tend, as almost all improvements do, to give new motives or new facilities to production.[39]

It is obvious that protective arrangements play a number of positive roles in these respects, especially if considered over the longer term and if one includes all indirect effects. Consequently, it is often possible to consider even the most economically inefficient of protective arrangements to be economically viable.[40]

Take the family. Families are certainly distorting markets in a number of ways. They provide services for free, and perversely they often provide them particularly abundantly to the least productive members, and hence to the least deserving.[41] Looked at from a broader perspective, however, this also means that the true potential of these unproductive family members will be properly explored. Often, no doubt, the handouts will turn out to be well spent. In addition, and as we pointed out above, families are superb at producing a wide range of services without which the market could not operate – education, health care, and support in times of hardship and loss. The economic benefits of such activities are incontrovertible.

A similar argument applies to the welfare state. As it turns out, European-style Social-Democratic welfare states have an excellent record of economic growth – at least as good, in fact, as that of countries embracing *laissez-faire*, and much better than the free market fundamentalists can explain.[42] One reason is that welfare states outperform others when it comes to resource mobilization. A universal system of free childcare will, for example, allow all women to work, and a universal system of free university education will make it possible for many more people to participate in a knowledge-based economy. In addition, welfare states provide social peace, stable political conditions and predictability – all features that businessmen and investors like.

The Japanese state, with its protectionist policies and corporate welfare programmes, is equally blatantly market-distorting. Yet as we know, Japan grew spectacularly quickly for some 40 years after World War II, and there are good reasons to believe that this was because of, and not despite, the market distortions.[43] Protection meant longer planning horizons, a better utilization of resources, and more money for research and development. By allowing them to take their eyes off the bottom line, protection made Japanese managers focus on goals other than profits, such as market share. In the short run the paybacks may have been meagre, but in the long run they were spectacular.[44]

An analogous argument could be made for trade unions.[45] Although it surely is the case that unions primarily look after the interests of their members and ignore the knock-on effects on consumers and on everyone else, much clearly depends on the position of the unions in society. Trade unions such as those in northern Europe, which encompass a large proportion of the population, will typically take a far broader view of the interests of their members.[46] These unions have an excellent record of supporting rather than resisting technological change, and they often suppress wage rises for the most productive groups of workers. And in any event, high wages might not be such a bad idea to the extent that they makes employers substitute labour for machinery.[47] Although this could lead to unemployment in the short run, trade unions may in this way unintentionally help spur technological innovation.

The personalized *guanxi* networks is another example. Often blamed for an assortment of ills by economic reformers, there are also, as we have discussed, substantial benefits to be derived from doing business with people one trusts. This is particularly the case wherever there is a shortage of information or where there is high uncertainty or risk. And you do not have to be Chinese to benefit from such personal connections. It is a long observed fact, for example, that members of religious sects often do surprisingly well for themselves economically.[48] The reason is that fellow sect members tend to be highly trustworthy, and that they for that reason make good business partners. Transaction costs are lower since people fulfil their obligations to each other without having to involve lawyers or explicit contracts.

As far as global markets are concerned, they too are surely risky and uncertain and low on information.[49] The more global the market becomes, in other words, the more difficult it would seem to be to find the right place to do business and the right people to do business with. Under such circumstances, personal contacts may make the difference between success and failure.[50] In an essentially unregulated world market only our friends can protect us. For this reason people in East Asia may be better prepared for global capitalism than people in Europe and North America – at least, better prepared than Europeans and North Americans who have no fellow sect members to fall back on.[51]

What this means, to briefly summarize, is first and foremost that we must try to keep our cool. There are plenty of good reasons to stay with our protective arrangements, and not to lose faith, regardless of what the market fundamentalists are saying. It is true, of course, that families, associations and states may have market-distorting effects, but the market distortion may indeed itself be what ultimately promotes economic growth.[52] To stand up for our protective arrangements would thus not be to disregard economic factors but to affirm them. Of course it would also be to stand up for our right to continue to be different from the global, and all-too-predictable, norm.

In Our Future Shells

But what if the worst still came to pass and the erosion continued? That the protective arrangements might one day simply disappear goes against our assumptions. We have assumed that people would always find a way of protecting themselves; that we would have no choice but to act and that protection would be more or less automatic. But perhaps it was a mistake to think only of a revival of the old arrangements; historically situated, like all things human, they are surely bound to disappear one day – and perhaps that day has now finally come. Yet this disappearance might itself not matter as long as there are other arrangements ready to replace them. For all we know, we may even be better off as a result.

The most readily available solution is simply to substitute one set of arrangements for another. The most commonly contemplated version is that colony-like arrangements would become more nest-like. As many observers have argued, this seems to be about to happen. People in Japan and China have reportedly become more individualistic of late, and society in Japan and China has become more atomized.[53] In line with this transformation, the state has taken on a larger responsibility for the welfare of its subjects, in particular in Japan, South Korea and Taiwan. Different East Asian societies have also developed more by means of horizontal, European-style, membership associations.[54] In Hong Kong and Singapore, distinctly European-style families live in distinctly European-style – if slightly more cramped – housing estates.

Yet such a substitution is unlikely to address the basic problem. A welfare state is still an alien concept to most people in East Asia, and in the one place where it has been tried – Communist China – it is now rapidly being dismantled. It is also unclear what actual impact, if any, new social movements and new family structures will have. The obvious eagerness with which foreign observers identify such cases of 'westernization' is in itself an indication that the changes are probably exaggerated.[55] Besides, the basic presumption is most likely false. It seems odd that people in China, Japan and Thailand would be content with solutions that people in Europe and North America are increasingly moving away from. Models that lose their attraction in Europe and North America are not necessarily all that appealing to people elsewhere.

We are probably better off looking for entirely new solutions. Consider for example the *deus ex machina* that is television. Although the technology itself is more than 50 years old, it is comparatively recently that TV-watching has come to completely dominate our lives.[56] Today, people spend nearly as much time watching television as they do working or sleeping. That is, television has virtually taken over all of our free time. The reason for this phenomenal impact is surely that TV-watching satisfies some basic human needs. For one thing, images on a screen create the illusion of presence; and as a result, when they appear in our living-rooms, we get a sense of participating in other people's lives.[57] Before long soap-opera actors and game-show hosts become people we know, people we care about, and it is tempting to think that they also know and care about us. Or we watch reality shows with people just like ourselves doing the things we also do. There is something utterly comforting about these images, and this is no doubt why we increasingly leave the TV on as a background soundtrack to our lives. Television has become our constant companion – as long as the telly is on we will be OK.

But there are also newer gadgets. While new technologies often separate people from one another, they clearly also unite us. One example is the mobile phone.[58] There are already something like 1 billion mobile phone users in the world, and when the day comes that everyone has a phone, and all costs approach that of a local call, we will be in constant touch with everyone everywhere. With picture-phones we can even see the person we are talking to. And there is of course also the internet. There has been a lot of talk in recent years about the internet as a tool for creating 'virtual communities', and perhaps such communities could serve as the functional equivalents of the protective arrangements we may be about to lose.[59] Instead of people gathering in the same parish halls or pubs, they would gather in the same chat-rooms or net-meetings. We would be protected by cyber-nests that would exist as easily accessible icons on our computer desktops; identifying completely with our on-screen avatars, recognition would only be a few clicks away.[60]

However, despite the contagious enthusiasm of their proponents, it is easy to see the social limitations of all of these technologies. Television is strictly communication in one direction only. The presence you feel as a TV viewer is the presence of others in your life, not your presence in theirs. Similarly, although mobile phones have made it easier and cheaper for people to stay in touch with each other, the technology is but a poor substitute for actual contacts. The same goes for the internet. Although it may be far easier to bare one's soul to a virtual person than to a person of flesh and blood, this fact is itself a sign that the virtual interaction is lacking a crucial human dimension.[61] While the internet makes it easier for people to meet, the meetings are low on social commitments. The internet is to actual social interaction what casual sex is to love.

But perhaps there is a still more ingenious alternative. Consider how elegantly the problem would be solved if markets were somehow able to create their own protective arrangements. Markets, in other words, would not only be responsible for the problem in the first place but also go on to help people deal with it, and money would be made in both steps. This is surely what is happening in our contemporary consumer societies where purchases concern not commodities and services but images and life-styles.[62] Today, consumption is not so much a matter of satisfying basic physical needs as a matter of the creation and affirmation of identities. As advertisements constantly assure us, there are people out there who care about who we are, how we look, and what products we employ in order to combat body odours. In this way companies prey on our anxieties while simultaneously making us think that social acceptance is dependent on the choices we make as consumers.[63]

The ultimate solution is of course to conclude that we no longer need all that much by means of protection. According to this argument, people are surely far better equipped today than ever before when it comes to dealing with the negative consequences of the expansion of markets. We are healthier, better educated, more sophisticated in economic matters and more adept at looking after ourselves. More attractive to the market, we are in a far better bargaining position. Besides, markets today are more orderly than ever before, and social statbility can be maintained without constant intervention by the state. Capitalism, in the twenty-first century, is an affair between consenting adults who only have themselves to blame if they get hurt. Hence the imminent demise of the various protective arrangements is an event to be celebrated, not to be bemoaned. There are now far fewer people around – government bureaucrats, church ladies, union bosses and family members – who can tell us what to think and what to do, and in the future there will be fewer still. Without their intrusive nosiness we will finally be free to maximize our utility.

But very few people would of course ever explicitly reason in such terms, and those who do do so only since they are blind to the many ways in which they depend on interaction with others. Yet this still highlights the degree to which people in the future will be differently exposed to markets and differently equipped to handle their effects. Some will no doubt work too many jobs, have too little money and time, and be too tired to go to meetings or even to socialize properly with their families.[64] People like this will form the new under-class. Others will be more than sufficiently well-equipped as individuals to thrive even under the harshest of market conditions, while simultaneously having both enough money and enough time to maintain their social networks in impeccable order.[65] People like this will form the new upper-class.

Between the under-class and the upper-class, a majority of us will cope through various half-measures. We will have some successes as market participants, but also plenty of failures. Our old protective arrangements will formally still be there, but we will rely on them only intermittently and increasingly hesitatingly. Instead, we will spend more time passively in front of our television sets, watching game-shows and televangelists, downloading pornography off the internet, do drugs and vote for politicians who promise national renewal through foreign military adventures. Or perhaps we will just quietly go crazy.

That is, we will in the future increasingly come to rely on protective arrangements built like shells. Opening ourselves sufficiently to receive external stimuli, and then spending the rest of our time fantasizing and hallucinating, we will be able to fashion some kind of a life for ourselves, albeit not a particularly attractive one. The problem is that for society as a whole this may very well result in an equilibrium from which there is no obvious impetus to move. Everyone gets by somehow, if in entirely different ways. A new class system is created, but not based on ancestry, wealth or education as in the past, but instead based on the amount and quality of the social interaction we have access to.

We are not there yet, and perhaps we never will get there. What is certain, however, is that markets will never ultimately outsmart societies. No one is actually prepared to live in a world where the logic of supply and demand is universally applied. Sooner or later we will all realize as much, and when we do, we will start to think of other ways of protecting ourselves. Eventually, society will reassert itself, and markets will once again be confined to their own delimited sphere. In the end we will no doubt learn from our mistakes, but that day may still be some way off and things may get a lot worse before they start to get better.

Notes

1. The Inevitability and Inhumanity of Capitalism

1 For various versions of the argument, see Luttwak, 1999, pp. 27–53; Head, 2003, pp. 1–16; Ehrenreich, 2002, pp. 193–221; Cappelli, 1999, pp. 113–57; Castells, 1996/2000, pp. 77–162.

2 It is a striking fact, for example, that real wages have remained largely stagnant in North America since the 1970s. The reason people feel richer is that they work more, above all as families. See Luttwak, 1999, pp. 63–7, 95–8. Compare the plight of the impoverished, neo-conservative, former farmers discussed in Frank, 2004, especially pp. 60–88.

3 Frank, 2004, p. 144–5, 166–9. Compare the idealism of the circle forming around Ayn Rand, including people like Alan Greenspan. See Madrick, 2001.

4 On China see Elvin, 1973, pp. 164–5; Gernet, 1972/1999, pp. 67–73; on Europe, see Pirenne, 1933/1947, pp. 15–38.

5 This is the 'great transformation' in the title of Polanyi, 1944/1957, see especially pp. 135–50. Polanyi's account is modified in Taylor, 1972, pp. 39–64; Hobsbawm, 1969, pp. 225–48.

6 It is instructive to compare an account of nineteenth-century capitalism such as 'Arbetarfrågan', *Nordisk familjebok*, 1904, web page, with the Report by the Democratic Staff of the House Committee on Education and the Workforce, 16 February 2004, web page. Compare Frank, 2004, p. 80; Toynbee, 2002, p. xiv.

7 On humiliation, see Ehrenreich, 2002, for example pp. 101–14.

8 Marx and Engels, 1848/1985, p. 83; and the elaboration in Berman, 1983, especially pp. 87–129.

9 On the relationship between capitalist development and democracy, see Lipset, 1959, pp. 69–105.

10 For a brief summary see Hirschman, 1982, pp. 1463–84.

11 This would among to something like a Scottian interpretation of Polanyi. See Scott, 1989, pp. 3–33, and Polanyi, 1944/1957, especially pp. 130–4.

12 Compare the surprisingly communitarian ethos of the self-proclaimed individualists gathering at the website www.theatlasphere.com, dedicated to the thought of Ayn Rand. See in particular the dating service.

13 There is no sense in which this discussion is exhaustive. Most obviously it ignores issues of inequality and the perpetuation of social and political privilege.

14 Friedman, 1953, pp. 3–43.

15 Smith, 1776/1981, I, pp. 6–36. On the division of labour see also Ferguson, 1767/1995, pp. 172–9. The classical sociological tract is Durkheim, 1893/1997, see especially pp. 147–75. Compare Honneth, 1995, pp. 88–91. For similar ideas in imperial China, see Wong, 1997, p. 134.

16 Smith, 1776/1981, I, pp. 429–72.

17 Ure, 1835/1967, pp. 19–20.
18 Simmel, 1900/1990, pp. 283–354.
19 Pirenne, 1933/1947, p. 71.
20 A famous early account is Merton, 1938, pp. 672–82.
21 Thompson, 1963/1991, pp. 366–72. as 'Arbetarfrågan', *Nordisk familjebok*, 1904, web page.
22 Pollard, 1968, pp. 189–244; Thompson, 1967, pp. 56–97; Braudel, 'Wheels', 1979/2002, pp. 231–373.
23 Ure, 1835/1967, pp. 13–14. Compare Thompson, 1963/1991, p. 395.
24 Ferguson, 1767/1995, p. 174.
25 Marx, 1866–67/1977, p. 483.
26 Ure strongly disputes this, see Ure, 1835/1967, pp. 23–4.
27 Sennett, 1998, pp. 68–70. Compare Ure, 1835/1967, pp. 19–21.
28 Quoted in Thompson, 1963/1991, p. 374.
29 Schulze, 1994, p. 141. Migration was limited, however, in countries such as England which were already heavily urbanized. Here the new factory workers were not peasants. Phillips, 1989, p. 19.
30 Harootunian, 2000, especially pp. 3–33.
31 Quoted in Clark, 2000, p. 157.
32 Quoted in Harootunian, 2000, p. 9. The subsequent quote is by the author Edogawa Rampo, *ibid*, p. 11.
33 Mulder paraphrasing the author Wo Winitchaikun. Mulder, 1997, p. 276.
34 Compare the frequent anxiety attacks which overcome Chinese migrants travelling by train for work away from home, discussed in Lee, 1998, pp. 1251–3.
35 On eighteenth-century London, see Clark, 2000, p. 154.
36 For a similar argument regarding the hand-loom weavers in Britain, see Thompson, 1963/1991, p. 346.
37 On 'efficient prices' compare Lindblom, 2002, pp. 134–9.
38 Commodification is not necessarily an irreversible process. Human beings and religious salvation, to take two examples, are no longer on sale. See Kopytoff, 1986, pp. 64–91. On the Japanese trade in children, see Ramseyer, 1995, pp. 127–49.
39 See for example Landes and Posner, 1978, pp. 323, 347. Compare the discussion in Radin, 1996, pp. 86–7.
40 Walzer, 1983, pp. 95–128.
41 Radin, 1996, pp. 109–10.
42 Polanyi, 1944/1957, pp. 163–77.
43 Hobbes, 1651/1981, I:10, pp. 151–2.
44 Esping-Andersen, 1990, pp. 36–7.
45 On 'efficient prices' see Lindblom, 2002, pp. 134–49.
46 Polanyi, 1944/1957, pp. 72–3; 178–91.
47 *Ibid*, pp. 131–2. Compare Kuttner, 1997, pp. 159–90.
48 More on the concept of recognition in Ringmar, 1996, pp. 13–14, 80–3.
49 Marx and Engels, 1848/1985, p. 84.
50 Schumpeter, 1942/1976, p. 124. Schumpeter himself acknowledges the similarities between his outlook and that of Marx, yet he also acknowledges the existence of a feedback loop from the 'superstructure' to the 'base'. See Swedberg, 1991, p. 155.
51 See, for example, Thatcher, 2004, pp. 1–30. Compare the contributions to Berger and Dore, 1996.
52 Waltz, 1979/1986. pp. 65–6.
53 Tudge, 2000, pp. 75–109.
54 *Ibid*, pp. 456–7.
55 Dore, 1973.
56 See, for example, Gilpin, 2001, p. 278–304.
57 Lindblom, 1982, pp. 324–36; Unger, 1987, pp. 100–20.
58 Hume, 1777/1987, pp. 312–13.

59 For the case of Thailand see Phongpaichit and Baker, 2000, pp. 35–68.
60 For two nineteenth-century prophecies, see de Tocqueville, 1840/1945, pp. 334–52, and Mill, 1856/1985, pp. 119–40. For two twentieth-century prophecies, see Ortega y Gasset, 1930/1994, pp. 11–18; Arendt, 1951/1973, pp. 305–64.
61 De Tocqueville speaking of the role of government in a democratic society in de Tocqueville, 1840/1945, p. 336.

2. How Society Protects Itself

1 This argument draws heavily on Polanyi's idea of 'self-protection'; see Polanyi, 1944/1957, pp. 130–5.
2 Streeten on a political economy which is 'good enough'; Streeten, 1996, pp. 353–65.
3 Compare Pizzorno's *'reductio in A mazoniam'*, in Pizzorno, 1986, pp. 355–73.
4 Kopytoff, 1986, pp. 73–7.
5 Walzer, 1983, pp. 95–128. Compare Honneth, 1995, especially pp. 92–139.
6 Franklin, 1784/1996, p. 65. Compare Weber, 1920–21/1996, pp. 47–78. On the importance of daydreaming, see Bachelard, 1960/1971, especially pp. 1–26.
7 Compare the way in which *kami*, Shinto gods, are sometimes thought to reside in the machinery of a Japanese factory. This is discussed in Kondo, 1990, p. 246.
8 That a relic is sacred did not, however, prevent it from being traded. The case is analogous to that of the Picasso painting. For a discussion see Geary, 1986, pp. 169–91.
9 On the concept of inalienability, see Radin, 1996. pp. 16–18.
10 Take for example the way German trade unions in the nineteenth century discriminated against Polish immigrants. Rosser, 1997, p. 29.
11 See for example Bronars and Lott, 1989, pp. 305–25; Stevens, 1995. pp. 190–202.
12 The more reflective among classically trained economists, including Adam Smith himself, always realized as much. See for example Smith, 1776/1981, pp. 463–6.
13 Compare Schumpeter on how the capitalist order 'rests on props and extra-capitalist material and derives its energy from extra-capitalist patterns of behaviour'. Schumpeter, 1942, pp. 157–62.
14 In addition, Boyer reaches this argument but via a different route. Boyer, 1996, pp. 29–59.
15 Compare Honneth's notion of a 'moral grammar'. Honneth, 1995, especially pp. 160–70.
16 On the far from unique case of Japan, see Dale, 1986, especially pp. 201–27.
17 Compare Polanyi, 1958, pp. 69–245.
18 An argument famously made in the context of the French Revolution in de Tocqueville, 1856/1955, pp. 19–21; 193–203. For a similar argument made in the context of Soviet Russia, see Biryukov and Sergeev, 1994, pp. 182–98; for Communist China, see Walder, 1986, pp. 1–27; 246–53.
19 Dawkins, 1996, pp. 135–7.
20 Tudge, 2000, pp. 456–7.
21 Kuttner, 1997, pp. 68–109.
22 The original use of this tripartite division is to be found in Hegel 1821/1957, pp. 110–223. Compare also Honneth, 1995, especially pp. 31–63.
23 Honneth, 1995, pp. 128–34.
24 On the intermediary position of pubs see Smith, 1983, pp. 383–4.
25 The classic description is de Tocqueville, 1840/1945, pp. 114–28. Compare the updated account in Putnam, 2000, pp. 31–64.
26 On Chinese lineages, see Stockman, 2000, pp. 69–93; on the incorrect view that Thailand lacks social organizations, see Embree, 1950, pp. 181–93.
27 Lindblom, 1982, pp. 324–36; Unger, 1987, pp. 100–20.
28 Offe, 1984, pp. 147–9.
29 Honneth, 1995, pp. 79–80.
30 See for example Albert, 1993; Dore, 2000, especially pp. 219–39; Coates, 2000, pp. 23–74.

3. The European Idea of the Home

1 Goody, 1996, pp. 169–70, and *Social Portrait of Europe*, p. 53.
2 A diversity discussed in Braudel, 'Structures', 1979/2002, pp. 266–333.
3 Schama, 1987, pp. 375–480.
4 Hareven, 1991, pp. 253–85; Ariès, 1973. For a dissenting view on the *palazzi* of Florence, see Golthwaite, 1972, especially pp. 1007–12.
5 Stone, 1991, pp. 229–30.
6 *Ibid*, pp. 231–3; Rybczynski, 1986, pp. 18–19; Hareven, 1991, p. 257.
7 Rybczynski, 1986, p. 26.
8 Compare Elias, 1939/1994, pp. 132–56.
9 Stone, 1991, p. 232; Braudel, 'Wheels', 1979/2002, p. 308.
10 On the Medici, see Strong, 1984, pp. 126–52.
11 Ford, 1994, pp. 128–30; Rybczynski, 1986, pp. 38–41.
12 Ariès, 1973, pp. 353–7; Braudel, 'Structures', 2002, p. 280.
13 Ford, 1994, p. 128.
14 Braudel, 'Structures', 2002, pp. 274–7.
15 Rybczynski, 1986, pp. 36, 131–2.
16 On the traditionalism of nineteenth-century families in France, see Weber, 1972, pp. 167–91.
17 Ariès, 1973, pp. 353–4.
18 Hareven, 1991, pp. 255–6.
19 Similarly the French *garçon* refers both to a 'boy' and to a 'waiter'. See 'garçon' in *Dictionnaire historique de la langue française*.
20 Rybczynski, 1986, pp. 51–75.
21 To mention but two pictures by Jan Vermeer. The *Young Woman Standing at a Virginal*, 1670, is in the National Gallery, London; *Woman with a Pearl Necklace*, 1664, is in the Gemäldegalerie, Berlin. Rybczynski, 1986, pp. 66–71; Schama, 1987, pp. 375–480.
22 Rybczynski, 1986, p. 60.
23 *Ibid*, p. 113.
24 Sir Edward Coke, Reports: 1600–1615, quoted in Rykwert, 1991, p. 53.
25 Segalen, 1996, pp. 382–3.
26 Braudel, 'Wheels', 1979/2002, pp. 320–9.
27 De Vries, 1992, p. 113.
28 Thompson, 1963/1991, pp. 352–6.
29 Daunton, 1983, p. 215; Segalen, 1996, pp. 386–9; Byington, 1909, p. 654.
30 Ariès, 1979, pp. 32–3.
31 Byington, 1909, pp. 649–50.
32 Compare the indictment of the tenements in New York's West Side in McLeod, 1996, p. 140; on overcrowding in German cities, see Geary, 2000, p. 396.
33 Byington estimates that families in the mill town of Homestead, Pennsylvania, in 1909 were deficient in protein and calories by about 20 per cent. Byington, 1909, p. 653.
34 Ariès, 1979, pp. 393–4; Laslett, 1973, p. 484; Morone, 2003, pp. 219–80.
35 Hareven, 1991, pp. 279–80; Daunton, 1983, pp. 226–8.
36 Clark, 1976, pp. 49–51.
37 Hareven, 1991, p. 259; Clark, 1976, pp. 40–2. Braudel, 'Structures', 1979/2002, pp. 306–11.
38 Welter, 1966, pp. 168–9; Ariès, 1979, pp. 32–3. On the retreat of the family from social obligations, see de Tocqueville, 1840/1945, pp. 104–6.
39 The home was, in the words of the American poet Robert Frost, 'the place where, when you have to go there, they have to take you in'. Quoted in Hollander, 1991, p. 31. Or what Fei calls a 'life fortress'. Fei. 1947/1992, p. 85.
40 Segalen, 1996, p. 396. On the changing roles of working-class mothers see Daunton, 1983, p. 228.
41 Quoted in Welter, 1966, pp. 162–3. Compare Morone, 2003, pp. 219–28.
42 Quoted in Hareven, 1991, p. 261.

43 *Ibid*, p. 261.
44 Welter, 1966, pp. 164–6.
45 Ariès, 1979, pp. 33–4; Welter, 1966, pp. 154–5; Morone, 2003, pp. 258–73.
46 Compare for example the scandal caused by Henrik Ibsen's *Hedda Gabler*, 1890, and *A Doll's House*, 1879.
47 In the United States several states passed laws in the 1840s and 1850s to allow women the right to own property.
48 Casey, 1989, p. 146; Ariès, 1973, pp. 60–97.
49 Casey, 1989, pp. 146–9; 160–1.
50 Hareven, 1991, pp. 258–9; Ariès, 1973.
51 Quoted in Rapson, 1965, p. 521.
52 De Tocqueville, 1840/1945, pp. 205–6. Compare Casey, 1989, p. 146.
53 Rapson, 1965, p. 534; Hareven, 1991, p. 257.
54 Daunton, 1983, pp. 221–5.
55 *Ibid*, p. 217. On the role of philanthropists, see Segalen, 1996, pp. 396–9.
56 Pollard, 1968, pp. 226–42; Segalen, 1996, p. 398.
57 Stone, 1991, pp. 233–48.
58 See for example Daly, 196, especially pp. 51–88, 128–62.
59 Compare the persistent contemporary myth of the hobo or the restless traveller. Hollander, 1991, p. 40.
60 Galbraith, 1958/1998, pp. 114–31.
61 *Ibid*, p. 109.
62 Douglas and Isherwood, 1979/1996. See also Douglas, 1991, p. 302.
63 Wright, 1991, p. 215. An argument famously discussed in Bourdieu, 1979/2002, especially pp. 260–317.
64 Ford, 1994, pp. 161–73.
65 Clark, 1986, p. 100; Clark, 1976. p. 40.
66 Quoted in Clark, 1976. p. 41.
67 Wright, 1991, pp. 222–3.
68 Clark, 1976. pp. 51–3. Compare the mid-nineteenth-century educational ideals of American families discussed in Rapson, 1965, pp. 523–7. For a contemporary illustration, see Kumar, 1997, pp. 204–36.
69 Clark, 1976. p. 53.
70 Kumar, 1997, pp. 221–31.
71 Luttwak, 1999, pp. 1–53.
72 Rybczynski, 1986, pp. 148–54; on the importance of gas for the working-class home, see Daunton, 1983, pp. 228–31.
73 For example, Christine Frederick, *Household Engineering*, 1915, or Mary Pattison, *The Principles of Domestic Engineering*, 1915. Discussed in Rybczynski, 1986, pp. 167–71. Compare Hareven, 1991, p. 265.
74 Compare de Vries, 1992, pp. 120–1, n. 124 on p. 132.
75 Kumar, 1997, pp. 227–31.
76 On the 'acceleration of consumption,' see Burenstam Linder, 1971, pp. 77–93.

4. The Chinese Family

1 Eastman, 1988, p. 15; Yang, 1959, p. 20.
2 Gernet, 1972/1999, pp. 67–73.
3 Elvin, 1973, pp. 84–90.
4 For an overview see Stockman, 2000, pp. 94–100; Cartier, 1996, pp. 505–6; Eastman, 1988, p. 15.
5 Liu, 1996, p. 95. Compare the doctrine of the 'five relationships', discussed in Stockman, 2000, p. 71.

6 In practice the monopoly was always far from complete. See Fu, 1996, pp. 107–26.

7 Cartier, 1996, pp. 505–6.

8 Eastman, 1988, pp. On this 'rule by elders', see Fei. 1947/1992, pp. 114–19.

9 The lack of primogeniture has been identified as an institutional reason for the prevalence of conflicts among brothers. Eastman, 1988, pp. 17–18; Wong, 1985, pp. 66–8.

10 *Ibid*, pp. 16–17.

11 Quoted in *ibid*, p. 24.

12 Fei. 1947/1992, pp. 80–6.

13 Potter and Potter, 1990, pp. 8–10.

14 Eastman, 1988, pp. 15–16.

15 Fei. 1947/1992, pp. 85–6. On the 'lack of encouragement for manifestations of material pleasure', see Gates, 1993, p. 264.

16 Hamilton, 1998, pp. 49–68; Eastman, 1988, pp. 136–57.

17 Elvin, 1973, pp. 285–316.

18 Compare Kuttner on Smithian as opposed to Schumpeterian efficiency. Kuttner, 1997, pp. 24–8.

19 Spence, 1990/1999, pp. 208–14.

20 Wyatt, 1982, pp. 210–15.

21 On discrimination against Chinese in Thailand see Skinner; on discrimination in the United States see Spence, 1990/1999, pp. 211–13, 235–6. Compare the recent pogrom in Jakarta in May 1998 when 1,000 Chinese were killed and some 168 women raped by angry mobs. Tuner and Seymour, 2002, pp. 175–80.

22 Siu, 1952. pp. 34–44.

23 At the end of the nineteenth century only 10 per cent of the Chinese population of Singapore was locally-born and only 20 per cent was female. Freedman, 1960, p. 26.

24 On the last, see Oxfeld, 1993, especially pp. 73–91.

25 These figures refer to parts of the American west coast. Spence, 1990/1999, p. 211.

26 Oxfeld, 1993, p. 76.

27 Greenhalgh, 1988, pp. 234–5; Mackie, 1998, pp. 133–43. For a general argument, see Wintrobe, 1996, pp. 48–55.

28 For a general explanation of the economic success of the Chinese family, see Whyte, 1996, pp. 1–30. On the Chinese in Thailand see Unger, 1998, pp. 47–51.

29 Phongpaichit and Baker, 2000, pp. 10–27.

30 In Thailand in the post-war period around 90 per cent of commercial and manufacturing investments have been made by Chinese. In the early 1980s, 23 out of 25 of the country's most influential businessmen were of Chinese origin. Formoso, 1996. pp. 245–60.

31 The importance of the distinction between kin and non-kin is emphasized in Wong, 1985, pp. 58–62.

32 Oxfeld, 1993, pp. 232–57.

33 Niehoff, 1987, pp. 302–3.

34 Hamilton, 1998, pp. 49–68; Greenhalgh, 1988, pp. 228–39. A general overview of entrepreneurship in Taiwan is Skoggard, 1996, especially pp. 111–71.

35 Lee and Sun, 1995, pp.102–8.

36 Greenhalgh, 1994, pp. 754 –64. Compare Hamilton, 1998, pp. 48–9. In 1988 Greenhalgh gave a figure of 97.4 per cent family-run businesses.

37 Hamilton, 1998, pp. 49–68; Greenhalgh, 1988, pp. 228–39. For a general argument, see Whyte, 1996, pp. 9–13.

38 Niehoff, 1987, pp. 291–6.

39 Greenhalgh, 1994, pp. 746–75; compare Whyte, 1996, pp. 17–20.

40 Gates provides an overview of the changing hopes of capital-owning women: Gates, 1993, pp. 251–74.

41 Greenhalgh, 1994, pp. 760–4; Gates, 1993, pp. 256–9.

42 On the economic reform process, see Meisner, 1996, pp. 221–7, 288–95.

43 Meisner, 1996, pp. 232–3; Goodkind and West, 2002, p. 2248. On the bad mental state of some of the migrants, see Lee, 1998, pp. 1251–3.

44 Goodkind and West, 2002, pp. 2238–9.

45 Meisner, 1996, p. 264; Goodkind and West, 2002, p. 2247; Lee, 1998, pp. 1258–9.

46 Xu, 2001, p. 309. Compare Meisner, 1996, pp. 492–523.

47 Meisner, 1996, pp. 478–81.

48 Cai, 2002, p. 327.

49 Chan and Qiu, 1999, pp. 315–17.

50 Yang, 1959, pp. 197–207 Schlesinger, 1966. pp. 221–8; Stockman, 2000, pp. 101–8.

51 Xu, 2001, p. 308; Bjorklund, 1986, pp. 19–29.

52 Compare the May 4th Movement discussed in Spence, 1990/1999, pp. 299–308; and the impact of early twentieth-century industrialization on the family, in Eastman, 1988, pp. 213–16.

53 See, for example, Hobbes, 1651/1981, II: 29, p. 368.

54 On the one-child policy, see for example, Wasserstrom, 1984, pp. 345–74; Li, 1995, pp. 563–85; Greenhalgh, 1993, pp. 219–50.

55 Wasserstrom, 1984, pp. 352–3; Li, 1995, pp. 563–5.

56 See Davis and Harrell, 1993, pp. 1–22 for an overview.

57 Wasserstrom, 1984, p. 358.

58 *Ibid* pp. 349–50; 368–70. Meanwhile the government has continued to insist that privatization of agriculture does not favour large families, *ibid*, pp. 362–5.

59 Li, 1995, p. 568; Greenhalgh, 1993, p. 220.

60 Greenhalgh, 1993, pp. 238–9.

61 *Ibid*. pp. 242–6.

62 See The Guardian, 14 April 2004, web page, on the partial liberalization of the one-child policy.

63 Potter and Potter, 1990, pp. 303–5; Stockman, 2000, pp. 112–14.

64 Xu, 2001, pp. 309–12; Davis and Harrell, 1993, pp. 17–18.

65 *Ibid*, pp. 316–17.

66 Meisner, 1996, pp. 232–3.

67 Unger, 1993, p. 25–49; Stockman, 2000, pp. 112–17.

68 Wang and Jones, 2002, p. 1790.

69 *Ibid*, p. 1789.

70 Davis and Harrell, 1993, p. 8; Unger, 1993, 40–9.

71 Compare de Tocqueville, 1840/1945, p. 105.

5. European Sects, Guilds and Trade Unions

1 For a nineteenth-century German illustration of these general principles of association, see Lidtke, 1985, pp. 25, 36.

2 For a classical account, see Pirenne, 1933/1947, pp. 15–38; a more extensive account is given by Braudel: 'Wheels', 1979/2002, pp. 25–137. On the social consequences, see also Cohn, 1970, pp. 56–9.

3 North, 1973/1996, pp. 79–84.

4 Prienne, 1933/1947, pp. 11–12; 27–28; le Goff, 1988, pp. 9–32.

5 The thirteenth-century *Tabula exemplorum* quoted in le Goff, 1988, p. 30.

6 Pirenne, 1933/1947, pp. 118–20. Compare Ekelund, 1996, pp. 113–30.

7 Geary, 1986, pp. 169–91. Some of the goings on in the fifteenth-century Church are discussed in Burckhardt, 1878/ 1958, pp. 444–72.

8 Extensively discussed in Cohn, 1970.

9 Compare the quasi-Communist ideals of More's Utopia, see More, 1516/1965, especially pp. 75–102.

10 These sects are exhaustively discussed in Cohn, 1970. pp. 148–222.

11 Cohn, 1970: on the Flagellants, see pp. 131–2; on the Adamites, pp. 219–20. On Waldensians and Albigenses, see *Catholic Encyclopaedia*, 1917, web page.

12 Cohn, 1970. pp. 29–36.

13 Compare the dream of a reversal of social hierarchies expressed in the medieval carnival. Bakhtin, 1965/1984, pp. 196–277.

14 Compare for example the sect of the Free Spirit discussed in Cohn, 1970, pp. 148–52.

15 Cohn, 1970, pp. 55–60.

16 Braudel, 1979/2002, 'Wheels', pp. 138–230; Jones, 1990, pp. 85–103.

17 Noell, 2001, pp. 475–81; Robertson, 1933, pp. 165–7.

18 Weber, 1920–21/1996, especially pp 95–154.

19 Robertson, 1933, pp. 111–32; 160–7.

20 Martin Luther, 'Martin Luther's Sermon on Trade and Usury', 1520, web page.

21 Weber, 1920–21/1996. When applied to politics, this came to be known as the doctrine of the 'two swords' or the 'two regiments'. See Skinner, 1978, pp. 65–73.

22 Martin Luther, 1620, quoted in Noell, 2001, p. 476.

23 Compare the discussion of Methodism in Thompson, 1963/1991, p. 390.

24 Compare for example John Wesley's use of this metaphor in *A Plain Account of Christian Perfection*, 1766.

25 Weber, 1924/1948/1991, pp. 302–22.

26 Thies, 2001, pp. 186–99.

27 *Ibid*, p. 197.

28 Marx, Introduction to *Contribution to the Critique of Hegel's Philosophy of Right*, 1844.

29 Thompson, 1963/1991, pp. 389–94.

30 *Ibid*, pp. 416–17.

31 McLeod, 1996, pp. 131–6.

32 *Ibid*, pp. 104–7. In a pre-war survey in Germany 50 per cent of metalworkers and 62 per cent of textile workers disclaimed a belief in god: Geary, 2000, p. 395. But parts of France show a similar pattern. In Limoges the percentage of unbaptized infants rose from 2.5 to 19.2 per cent between 1899 and 1904, civil marriages from 14 to 32.8 per cent. Magraw, 1989, p. 57.

33 Göhre, 1891/1895, p. 112.

34 Despite the recent decline in religious participation which Putnam documents, 'Virtually all Americans say they believe in God, and three out of four say they believe in immortality.' Putnam, 2000, p. 69.

35 Frank, 2004, especially pp. 28–77.

36 Pirenne, 1933/1947, pp. 176–88.

37 Rosser, 1997, pp. 4–6.

38 They were, however, far from being 'monopolies' in the current sense: Richardson, 2001, pp. 220–5.

39 Rosser, 1997, pp. 24–6.

40 See for example North, 1981, p. 134; Pirenne, 1933/1947, pp. 177–9.

41 Richardson, 2001, pp. 233–8.

42 On the prevalence of this metaphor in medieval economic life, see Maitland, 1900/1996, pp. xx–xxiv.

43 Rosser, 1997, pp. 9–10.

44 Smith, 1776/1981, I: 10, p. 145. On 'asceticism' descending 'like a frost on the life of "Merrie old England"', see Weber, 1920–21/1996, p. 168.

45 Smith, 1776/1981, I: 10, pp. 142–5.

46 It is doubtful whether these acts really accomplished any of their aims. They were repealed in 1824. See Phillips, 1989, pp. 24–5.

47 Sewell, 1980, pp. 62–91. On the last set of legislation, see Fitzsimmons, 1996, pp. 149–53.

48 Quoted in Fitzsimmons, 1996, p. 150.

49 Clark, 2000, pp. 350–87; Phillips, 1989, pp. 20, 37.

50 Sewell, 1980, pp. 162–93.
51 On the language of the labour movement, see *ibid*, pp. 199–206.
52 For a general overview, see Phillips, 1989, pp. 11–47.
53 Phillips, 1989, p. 36. The *Encyclopaedia of the Social Sciences* gives a figure of 8 million by 1914.
54 For an overview, see Geary, 1989, pp. 101–35.
55 Phillips, 1989, pp. 11–12; Lidtke, 1985, pp. 11–13. There were some 3 million Polish workers in the Reich.
56 Guttsman, 1990, p. 2.
57 More than 60 per cent of the population was 'rural' in 1914: see Magraw, 1989, p. 49.
58 On the US experience of unionization, see Lipset, 1996, pp. 77–109.
59 Kautsky, 'Der Alkoholismus and seine Bekämpfung', 1891, quoted in Geary, 2000, pp. 396–7. For a discussion, see also Guttsman, 1990, p. 14.
60 Geary, 2000, p. 394. More union-friendly sentiments were reported from England. See Phillips, 1989, pp. 39–40.
61 On the role of the café in French working-class districts, see Ariès, 1979, pp. 35–6.
62 Smith, 1983, p. 384.
63 Geary, 2000, pp. 396–7; Smith, 1983, pp. 372–8. See also Guttsman, 1990, p. 14; Segalen, 1996, p. 400.
64 The *Sprechchor*, or the declamatory chorus, was a particular favourite among avant-garde directors. It was later used also by the Nazis. See Guttsman, 1990, p. 317.
65 *Ibid*, p. 314.
66 *Ibid*.
67 As Geary points out, however, this trend started already as at the turn of the twentieth century with commercial movie theatres and sports events like football games. Geary, 2000, pp. 401–2.
68 The seminal account is Yang, 1994, especially pp. 47–145. See also Gold, Guthrie and Wank, 2002, especially pp. 3–34.
69 Gold, Guthrie and Wank, 2002, pp. 10–13.
70 Fei. 1947/1992, pp. 60–70; Hamilton and Zheng, 1992, pp. 21–4; Eastman, 1988, pp. 34–9.
71 Nakane, 1970, pp. 50–1.
72 For a discussion, see Yang, 1994, pp. 130–2; Stockman, 2000, pp. 85–90.
73 This theme was treated by a number of continental social philosophers: see Simmel, 1900/1990, pp. 343–7; Durkheim, 1893/1997, pp. 147–75. The original source for the discussion of the move from 'status to contract' is Sir Henry Maine, *Ancient Law*, 1861.
74 Yang, 1994, pp. 58–64.
75 Guthrie, 1998, pp. 254–82.
76 Wintrobe, 1996, pp. 48–55; Fukuyama, 1995, pp. 3–57.
77 Gernet, 1972/1999, p. 318.
78 Eastman, 1988, pp. 107–14.
79 Yang provides a list of goods and services made available in China in the 1980s in Yang, 1994, pp. 91–9.
80 A strong argument in favour of this thesis is Guthrie, 1998, pp. 254–82.
81 Gold, Guthrie and Wank, 2002, pp. 7–9.
82 Compare Kipnis, 1997, p. 23; Smart, 1993, pp. 402–4.
83 Gernet, 1972/1999, p. 318.
84 Eastman, 1988, p. 222.
85 Yang, 1975, p. 286.
86 Freedman, 1960, p. 30. Compare Spence, 1990/1999, pp. 211–12.
87 Formoso, 1996. p. 245.
88 Phongpaichit and Baker, 1998, pp. 10–27.
89 On the role of *danwei*, or work units, see Bjorklund, 1986, pp. 19–29; Francis, 1996, pp. 839–59.

6. Japanese Business Corporations

1 Braudel, 'Wheels', 1979/2002, pp. 433–55. On the VOC, see de Vries and van der Woude, 1997, pp. 382–96.
2 Braudel, 'Wheels', 1979/2002, p. 436; Carruthers, 1996, p. 133.
3 For a contemporary discussion, see Putnam, 2000, pp. 80–92.
4 Coase, 1937/1993, pp. 18–33.
5 'Career' originally referring to a 'road for carriages'. Compare Sennett, 1998, p. 9.
6 Some of the artisan bakers Kondo met would occasionally work up to 20 hours a day. Kondo, 1990, pp. 214–15.
7 For an overview see Keys and Miller, 1984/1998, pp. 344–61. For a highly critical account, see van Wolferen, 988/1990, pp. 159–80.
8 Van Wolferen, 1988/1990, p. 68.
9 Dore, 2000, p. 123.
10 See the discussion in Dore, 2000, p. 107.
11 Fukutake, 1989, pp. 32, 50; Nakane, 1970, pp. 40–63.
12 Nakane, 1970, p. 38.
13 *Ibid*, p. 83.
14 Van, Wolferen, 1988/1990, p. 65–72.
15 Nakane, 1970, p. 121.
16 Lincoln, 1989/1998, pp. 366–7.
17 Peng, 2000, pp. 94–7.
18 Nakane, 1970, p. 55.
19 See, also Kondo, 1990, pp. 280–5. Although they socialize far less with their children than their European counterparts, Japanese fathers still occupy a position of authority in the family. Ishii-Kuntz, 1992, p. 108.
20 On ways to resolve this contradiction, see Kimoto, 1997, pp. 13–15. On the company as a family, see *Ibid*, pp. 161–225; on the ability of workers to resist this official view, see pp. 199–202, 298–9.
21 Lincoln, 1989/1998, pp. 363–5.
22 Ogasawara, 1998, pp. 17–43; Kondo, 1990, pp. 258–99.
23 Houseman and Abraham, 1993, pp. 45–51.
24 Vogel, 1979, pp. 9–23. For a highly sceptical view of Japanese uniqueness, see Dale, 1986, especially pp. 201–27.
25 On the early Meiji period, see Jansen, 1975/1995, pp. 41–73; on the post-war period see van Wolferen, 1988/1990, pp. 67–8.
26 Fukutake, 1989, p. 6.
27 For two accounts of the history of the ie, see Nakane, 'Ie', 1970, pp. 259–60; Dore, 1958, pp. 136–56.
28 Kondo, 1990, pp. 162–9; Nakane, 1970, pp. 5–6; Dore, 1958/1999, pp. 136–56; Bachnik, 1983, pp. 160–82.
29 Pye, 1985, pp. 163, 170.
30 Jansen, 2000, pp. 237–56; Nakai and McLain, 1998, pp. 568–75.
31 The most general account is Murakami, 1984, pp. 281–363. See also Shimizu, 1987, pp. 85–90. Compare Fukutake, 1989, pp. 25–32. The term *iemoto* groups refers specifically to groups of kabuki dancers or other artists assembling around a master. See Hsu, 1970, p. 260.
32 Kondo pp. 162–6.
33 Nakane, 1970, p. 58. Compare Fukuyama, 1995, pp. 53–4; 176–7.
34 Fukutake, 1989, p. 32.
35 *Ibid*, pp. 91–113.
36 Dore, 1969, p. 442.
37 Taira, 1997, pp. 259–62; Yamamura, 1997, pp. 342–9; van Wolferen, 1988/1990, pp. 65–6.
38 Weiss, 1993, p. 328.

39 Daisankai Noshoko Koto Kaigi, quoted in Dore, 1969, p. 442.

40 Taira, 1997, pp. 265–71.

41 Extensively discussed in Nakane, 1970, pp. 40–63.

42 As neatly demonstrated in the case of the Kikkoman soy factory in Totten, 1974/1999, pp. 400–1. On the conservative political implications of Japanese sociology which emphasizes the immutability of structural patterns, see Hata and Smith, 1983, pp. 361–88.

43 In George W. Bush's memorable, possibly apocryphal, phrase: 'The problem with the French is that they don't have a word for entrepreneur.' Garton Ash, 2003, p. 32. Compare Luttwak, 1999, pp. 4–7.

44 There is a growing number of books discussing this new economy from a bottom-up perspective. For a representative example, see Ehrenreich, 2002.

45 Cappelli, 1999, pp. 51–7; Chandler, 1977, pp. 50–80.

46 As argued by Marsh and Mannari, 1971, pp. 795–812. Compare Cappelli, 1999, p. 51.

47 Chandler, 1977, pp. 272–314.

48 *Ibid*, pp. 484–500.

49 Demsetz, 1993, pp. 159–78.

50 Cappelli, 1999, pp. 57–62.

51 *Ibid*, pp. 64–7; Sennett, 1998, pp. 107–8.

52 As late as in 1982 in the United States 'most workers do wind up in lifetime work.' Hall, 1982, p. 721.

53 Cappelli, 1999, p. 51.

54 A genre represented above all by William Whyte's *The Organization Man*, 1956, partly reprinted in Whyte, 1956/2000, pp. 75–101.

55 As Whyte reported regarding the graduating class of 1949: 'Looking to big business for security, a cautious generation turns its back on venture.' ... 'It is the floor, not the ceiling, that the men of '49 are concerned about.' Whyte, 1949/2000, quotes, p. 3, 5.

56 At times Whyte comes close to conceding as much. See Whyte, 1956/2000, pp. 94–101.

57 As Nakane argues, the 'attributes' of social relations have changed while the 'frames' have remained the same. Nakane, 1970, pp. 1–22.

7. Personal Thais, and How They Survived the Boom

1 Phongpaichit and Baker, 1998, pp. 1–7.

2 *Ibid*, pp. 281–7. For a slightly alarmist account of Thailand's development, see Laird, 2000, especially pp. 85–142.

3 For a charming, romanticized account by a foreigner, see Hollinger, 1965/2001; for a charming, romanticized account by a Thai, see Nartsupha, 1984/1999, especially pp. 16–43.

4 Phongpaichit and Baker, 2000, pp. 69–106.

5 Nartsupha, 1984/1999, pp. 23–6. For an alternative view, see Bowie, 1992, pp. 797–824.

6 Wyatt, 1982, p. 215.

7 Nartsupha, 1984/1999, p. 25.

8 Shigetomi, 1992, p. 159. For a moral interpretation of labour-sharing schemes, see Scott, 1976, p. 168; for a rationalistic one, see Popkin, 1979, pp. 47–8.

9 Kemp, 1991, pp. 101–2.

10 Embree, 1950, pp. 181–93. For a devastating critique, see Potter, 1976, especially pp. 147–223; Mulder, 2000, pp. 56–68.

11 Embree, 1950, pp. 181–93.

12 Mulder, 2000, pp. 62–3.

13 *Ibid*, pp. 53, 88.

14 *Ibid*, pp. 85–7. On the difficulties of expressing egalitarian relationships in Thai, see Wyatt, 1982, p. 188; Kemp, 1991, pp. 104–5; Potter, 1976, pp. 158–62.

15 Mulder, 2000, pp. 69–73.
16 Shigetomi, 1992, pp. 157–62; on the difference between 'friends to death' and 'eating friends', see Foster, 1976, pp. 251–67.
17 Mulder, 2000, pp. 54, 65; Klausner, 2000, pp. 290–2.
18 Mulder, 2000, 90-91; Kemp, 1991, p. 93.
19 Potter, 1976, pp. 188–98. On clientalism in politics, see Phongpaichit and Baker, 1998, pp. 256–64; Phongpaichit and Baker, 2000, pp. 127–31; as a source of corruption, see Laird, 2000, pp. 242–59.
20 Mulder, 2000, pp. 47–8.
21 Shigetomi, 1992, p. 159–60.
22 *Ibid.* p. 163. Compare Nartsupha, 1984/1999, pp. 38–41; Klausner, 2000, 358–64.
23 Shigetomi, 1992, pp. 162–6.
24 Wyatt, 1982, pp. 109–12.
25 Nartsupha, 1984/1999, pp. 23–4.
26 Phongpaichit and Baker, 2000, pp. 188–93.
27 Chiengkul, 1983, 342–4.
28 Phongpaichit and Baker, 1998, pp. 287–93.
29 Nartsupha, 1984/1999, pp. 73–7; Chiengkul, 1983, 348–9.
30 Bowie, 1997, pp. 59–79.
31 Shigetomi, 1992, pp. 166–75.
32 *Ibid*, pp. 167–71.
33 On collective risk-pooling in the north-east, see Bryant and Prohmmo, 2002, pp. 63–75.
34 Shigetomi, 1992, pp. 166–7.
35 Askew, 1994, p. 85; Askew, 2002, especially pp. 48–106.
36 Well chronicled in Askew, 2002, pp. 86–106; on the Khlong Toei slum, pp. 139–69. Compare Laird, 2000, pp. 401–40.
37 Phongpaichit and Baker, 1998, quote p. 291.
38 Mills, 1998, pp. 34–7.
39 See Textor, 1961, and Phongpaichit, 1982.
40 Fuller and Lightfoot, 1990, pp. 534–6.
41 Phongpaichit and Baker, 1998, pp. 181–5, 324–5.
42 Askew, 1994, pp. 175–6.
43 Phongpaichit and Baker, 1998, pp. 172–6.
44 Phongpaichit and Baker, 2000, pp. 161–92.
45 Jackson, 1999, pp. 254–6.
46 'Prosperity faith' is here defined as 'popular movements that emphasize wealth acquisition as much as salvation' and that 'attach spiritual meanings to the prevailing consumerism of the period': Jackson, 1999, p. 246. On new Buddhist movements, see Taylor, 1990, pp. 135–53.
47 Jackson, 1999, pp. 266–8, 293–6; Phongpaichit and Baker, 1998, pp. 170–1.
48 Siu, 1952. pp. 34–44.
49 Goldstein, 1993, pp. 206–9; Ogena and de Jong, 1999, pp. 423–4; Nakanishi, 1976, pp. 487–92; Singhanetra-Renard, 1981, pp. 137–66.
50 Nakanishi, 1976, pp. 474–6.
51 Singhanetra-Renard, 1981, pp. 151–65.
52 Phongpaichit and Baker, 2000, pp. 69–106.
53 *Ibid*, pp. 86–94.
54 Phongpaichit and Baker, 2000, pp. 92–7.
55 Archavnitkul and Guest, 1994, p. 274; Walker and Ehrlich, 2000, p. 25, have 250,000; Askew, 2000, p. 262, between 150,000 and 800,000; Hantrakul, 1988, p. 121, gives the almost certainly inflated figure of 500,000–700,000.
56 Archavnitkul and Guest, 1994, pp. 282–3.
57 This was true at least in the late 1980s, and it might say more about academic salaries than about the income of sex workers. See Hantrakul, 1988, p. 120. Walker and Ehrlich,

2000, p. 240, give a top figure of 50,000 to 100,000 baht. On whether sex work can be considered *sanuk*, see van Esterik, 2000, pp. 194–5.

58 Askew, 2000, pp. 251–3. For a collection of contradictory views on Thai prostitution, see van Esterik, 2000, pp. 164–5.

59 On the history of prostitution in Thailand, see van Esterik, 2000, pp. 172–81; Askew, 2000, pp. 257–8.

60 On the relative weakness of the wife-husband link, see van Esterik, 2000, pp. 188–92.

61 Muecke, 1992. pp. 891–901.

62 Until the 1950s, 80 per cent of the prostitutes in Thailand were Chinese: van Esterik, 2000, p. 174.

63 Hantrakul, 1988, p. 132.

64 Podhisita *et al*, 1994, p. 307.

65 Lyttleton, 1994, p. 261; van Esterik, 2000, p. 180; Walker and Ehrlich, 2000, pp. 9–10; Peracca, Knodel and Saengtienchai, 1998, pp. 259–65.

66 Archavnitkul and Guest, 1994, p. 275; Hantrakul, 1988, p. 120.

67 Muecke, 1992, pp. 891–901; Phongpaichit, 1982, p. 75; Walker and Ehrlich, 2000, p. 225.

68 Walker and Ehrlich, 2000, p. 232.

69 Van Esterik, 2000, p. 177.

70 Lyttleton, 1994, pp. 259–60.

8. Versions of the European State

1 Weber, 'Politics as a vocation', in Weber, 1948/1991, pp. 77–8.

2 This was most dramatically expressed through the late medieval notion of the 'two bodies of the state', one temporal and the other eternal. See Kantorowicz,1957/1981, especially pp. 207–32. For an indictment of Hegel's view of the state, see Cassirer, 1946/1973, pp. 248–76.

3 Honneth, 1995, pp. 31–63; Pizzorno, 1986, pp. 355–73.

4 Compare for example 'Another theory of democracy', in Schumpeter, 1942/1976, pp. 269–83.

5 A standard argument well developed in Lindblom, 1982, pp. 324–36; Unger, 1987, pp. 100–20.

6 Van Caenegem, 1995, pp. 108–93; Oestreich, 1982, pp. 166–86.

7 Oestreich, 1982, pp. 173–4.

8 As Tribe points out, there were differences between Cameralism and *Polizeiwissenschaft*: the former dealt more with state administration and the latter primarily with matters of social order. See Tribe, 1984, p. 266. Compare Koselleck, 1959/1988, pp. 23–40.

9 Quoted in Mayr, 1986, p. 111.

10 Raeff, 1983, pp. 1–42.

11 *Ibid*, pp. 92–119.

12 Tribe, 1984, pp. 263–7. Compare Horváth and Szakolczai, 1989, pp. 168–71.

13 Günther Heinrich von Berg, *Handbuch des Teutschen Policeyrechts*, 1802, quoted in Tribe, 1984, p. 274.

14 Tribe, 1984, pp. 277–8. On the German critique of the Cameralist outlook and on Justus Möser's notion of *Lokalvernunft*, see Parry, 1963, pp. 185–91.

15 For a contemporary statement, see North and Weingast, 1989, pp. 803–32.

16 North and Weingast, 1989, pp. 805–7; van Caenegem, 1995, pp. 109–25.

17 van Caenegem, 1995, pp. 150–93.

18 Robespierre, 'Sur la constitution', 10 May 1793, in Robespierre, 1965, p. 131. On recognition through the legal system, see Honneth, 1995, pp. 107–21.

19 Article 21 of the abortive Jacobin Declaration of Rights of 1793 had proclaimed assistance to the poor to be a sacred national duty. Weiss, 1983, p. 56.

20 On constitutional neutrality between economic doctrines, see Hardin, 1999, pp. 228–36.

21 Honneth, 1995, pp. 107–21.

22 Chang provides a useful summary: see Chang, 2002, pp. 104–10; French legislation is discussed in Magraw, 1989, pp. 55–8. Marshall, 1950/2000, pp. 32–41, provides a general discussion of the logic behind the legislation.

23 R. Pinot quoted in Magraw, 1989, p. 65.

24 On French reactions along these lines, see Weiss, 1983, p. 57.

25 Marshall, 1950/2000, pp. 32–41.

26 Connor, 1994, pp. 196–209.

27 Herder was more specifically referring to 'the heart of the cosmopolite,' *Letters for the Advancement of Humanity*, (1793–7, quoted in Kedourie, 1960/1994, p. 51.

28 Koselleck, 1959/1988, pp. 62–85. This 'personalization of public space' is the leading theme of Sennett, 1974/86, especially pp. 150–94. Compare Ringmar, 1998, pp. 540–45.

29 Nora, 1988, pp. 801–12; Brubaker, 1992, pp. 43–48.

30 On the definition of the nation see Abbé Sieyès, *Qu´est-ce que le tiers état?*, 1789, web page; on terror, see Robespierre, 1794, 'Sur les principes de morale politique qui doivent guider la convention nationale dans l'administration intérieure de la république,' in Robespierre, 1965, pp. 221–23.

31 On the idea of a 'national economy' see Hobsbawm, 1990, pp. 27–30, 181–83.

32 Hobsbawm, 1983, pp. 1–14.

33 Hobsbawm, 1990, pp. 46–79.

34 An argument made famous by Gellner, 1983, especially pp. 19–52.

35 Weber, 1972, pp. 78–94.

36 The figure from France is from Weber, 1972, p. 70; for Italy from Hobsbawm, 1990, pp. 60–1.

37 Quoted in Hobsbawm, 1990, p. 44. On the unification of France, see Weber, 1972, the construction of roads and railroads pp. 195–220; conscription, pp. 292–302; schooling, pp. 303–38.

38 Hobsbawm, 1990, pp. 91–6.

39 Anderson, 1982, pp. 14–16.

40 *Ibid*, p. 15.

41 Connor, 1994, pp. 196–209.

42 Deutsch, 1969, pp. 3–36. See also Schulze, 1994, pp. 139–41. On fascism as an integrative social force, see Polanyi 1944/1957, pp. 237–48.

43 Compare the seminal work by Bellah, 1967, pp. 1–21; for a recent discussion, see Lieven, 2004, pp. 39–45, 91–5.

44 On nationalism as a liberal idea see Schulze, 1994, pp. 197–230.

45 Marx and Engels, 1848/1967, p. 102. Compare Szporluk, 1988, pp. 61–75, 225–40.

46 Göhre, 1891/1895, pp. 120–4, quote on p. 120.

47 Magraw, 1989, pp. 58–9.

48 Ferry, 'Speech before the French Chamber of Deputies, 28 March 1884', web page.

49 Magraw, 1989, p. 58.

50 On American anti-Semitism, see Lieven, 2004, pp. 202–7.

51 A German example is provided by Peukert, 1991, p. 11; a US example by Hofstadter, 1955, pp. 23–36; a Swiss example by Berthoud, 2001, pp. 85, 89–94.

52 Compare the 'legibility' imposed on rural society by the state, discussed in Scott, 1998, especially pp. 35–45.

53 On protectionism in nineteenth-century Germany, see Friedrich List, discussed in Szporluk, 1988, pp. 115–51; Friedrich List, *The National System of Political Economy*, 1885, quoted in Hobsbawm, 1990, p. 30.

54 Peukert, 1991, pp. 107–28, 275–82.

55 Reich, 1990, pp. 43–5; Garraty, 1973, pp. 907–44.

56 Quoted in Garraty, 1973, p. 917.

57 Reich, 1990, pp. 45–6.

58 As Frank points out, capitalism is the driving force here rather than 'liberal values'. Frank, 2004, pp. 129–31, 134–5.

59 Frank, 2004, pp. 113–37; Lieven, 2004, especially pp. 92–3.
60 Compare the definition in David Wilensky, *The Welfare State and Equality*, 1975, quoted in Wolin, 1987, p. 493.
61 Compare Polanyi, 1944/1957, pp. 77–85.
62 For Senior's views, see Senior, 1830, web page. For a discussion, see Persky, 1997, pp. 182–7. In France, additionally, liberals declared that the old and the sick should be 'returned to their homes', and all the 'merely idle' should be enrolled in the army. See Weiss, 1983, p. 55.
63 Authored by Senior, quoted in Persky, 1997, p. 183.
64 Phillips, 1989, pp. 24–5; Hobsbawm, 1969, p. 229.
65 This and the following quote are from Dickens, 1850, web page.
66 Guttsman, 1990, p. 1.
67 Briggs, 1969/2000, pp. 21–5; Tampke, 1981, pp. 71–83.
68 Briggs, 1969/2000, pp. 21–9.
69 Weiss, 1983, pp. 55–60.
70 In 1910 Britain spent about five times as much on aid for the poor. Weiss, 1983, pp. 72–3.
71 Ruggie, 1982, pp. 379–415. The idea of a post-war consensus in Britain is defended in Hickson, 2004, pp. 142–55.
72 On the consensus on Keynesianism in Britain, see Hickson, 2004, p. 148.
73 Compare Pateman, 1989/2000, pp. 133–50.
74 Esping-Andersen, 1990, pp. 9–34.
75 The metaphor originated with the proto-fascist Rudolf Kjellén in the 1890s but was recycled by Prime Minister Per Albin Hansson in the 1930s. See Trägårdh, 2002, pp. 84–5. The foreign image of Sweden was decisively determined by Marquis Childs, *Sweden: The Middle Way*, 1936.
76 As persuasively argued by Trägårdh, 2002, pp. 80–5.
77 There is no doubt, for example, that the restrictive, and much despised, alcohol policy pursued by the Swedish government was backed by solid medical evidence. On 'real interest', see Connolly, 1974, p. 63.
78 Wolin, 1987, p. 494–5; Offe, 1984, pp. 147–9.

9. The State in China and Japan

1 See for example Cooper, 1965, pp. 56, 93–127.
2 Spence, 1990/99, pp. 118–22, 147–50. Compare Mill, 1859/1985, pp. 137–40.
3 Compare Arendt, 1951/1979, pp. vvi–vvii.
4 Pye, 1985, pp. 55–89; Fei. 1947/1992, especially pp. 60–86.
5 Hamilton and Zheng, 1992, p. 30.
6 Elvin, 1973, pp. 28–31.
7 On the enormous sums the salt tax yielded to the state in the early fourteenth century, see Polo, 1298/1903/1993, pp. 215–18.
8 Gernet, 1972/1999, pp. 144–5.
9 Elvin, 1973, pp. 47–51.
10 Quoted in *ibid*, p. 48.
11 *Ibid*, pp. 67, 149–50; Gernet, 1972/1999, pp. 312–19.
12 Balazs, 1964, p. 77; Gernet, 1972/1999, pp. 322–3; Feuerwerker, 1984, p. 304.
13 Elvin, 1973, pp. 113–63. The question of why these activities were not repeated is treated in Jones, 1990, pp. 5–22.
14 This is the city Marco Polo referred to as Hangchow. Polo, 1298/1903/1993, p. 185.
15 *Ibid*, pp. 200–6.
16 Elvin, 1973, p. 177; Wong, 1997, p. 102.
17 As Feuerwerker points out, however, because the tax system was highly inefficient it was always difficult to raise large additional revenue quickly. Feuerwerker, 1984, pp. 305–6.

18 Compare the influence which its creditors had over the British state, discussed in Carruthers, 1996, pp. 195–207.

19 Gernet, 1972/1999, pp. 304–5; Balazs, 1964, pp. 23, 42–4, 78; Finer, 1999, II, 1999, p. 810.

20 For a general overview, see Yang, 1959; on the anti-family propaganda, see pp. 197–207; Myers, p. 607; Eastman, 1988, pp. 101–3; Wong, 1997, p. 96.

21 Quoted in Eastman, 1988, p. 101.

22 Myers and Wang, 2002, p. 607; Balazs, 1964, p. 153; Wong, 1997, p. 92.

23 Wong, 1997, p. 134. Eastman, 1988, pp. 101–3.

24 This policy of 'active inactivity' was known as the *wu wei* doctrine: Chan, 1963, p. 139. Compare Ringmar, 2005.

25 Quoted in Fu, 1996, p. 89.

26 Wong, 1997, pp. 92–100.

27 Polo, 1298/1903/1993, p. 188.

28 Balazs, 1964, p. 17. Compare Wong, 1997, pp. 99–100. The realist, anti-Confucian tradition of Chinese statecraft is discussed in Fu, 1996, especially pp. 35–56.

29 Eastman, 1988, pp. 136–57.

30 *Ibid*, pp. 170–80.

31 *Ibid*, pp. 206–7.

32 Fei, pp. 101–13.

33 Eastman, 1988, p. 207.

34 Wong, 1997, pp. 168–74; Spence, 1990/1999, pp. 229–47.

35 Van Wolferen, 1988/1990, p. 164; Hall, 1974, pp. 39–49; Pye, 1985, p. 162.

36 Berry, 1997, pp. 547–61.

37 Compare for example Schrecker, 1980, pp. 96–106.

38 Nakai and McLain, 1998, pp. 554–68.

39 Jansen, 2000, pp. 237–56; Nakai and McLain, 1998, pp. 568–75.

40 Jansen, 2000, pp. 43–51. Two informative articles are Totman, 1980, pp. 1–19; Ericson, 1979, pp. 383–407.

41 Jansen, 1975/1995, pp. 43–51; Hirakawa, 1989, pp. 455–61.

42 Smith, 1986, especially pp. 184–94.

43 Yamamura, 1997, pp. 294–322.

44 See the contributions to Vlastos, 1997, for an overview; Berry, 1997, pp. 555–7.

45 Quoted in Hirakawa, 1989, p. 496. Compare Jansen, 1980/1995, pp. 70–1.

46 Quoted in Ito, 1998, p. 46.

47 In some places the turnover rate of labour approached 200 per cent per year. Dore, 1969, p. 443.

48 Quoted in Gordon, 1998, p. 22.

49 Weiss, 1993, pp. 333–7.

50 Taira, 1997, pp. 287–91.

51 Gordon, 1998, p. 24.

52 Totten, 1974/1999, p. 401. Fukutake, 1989, pp. 113, 166. On the unionization of female textile workers, see Tsurumi, 1984, pp. 3–27.

53 Extensively discussed in Weiss, 1993, pp. 337–46.

54 Totten, 1974/1999, p. 400.

55 Johnson, 1982, pp. 83–115.

56 Weiss, 1993, p. 342; van Wolferen, 1988/1990, p. 66.

57 Weiss, 1993, pp. 343–4.

58 Johnson, 1982, pp. 41–5, 199–225.

59 *Ibid*, pp. 173–4; van Wolferen, 1988/1990, p. 67.

60 Johnson, 1982, pp. 216–17.

61 Van Wolferen, 1988/1990, p. 49.

62 Van Wolferen, pp. 348–51, 389–90; Gao, 2001, pp. 68–100.

63 Johnson, 1982, pp. 215–30; Weiss, 1993, pp. 346–54; Hamilton and Biggart, 1988, pp. 75–87.

64 On the transformation of the family, see Fukutake, 1989, pp. 123–5; on the transformation of neighbourhoods, see Dore, 1958/1999, pp. 285–7; Kondo, 1990, pp. 58–62.

65 Van Wolferen, 1988/1990, pp. 109–58.

66 Johnson, 1982, pp. 242–74. The 1986 legislation against sex discrimination is an example. The law was clearly only enacted for the purposes of impressing foreign audiences. Van Wolferen, 1988/1990, pp. 172–3.

67 On the official 'neo-nationalism' of the 1990s, see McCormack, pp. 154–8.

68 Fukutake, 1989, pp. 195–202.

69 Compare Kimoto, 1997, pp. 1–2.

70 For an overview, see Gilpin, 2001, pp. 156–68.

71 Johnson, 1982, p. 78.

72 *Ibid*, pp. 242–74; Weiss and Hobson, 1995, pp. 171–5; Reich, 1990, pp. 288–91.

73 There may have been 1 million workers in 1920, see Eastman, 1988, p. 206; on the conditions of the peasantry before the revolution, see Potter and Potter, 1990, pp. 1–35.

74 Compare the idea of 'the great leap forward', discussed in Yang, 1996, pp. 33–67. An early critic was of course Hayek, 1944, see especially pp. 43–100.

75 Elvin, 1973, pp. 48–9; Wong, pp. 113–16. On the cultural and institutional underpinnings of this model, see Hamilton and Biggart, 1988, pp. 75–87.

76 Fu, 1996, p. 127–49; on Mao's fascination with the Qin emperor Shi Huangdi, see Li, 1996, p. 122.

77 See, for example, Hobbes, 1651/1981, II: 29, p. 368.

78 In February 2000, more than 20,000 mineworkers in Liaoning province in north-eastern China smashed windows, blocked traffic, burned cars and fought with armed police for several days. See Cai, 2002, p. 339. More generally on the social consequences of capitalism, see Meisner, 1996, pp. 492–523.

10. How we Survived Capitalism

1 Compare Ringmar, 2005.

2 Gould & Gould, 1988, pp. 27–28; 51–54.; Wilson, 1980, pp. 189–206.

3 The caveats are obvious. Societies are not monoliths and not all social arrangements operate in the same manner. Rather, it is a matter of a continuum where European and North American societies contain comparatively more nest-like arrangements and China and Japan comparatively more colony-like ones. It is clearly possible to find counter-examples in both parts of the world. For a similar argument see Dore, 2000, pp. 57–59.

4 A seminal statement is Mauss, 1938/1985, pp. 1–25.

5 De Tocqueville, 1840/1945, p. 104.

6 For a discussion of this Rousseauian doctrine see Blum, 1986, pp. 98–100.

7 Mill, 1856/1985, pp. 119–40. Compare also Sumner Maine, 1861, pp. 144–74.

8 On Japan, see Hirakawa, 1989, pp. 455–61; on China, see Wood, 1995, pp. 8–12; Spence, 1990/1999, pp. 299–308.

9 Ringmar, 2005.

10 Goody, 1996, pp. 151–61.

11 Compare the 'November Tree Principle', discussed in Ringmar, 2002, pp. 42–4; see also Ringmar, 2005.

12 Miyanaga, 1991, pp. 1–26. While largely purged from serious academic writing, this kind of Orientalism still leads a subterranean existence, for example in books on 'management theory' for sale in airports. Compare for example Hickson, 1997, pp. 287–421.

13 The seminal statement is Mill, 1856/1985, pp. 119–40. Compare Ringmar, 2001, pp. 64–6.

14 Fei. 1947/1992, pp. 64–73.

15 For two seminal statements, see Mead, 1934/1967, pp. 135–226; Pizzorno, 1986, pp. 355–73. Compare Honneth, 1995, pp. 71–91.

16 The relational conception of the self in Chinese culture is discussed in Fei. 1947/1992, pp. 60–70; in Japan in Miller and Kanazawa, 2000, especially pp. 105–17; Kondo, 1990, pp. 119–60.

17 Bachelard, 1958/1969, pp. 105–35.

18 For a biologist's perspective on this Aristotelian insight, see Wilson, 1980, pp. 271–301.

19 Compare the 'experience machine' discussed in Nozick, 1974, pp. 42–5.

20 On 'formative moments' and 'rhetorical battles', see Ringmar, 1996, pp. 83–7.

21 For a similar argument made in relation to Nakane's sociology, see Hata and Smith, 1983, pp. 361–88.

22 Greenhalgh, 1994, especially pp. 746–51; on the paternalism of the family firm, see Wong, 1985, pp. 65–74.

23 Chang, 2001, 155–74.

24 *Ibid*, pp. 170–1.

25 Compare for example Smith's attempt to provide an 'ethno-symbolic' core for a nation that is continuous over time. Smith, 1986, especially pp. 6–18.

26 Compare Brubaker on the nation as 'event'. Brubaker, 1996, pp. 18–19.

27 On the Communist version, see Horváth and Szakolczai, 1989, pp. 195–7.

28 The parallel between developments in Germany and Sweden in the 1930s is developed in Berman, 1998, especially pp. 201–30; Ringmar, 2002, pp. 39–42; Trägårdh, 2002, pp. 84–91.

29 Pateman, 1989/2000, pp. 133–50; Esping-Andersen, 1990, pp. 58–61.

30 On the possibility of resistance by *oerufu* – 'office ladies' – to the patriarchal practices of Japanese companies, see Ogasawara, 1998, pp. 114–38.

31 Compare Walzer, 1983, pp. 31–51.

32 On the unique case of the Venetian guild of cripples, see Rosser, 1997, pp. 29–30.

33 This is particularly the case for a Continental welfare state with a Catholic legacy. Esping-Andersen, 1990, pp. 144–61.

34 Van Wolferen, 1988/1990, p. 68.

35 For a general overview, see Ogasawara, 1998, especially pp. 155–68; Houseman and Abraham, 1993, pp. 45–51. A sensitive account is Kondo, 1990, pp. 258–99.

36 An interesting case study here is provided by the working conditions in Japanese companies that operate abroad, such as in the United States. See Lincoln, Olson and Hanada, 1978, pp. 829–47.

37 On the impact on the village of the recession of 1997, see Phongpaichit and Baker, 2000, pp. 82–6.

38 See, again, Frank, 2004, especially pp. 60–88, For recent immigrants' perception of 'the American dream', see Talwar, 2002.

11. The Coming Crisis

1 For an early version of the argument, see Herz, 1976, pp. 96–108; for a passionate version, see Strange, 1995, pp. 55–74; Strange, 1996, pp. 66–87; for a sceptical version, see Micklethwait and Wooldridge, 2000, pp. 143–63.

2 A good brief summary is Wallace, 1999, especially pp. 217–23.

3 Fawcett and Hurrell, 1995; on Pacific Asia, pp. 228–49; on the Americas, pp. 250–82.

4 On the kitsch versions of nationalism remaining, see Billig, 1995, especially pp. 93–127; compare the utter failure of the 'Cool Britannia' project; on the symbolic use of ethnic markers, see Gans, 1979, pp. 13–17.

5 A partial exception is Jörg Heider's Freedom Party which received 26.9 per cent of the vote in Austria in 1999 – but the election in 2002 took the Party down to 10 per cent.

6 Dogan, 1994, pp. 285–97.

7 Lieven, 2004, pp. 39–45, 91–5.

8 On the imminent demise of the welfare state, see Gray, 1998, pp. 87–92; on reasons for its longevity, see Garrett, 1998, pp. 787–824.

9 Scarbrough, 2000, p. 233; Rodrik, 1998, pp. 997–1032.

10 Social spending in OECD countries, which in 1980 was around 21 per cent of GDP, continued to grow until about 1993, and it has since then stabilized at around 24 per cent. See Social Expenditures Database, 1980–1997.

11 In the 1990s this has above all taken the form of state-level opt-outs from the Aid to Families with Dependent Children programme. See Zylan and Soule, 2000, pp. 624–6.

12 At most the government may lend a hand in organizing companies into 'research clubs' in order to coordinate scarce intellectual resources. Dore, 2000, pp. 156–67.

13 See speech by Kaoru Yosano, MITI Minister, before the Council on Foreign Relations in New York in January 1999. Asia Times, web page.

14 Chan and Qiu, 1999, pp. 315–17.

15 This is the guiding theme of Putnam, 2000; see for example pp. 31–133.

16 Visser, 2002, pp. 403–6.

17 Scarbrough, 2000, p. 81.

18 Putnam, 2000, pp. 48–64.

19 *Ibid*, p. 72.

20 On Britain, see Smith, 1983, p. 369; British Beer and Pub Association website. On Germany, see Geary, 2000, p. 397.

21 Cappelli, 1999, pp. 17–48; Luttwak, 1999, pp. 46–50; Castells, 1996/2000, pp. 216–302.

22 Putnam, 2000, p. 90.

23 Eurostat, 1998. pp. 119–25.

24 Putnam, 2000, p. 92. On monitoring staff in call centres, see Head, 2003, pp. 100–16; on computerization, see Sennett, 1998, pp. 68–70.

25 Compare the Wal-Mart corporation's notion of 'time theft' by employees. Head, 2004, p. 85.

26 For a comprehensive overview, see Chuma, 2002, pp. 653–82; Lincoln and Nakata, 1997, pp. 33–55.

27 Dore, 2000, pp. 73–7.

28 *Ibid*, p. 74. A similar argument is made in Berggren and Nomura, 1997, pp. 66–94.

29 Dore, 2000, p. 109. Lincoln and Nakata, 1997.

30 Lincoln and Nakata, 1997, pp. 38–43.

31 Eurostat, 1998. pp. 65–6.

32 OECD, 2001, p. 33. In some countries, such as Belgium and Sweden, almost seven out of every 10 marriages are dissolved.

33 Eurostat, 1998. pp. 53, 69. On the 'erosion of the American dream', see Coates, 2000, p. 24–6.

34 Kumar, 1997, pp. 221–31. On the 'declining pleasures of the table and the bed', see Burenstam Linder, 1971, pp. 83–9.

35 In Douglas' vocabulary, the home has become a 'household'. Douglas, 1991, pp. 297–8.

36 Schumpeter, 1942, pp. 188–90; Kuttner, 1997, pp. 191–224. For a series of historical illustrations of this principle, see Chang, 2002, pp. 13–68.

37 Kuttner, 1997, pp. 24–8.

38 More on potentiality in Ringmar, 2005.

39 Mill, 1848, I.13.6, web page. Compare Abramovitz, 1989, p. 7; Murakami, 1996, pp. 95–143.

40 Schumpeter, 1942, pp. 157–62. For a kindred argument, see Hirsch, 1977, pp. 115–54.

41 Compare Becker on family altruism: Becker, 1991, pp. 277–304.

42 Goodin, 1999/2000, pp. 182–5.

43 Johnson, 1982, pp. 83–115; Gao, 2001, pp. 68–100; Murakami, 1996, pp. 95–143.

44 The 'hollowing out' of Japan's industrial sector did not mean that individual companies did badly. Berggren and Nomura, 1997, pp. 51–65.

45 Coates, 2000, pp. 94–101.

46 Olson, 1982, pp. 49–50, 90–1.

47 Compare the abundance of cheap labour in Ming China as an obstacle to technological innovation, see Elvin, 1973, pp. 312–15.

48 Weber, 1924/1948/1991, pp. 302–22. Note that this argument is quite independent of the famous one in Weber, 1920–21/1996. Compare Fukuyama, 1995, pp. 43–8.

49 Baba and Imai, 1992, p. 141. Castells, 1996/2000, pp. 409–17.

50 Compare Greenhalgh, 1988, pp. 233–4; Crawford, 2001, pp. 45–6.

51 On the virtues of East Asian network capitalism, see Castells, 1996/2000, pp. 169–205. On the many advantages of Chinese family firms in global markets, see Shapiro, Gedajlovic and Erdener, 2003, pp. 112–19.

52 Schumpeter, 1942, pp. 98–106.

53 This is the guiding theme of Miyanaga, 1991, especially pp. 27–48. Dore notices a change but is far less convinced regarding its magnitude. Dore, 2000, pp. 57–9.

54 A good summary of East Asian welfare regimes is Kwon, 1998, pp. 27–75; on Thai farmers' movements, see Phongpaichit and Baker, 2000, pp. 143–51.

55 A point nicely developed in van Wolferen, 1988/1990, p. 15.

56 Bowden and Offer, 1994, pp. 736–9; bemoaned in Putnam, 2000, pp. 216–46. More generally, on television as a medium, see McLuhan, 1964/1998, pp. 308–37.

57 McLuhan, 1964/1998, p. 317. On television as religion, see Postman, 1987, pp. 116–27.

58 Agar, 2002, pp. 3–27; 153–68.

59 See Wellman and Gulia, 1998, especially pp. 185–8; or Holmes, 1997, pp. 33–43. For an optimistic view of the internet as a tool for trade unions, see Diamond and Freeman, 2002, pp. 569–96. For an example of such neo-collectivism, see www.theatlasphere.com.

60 Donath, 1998, pp. 29–59.

61 On identity deception on the web, see Donath, 1998, pp. 29–59.

62 Baudrillard, 1970/1998, pp. 99–128.

63 *Ibid*, p. 161.

64 Ehrenreich, 2002, explains the logic; see for example pp. 193–221.

65 Compare 'the cosmocrats' discussed in Micklethwait and Wooldridge, 2000, pp. 225–45.

Bibliography

Abramovitz, Moses, 1989, 'Thinking about growth', *Thinking about Growth: And Other Essays on Economic Growth and Welfare*, Cambridge, Cambridge University Press.

Agar, Jon, 2003, *Constant Touch: A Global History of the Mobile Phone*, Duxford, Icon Books.

Albert, Michel, 1993, *Capitalism against Capitalism*, London, Whurr.

Anderson, Benedict, 1982, *Imagined Communities: Reflections on the Origin and Spread of Nationalism*, London, Verso.

Appadurai, Arjun and Breckenridge, C A, 1995, 'Public modernity in India', *Consuming Modernity: Public Culture in a South Asian World*, Minneapolis, University of Minnesota Press.

Archavnitkul, Kritaya and Guest, P, 1994, 'Migration and the commercial sex sector in Thailand,' *Health Transition Review*, 4, Supplement.

Arendt, Hannah, 1973 [1951], *The Origins of Totalitarianism*, San Diego, Harcourt, Brace, Jovanovich.

Arendt, Hannah, 1998 [1958], *The Human Condition*, Chicago, University of Chicago Press.

Ariès, Philippe, 1973, *Centuries of Childhood: A Social History of Family Life*, Harmondsworth, Penguin.

Ariès, Philippe, 1979, 'The family and the city in the Old World and the New', *Changing Images of the Family*, Tufte, V and Myerhoff, B (eds), New Haven, Yale University Press.

Askew, Marc, 1994, *Interpreting Bangkok: The Urban Question in Thai Studies*, Bangkok, Chulalongkorn University Press.

Askew, Marc, 2002, *Bangkok: Place, Practice and Representation*, London, Routledge.

Attané, Isabelle, 2002, 'A half century of Chinese Socialism: the changing fortunes of peasant families', *Journal of Family History*, 27: 2, 150–71.

Baba, Yasunori and Imai, Ken-ichi, 1992, 'Systemic innovation and cross-border networks: the case of the evolution of the VCR System', *Entrepreneurship, Technical Innovation, and Economic Growth: Studies in the Schumpeterian Tradition*, Scherer, F M and Perlman, M (eds), Ann Arbor, University of Michigan Press.

Bachelard, Gaston, 1969 [1958], *The Poetics of Space*, Boston, Beacon Press.

Bachelard, Gaston, 1971 [1960], *The Poetics of Reverie: Childhood, Language, and the Cosmos*, Boston, Beacon Press.

Bachnik, Jane M, 1983, 'Recruitment strategies for household succession: rethinking Japanese household organziation', *Man*, 18:1, 160–82.

Bakhtin, Mikhail, 1984 [1965], *Rabelais and His World*, Bloomington, Indiana University Press.

Balazs, Etienne, 1964, *Chinese Civilization and Bureaucracy*, New Haven, Yale University Press.

Baudrillard, Jean, 1998 [1970], *The Consumer Society: Myths and Structures*, London, Sage; 161.

Becker, Gary S, 1991, *A Treatise on the Family*, Cambridge MA, Harvard University Press.

Bell, Duran, 2000, 'Guanxi: A nesting of groups', *Current Anthropology*, 41:1.

Bellah, Robert N, 1967, 'Civil religion in America', *Daedalus*, 96:1, 1–21.

Berger, Suzanne and Dore, R (eds), 1996, *National Diversity and Global Capitalism*, Ithaca, Cornell University Press.

Berggren, Christian and Nomura, M, 1997, *The Resilience of Corporate Japan: New Competitive Strategies and Personnel Practices*, London, Paul Chapman.

Berman, Marshall, 1983, *All that is Solid Melts into Air: The Experience of Modernity*, London, Verso.

Berman, Sheri, 1998, *The Social Democratic Moment: Ideas and Politics in the Making of Interwar Europe*, Cambridge, Harvard University Press.

Berry, Mary Elizabeth, 1997, 'Was early modern Japan culturally integrated?', *Modern Asian Studies*, 31: 3, 547–81.

Berthoud, Gérald, 2001, 'The "Spirit of the Alps" and the making of political and economic modernity in Switzerland', *Social Anthropology*, 9: 1, 81–94.

Bian, F, Logan, J R and Bian, Yanjie, 1998, 'Intergenerational relations in urban China: proximity, contact, and help to parents', *Demography*, 35: 1, 115–24.

Billig, Michael, 1995, *Banal Nationalism*, London, Sage.

Biryukov, Nikolai and Sergeev, V, 1994, 'The idea of democracy in the West and in the East', in *Defining and Measuring Democracy*, Beetham, D (ed.), London, Sage.

Bjorklund, E M, 1986, 'The *Danwei*: socio-spatial characteristics of work units in China's urban society', *Economic Geography*, 62: 1, 19–29.

Blau, Peter M, Ruan, D and Ardelt, M, 1991, 'Interpersonal choice and networks in China', *Social Forces*, 69: 4, 1037–62.

Blum, Carol, 1986, *Rousseau and the Republic of Virtue: The Language of Politics in the French Revolution*, Ithaca, Cornell University Press.

Bourdieu, Pierre, 2002 [1979], *Distinction: A Social Critique of the Judgement of Taste*, London, Routledge.

Bowden, Sue and Offer, A, 1994, 'Household appliances and the use of time: the United States and Britain since the 1920s', *Economic History Review*, 47.

Bowie, Katherine A, 1997, *Rituals of National Loyalty: An Anthropology of the State and the Village Scout Movement in Thailand*, New York, Columbia University Press.

Bowie, Katherine A, 1992, 'Unravelling the myth of the subsistence economy: textile production in nineteenth-century Northern Thailand', *Journal of Asian Studies*, 51: 4, 797–824.

Boyer, Robert, 1996, 'The convergence hypothesis revisited: globalization but still the century of nations', *National Diversity and Global Capitalism*, Berger, S and Dore, R (eds), Ithaca, Cornell University Press.

Braudel, Fernand, 2002 [1979], *Civilization and Capitalism, 15th–18th Century: Volume II, The Wheels of Commerce*, Reynolds, S (trans.), London, Phoenix Books.

Braudel, Fernand, 2002 [1979], *The Structures of Everyday Life: Volume I. Civilization and Capitalism, 15th–18th Century*, London, Phoenix.

Briggs, Asa, 2000 [1969], 'The welfare state in historical perspective', *The Welfare State Reader*, Pierson, C and Castles, F G (eds), Cambridge, Polity.

Bronars, S G and Lott, J R, 1989, 'Why do workers join unions?: the importance of rent-seeking', *Economic Inquiry*, 27: 2, 305–25.

Brubaker, Rogers, 1992, *Citizenship and Nationhood in France and Germany*, Cambridge MA, Harvard University Press.

Brubaker, Rogers, 1996, 'Rethinking nationhood: nation as institutionalized form, practical category, contingent event', *Nationalism Reframed: Nationhood and the National Question in the New Europe*, Cambridge, Cambridge University Press.

Bryant, John and Prohmmo, A, 2002, 'Equal contributions and unequal risk in a north-east Thai village funeral society', *Journal of Development Studies*, 38: 3.

Burckhardt, Jacob, 1958 [1878], *The Civilization of the Renaissance in Italy: Volume II*, New York, Harper & Row.

Burenstam Linder, Staffan, 1971, *The Harried Leisure Class*, New York, Columbia University Press.

Byington, Margaret F, 1909, 'The family in a typical mill town', *American Journal of Sociology*, 14: 5, 648–59.

Cai, Yongshun, 2002, 'The resistance of Chinese laid-off workers in the reform period', *China Quarterly*, 170, 327–44.

Cappelli, Peter, 1999, *The New Deal at Work: Managing the Market-driven Workforce*, Boston, Harvard Business School Press.

Carruthers, Bruce G, 1996, *City of Capital: Politics and Markets in the English Financial Revolution*, Princeton, Princeton University Press.

Cartier, Michel, 1996, 'China: the family as a relay of government', *A History of the Family: Volume 1, Remote Worlds and Ancient Worlds*, Burguière, A (ed.), Cambridge, Polity.

Casey, James, 1989, *The History of the Family*, Oxford, Blackwell.

Cassirer, Ernst, 1973 [1946], *The Myth of the State*, New Haven, Yale University Press.

Castells Manuel, 2000 [1996], *The Rise of Network Society*, Oxford, Blackwell.

Chan, Kin-man and Qiu, Haixiong, 1999, 'When the lifeboat is overloaded: social support and state enterprise reform in China', *Communist and Post-Communist Studies*, 32, 305–18.

Chandler, Alfred D, Jr, 1977, *The Visible Hand: The Managerial Revolution in American Business*, Cambridge, Harvard University Press.

Chang, Ha-Joon, 2002, *Kicking Away the Ladder: Development Strategy in Historical Perspective*, London, Anthem.

Chang, Ly-yun, 2001, 'Family at the bedside: strength of the Chinese family or weakness of hospital care?', *Current Sociology*, 49: 3, 155–74.

Chiengkul, Witayakorn, 1983, 'The transformation of the agrarian structure of central Thailand, 1960–1980', *Journal of Contemporary Asia*, 13: 3, 340–60.

Chuma, A Hiroyuki, 2002, 'Employment adjustments in Japanese firms during the current crisis', *Industrial Relations*, 41: 4.

Clark, Clifford E, 1976, 'Domestic architecture as an index: the romantic revival and the cult of domesticity in America, 1840–1870', *Journal of Interdisciplinary History*, 7, 33–56.

170   *Surviving Capitalism*

Clark, Clifford E, 1986, *The American Family House, 1800–1960*, Chapel Hill, University of North Carolina Press.

Clark, Peter, 2000, *British Clubs and Societies, 1580–1800: The Origins of an Associational World*, Oxford, Clarendon.

Clegg, Stewart R, Higgins, W and Spybey, T, 1990, '"Post-Confucianism," social democracy and economic culture', *Capitalism in Contrasting Cultures*, Clegg, S R and Redding, S G (eds), Berlin, Walter de Gruyter.

Coase, Ronald, 1993 [1937], 'Theory of the firm', (reprinted), *The Nature of the Firm: Origins, Evolution, and Development*, Williamson, O E (ed.), New York, Oxford University Press.

Coates, David, 2000, *Models of Capitalism: Growth and Stagnation in the Modern Era*, Cambridge, Polity.

Cohn, Norman, 1970, *The Pursuit of the Millennium: Revolutionary Millenarians and Mystical Anarchists of the Middle Ages*, New York, Oxford University Press.

Connolly, William, 1974, 'The import of contests over interests', *The Terms of Political Discourse*, Princeton, Princeton University Press.

Connor, Walker, 1994, 'Beyond reason: the nature of the ethnonational bond', *Ethnonationalism*, Princeton, Princeton University Press.

Cooper, Michael (ed.), 1965, *They Came to Japan: An Anthology of European Reports on Japan, 1543–1640*, Berkeley, University of California Press.

Crawcour, E S, 1968, 'Changes in Japanese commerce in the Tokugawa period', *Studies in the Institutional History of Early Modern Japan*, Hall, J W and Jansen, M B (eds), Princeton, Princeton University Press.

Crawford, Darryl, 2001, 'Globalisation and *Guanxi*: the ethos of Hong Kong finance', *New Political Economy*, 6: 1, 45–65.

Dale, Peter N, 1986, *The Myth of Japanese Uniqueness*, London, Routledge.

Daly, Gerald, 1996, *Homeless: Policies, Strategies, and Lives on the Street*, London, Routledge.

Daunton, M J, 1983, 'Public and private sphere: the Victorian city and the working-class household', *Pursuit of Urban History*, Frazer, D and Sutcliffe, A (eds), London, Edward Arnold.

Davis, Deborah and Harrell, S, 1993, 'Introduction', *Chinese Families in the Post-Mao Era*, Davis, D and Harrell, S (eds), Berkeley, University of California Press.

Dawkins, Richard, 1996, *Climbing Mount Improbable*, New York, W.W. Norton.

de Tocqueville, Alexis, 1994 [1835–40], *Democracy in America: Volume II*, London, David Campbell.

de Tocqueville, Alexis, 1955 [1856], *The Old Régime and the French Revolution*, New York, Doubleday.

de Vries, Jan and van der Woude, A M, 1997, *The First Modern Economy: Success, Failure, and Perseverance of the Dutch Economy, 1500–1815*, Cambridge, Cambridge University Press.

de Vries, Jan and van der Woude, A M, 1992, 'Between purchasing power and the world of goods: understanding the household economy in early Modern Europe', *Consumption and the World of Goods*, Brewer, J and Porter, R (eds), London, Routledge.

Demsetz, Harold, 1993, 'Theory of the firm revisited', *The Nature of the Firm: Origins, Evolution, and Development*, Williamson, O E (ed.), New York, Oxford University Press.

Deutsch, Karl, 1969, *Nationalism and Its Alternatives*, New York, Knopf.

Dewey, John, 1946, *The Public and Its Problems: An Essay in Political Inquiry*, Chicago, Gateway.

Diamond, W J and Freeman, R B, 2002, 'Will unionism prosper in cyberspace?: the promise of the internet for employee organization', *British Journal of Industrial Relations*, 40: 3. 569–96.

Dictionnaire historique de la langue française, 1993, Paris, Robert.

Dogan, Mattei, 1994, 'The decline of nationalisms within European Europe', *Comparative Politics*, 2, 281–305.

Donath, Judith S, 1998, 'Identity and deception in the virtual community', *Communities in Cyberspace*, Kollock, P and Smith, M (eds), New York, Routledge.

Dore, Ronald P, 1999 [1958], *City Life in Japan: A Study of a Tokyo Ward*, Richmond, Japan Library.

Dore, Ronald P, 1969, 'The modernizer as special case: Japanese Factory Legislation, 1882–1922', *Comparative Studies in Society and History*, 11: 4.

Dore, Ronald P, 1973, *British Factory, Japanese Factory: The Origins of National Diversity in Industrial Relations*, London, Allen & Unwin.

Dore, Ronald P, 2000, *Stock Market Capitalism; Welfare Capitalism: Japan and Germany versus the Anglo-Saxons*, Oxford, Oxford University Press.

Douglas, Mary, 1991, 'The idea of a home: a kind of place', *Social Research*, 58: 1.

Douglas, Mary and Isherwood, B, 1996 [1979], *The World of Goods: Towards an Anthropology of Consumption*, London, Routledge.

Durkheim, Émile, 1997, [1893], *The Division of Labor in Society*, New York, Free Press.

Eastman, Lloyd E, 1988, *Family, Fields, and Ancestors: Constancy and Change in China's Social and Economic History*, New York, Oxford University Press.

Ehrenreich, Barbara, 2002, *Nickel and Dimes: Undercover in Low-wage USA*, London, Granta.

Ekelund, Robert B and Hébert, R F, 1997, *A History of Economic Theory and Method*, New York, McGraw-Hill.

Ekelund, Robert B, Hébert, R F, Tollison R D, Anderson, G M and Davidson, Audrey B, 1996, *Sacred Trust: the Medieval Church as an Economic Firm*, Oxford, Oxford University Press.

Elias, Norbert, 1994 [1939], 'The history of manners', *The Civilizing Process*, Oxford, Blackwell.

Elvin, Mark, 1973, *The Pattern of the Chinese Past: A Social and Economic Interpretation*, Stanford, Stanford University Press.

Embree, John F, 'Thailand: a loosely structured social system', *American Anthropologist*, 52, 181–93.

Ericson, Mark D, 1979, 'The Bakufu looks abroad: the 1865 mission to France,' *Monumenta Nipponica*, 34: 4, 383–407.

Esping-Andersen, Gøsta, 1990, *The Three Worlds of Welfare Capitalism*, Princeton, Princeton University Press, 36–7.

Fawcett, Louise and Hurrell, A (eds), 1995, *Regionalism in World Politics: Regional Organization and International Order*, New York, Oxford University Press.

Fay, S B, 1950, 'Bismarck's welfare state', *Current History*, 43.

Fei, Xiaotong, 1992 [1947], *From the Soil: The Foundations of Chinese Society*, Hamilton, G G and Wan Zheng (trans.), Berkeley, University of California Press.

Ferguson, Adam, 1995 [1767], *An Essay on the History of Civil Society*, Cambridge, Cambridge University Press.

Feuerwerker, Albert, 1984, 'The state and the economy in late imperial China', *Theory and Society*, 13, 297–326.

Fitzsimmons, Michael P, 1996, 'The national assembly and the abolition of guilds in France', *The Historical Journal*, 39: 1, 133–54,

Ford, Larry R, 1994, *Cities and Buildings: Skyscrapers, Skid Rows, and Suburbs*, Baltimore, Johns Hopkins University Press.

Formoso, Bernard, 1996, 'Chinese temples and philanthropic associations in Thailand', *Journal of Southeast Asian Studies*, 27: 2, 245–60.

Foster, Brian L, 1976, 'Friendship in rural Thailand', *Ethnology*, 15: 3, 251–67.

Francis, Corinna-Barbara, 1996, 'Reproduction of *Danwei* institutional features in the context of China's market economy: the case of Haidian district's high-tech sector', *China Quarterly*, 147, 839–59.

Frank, Thomas, 2004, *What's the Matter with America?: The Resistible Rise of the American Right*, London, Secker & Warburg.

Franklin, Benjamin, 1996 [1784], *The Autobiography of Benjamin Franklin*, New York, Dover.

Fraser, Derek, 1981, 'The English poor laws and the origins of the British welfare state', *The Emergence of the Welfare State in Britain and Germany, 1850–1950*, Mommsen, W J (ed.), London, Croom Helm.

Freedman, Maurice, 1960, 'Immigrants and associations: Chinese in nineteenth-century Singapore', *Comparative Studies in Society and History*, 3: 1, 25–48.

Friedman, Milton, 1953, 'The methodology of positive economics', *Essays in Positive Economics*, Chicago, University of Chicago Press.

Fu, Zhengyuan, 1996, *China's Legalists: The Earliest Totalitarians and Their Art of Ruling*, Armonk NY, M.E. Sharpe.

Fukutake, Tadashi, 1989, *The Japanese Social Structure: Its Evolution in the Modern Century*, Dore, R P (trans.), Tokyo, University of Tokyo Press.

Fukuyama, Francis, 1995, *Trust: the Social Virtues and the Creation of Prosperity*, Harmondsworth, Penguin.

Fuller, Theodore D, Kamnuansilpa, Peerasit and Lightfoot, P, 1990, 'Urban ties of rural Thais', *International Migration Review*, 24: 3.

Fung, Hi, 2001, 'The making and melting of the "Iron Rice Bowl" in China 1949 to 1995', *Social Policy and Administration*, 35: 3, 258–73.

Galbraith, John Kenneth, 1998 [1958], *The Affluent Society*, Harmondsworth, Penguin.

Gans, Herbert J, 1979, 'Symbolic ethnicity: the future of ethnic groups and cultures in America', *Ethnic and Racial Studies*, 2: 1, 1–20.

Gao, Bai, 2001, *Japan's Economic Dilemma: The Institutional Origins of Prosperity and Stagnation*, Cambridge, Cambridge University Press.

Garraty, John A, 1973, 'The new deal, national socialism, and the great depression', *American Historical Review*, 78: 4, 907–44.

Garrett, Geoffrey, 1998, 'Global markets and national politics: collision course or virtuous circle?', *International Organization*, 52: 4, 787–824.

Garton Ash, Timothy, 2003, 'Anti-Europeanism in America', *New York Review of Books*, February 13, 32–34.

Gates, Hill, 1993, 'Cultural support for birth limitation among urban capital-owning women', *Chinese Families in the Post-Mao Era*, Davis, D and Harrell, S (eds), Berkeley, University of California Press.

Geary, Dick, 1989, 'Socialism and the German labour movement before 1914', *Labour and Socialist Movements in Europe Before 1914*, Geary, D (ed.), Oxford, Berg.

Geary, Dick, 2000, 'Beer and skittles?: workers and culture in early twentieth-century Germany', *Australian Journal of Politics and History*, 46: 3.

Geary, Patrick, 1986, 'Sacred commodities: the circulation of medieval relics', *The Social Life of Things: Commodities in Cultural Perspective*, Appadurai, A (ed.), Cambridge, Cambridge University Press.

Gellner, Ernest, 1983, *Nations and Nationalism*, Ithaca, Cornell University Press.

Gernet, Jacques, 1999 [1972], *A History of Chinese Civilization*, Cambridge, Cambridge University Press.

Gil, Tom, 2000, '*Yoseba* and *Ninpudashi*: changing patterns of employment on the fringes of the Japanese economy', *Globalization and Social Change in Contemporary Japan*, Eades, J S, Gill, T and Befu, H (eds), Melbourne, Trans Pacific Press.

Gilpin, Robert, 2001, *Global Political Economy: Understanding the International Economic Order*, Princeton, Princeton University Press.

Göhre, Paul, 1895 [1891], *Three Months in a Workshop: A Practical Study*, London, Swan Sonnenschein.

Gold, Thomas, Guthrie, D and Wank, D (eds), 2002, *Social Connections in China: Institutions, Culture, and the Changing Nature of Guanxi*, Cambridge, Cambridge University Press.

Gold, Thomas, Guthrie, D and Wank, D, 2002, 'An introduction to the study of *Guanxi*', *Social Connections in China: Institutions: Culture, and the Changing Nature of Guanxi*, Gold, Thomas, Guthrie, D and Wank, D (eds), Cambridge, Cambridge University Press.

Goldstein, Sidney, 1993, 'The impact of temporary migration on urban places: Thailand and China as case studies', *Third World Cities: Problems, Policies, and Prospects*, Karnada, J D and Parnell, A M (eds), Newbury Park, Sage.

Goldthwaite, Richard A, 1972, 'The Florentine palace as domestic architecture', *American Historical Review*, 77: 4, 977–1012.

Goodin, Robert E, Headey, B, Muffels, R and Dirven, Henk-Jan, 2000 [1999], 'The real worlds of welfare capitalism', *The Welfare State Reader*, Pierson, C and Castles, F G (eds), Cambridge, Polity.

Goodkind, Daniel and West, L A, 2002, 'China's floating population: definitions, data and recent findings', *Urban Studies*, 39: 12, 2237–50.

Goody, Jack, 1996, *The East in the West*, Cambridge, Cambridge University Press.

Gordon, Andrew, 1998, 'The invention of Japanese-style labor management', *Mirror of Modernity: Invented Traditions of Modern Japan*, Vlastos, S (ed.), Berkeley, University of California Press.

Gould, James L and Gould, C G, 1988, *The Honey Bee*, New York, Scientific American.

Gray, John, 1998, 'The passing of social democracy', *False Dawn: The Delusions of Global Capitalism*, London, Granta.

Greenhalgh, Susan, 1988, 'Families and networks in Taiwan's economic development', *Contending Approaches to the Political Economy of Taiwan*, Winckler, E A and Greenhalgh, S (eds), Armonk NY, M.E. Sharpe.

Greenhalgh, Susan, 1993, 'The peasantization of the one-child policy in Shaanxi', *Chinese Families in the Post-Mao Era*, Davis, D and Harrell, S (eds), Berkeley, University of California Press.

Greenhalgh, Susan, 1994, 'De-orientalizing the Chinese family firm', *American Ethnologist*, 21: 4.

Guthrie, Doug, 1998, 'The declining significance of *Guanxi* in China's economic transition', *China Quarterly*, 154, 254–82.

Guttsman, W L, 1990, *Workers' Culture in Weimar Germany: Between Tradition and Commitment*, Oxford, Berg.

Hall, John W, 1974, 'Rule by status in Tokugawa Japan', *Journal of Japanese Studies*, 1: 1.

Hall, Robert E, 1982, 'The importance of lifetime jobs in the US economy', *American Economic Review*, 72: 4, 716–24.

Hamilton, Gary G and Biggart, N W, 1988, 'Market culture, and authority: a comparative analysis of management and organization in the Far East', *American Journal of Sociology*, 52–94.

Hamilton, Gary G, Biggart, N W and Wang Zheng, 1992, 'Introduction: Fei Xiaotong and the beginnings of a Chinese sociology', *Fei Xiaotong*, [1947], *From the Soil: The Foundations of Chinese Society*, Berkeley, University of California Press; 30.

Hamilton, Gary G and Biggart, N W, 1998, 'Culture and organisation in Taiwan's market economy', *Market Cultures: Society and Morality in the New Asian Capitalisms*, Hefner, R W (ed.), Boulder, Westview.

Hanks, L M, 1962, 'Merit and power in the Thai social order', *American Anthropologist*, 64, 1247–61.

Hantrakul, Sukanya, 1988, 'Prostitution in Thailand', *Development and Displacement : Women in Southeast Asia*, Chandler, G, Sullivan, N and Bransom, J (eds), Clayton, Centre of Southeast Asian Studies, Monash University.

Hardin, Russell, 1999, *Liberalism, Constitutionalism, and Democracy*, Oxford, Oxford University Press.

Hareven, Tamara, 1991, 'The home and family in historical perspective', *Social Research*, 58: 1.

Harootunian, Harry, 2000, *Overcome by Modernity: History, Culture, and Community in Interwar Japan*, Princeton, Princeton University Press.

Hata, Hironi and Smith, W A, 1983, 'Nakane's Japanese society as utopian thought', *Journal of Contemporary Asia*, 13: 3, 361–88.

Hayek, Friedrich A, 1986 [1944], *The Road to Serfdom*, London, Ark Paperbacks.

Head, Simon, 2003, *The New Ruthless Economy: American Workers in the Information Age*, Oxford, Oxford University Press.

Head, Simon, 2004, 'Inside Leviathan', *New York Review of Books*, December 16, 51: 20.

Hegel, G W F, 1957 [1821], *Hegel's Philosophy of Right*, Knox, T M (trans.), New York, Oxford University Press.

Henderson, Charles R, 1909, 'Are modern industry and city life unfavorable to the family?', *American Journal of Sociology*, 14: 5, 668–80.

Herman, Edward and McChesney, R, 2000, 'The global media', *The Global Transformations Reader*, Held, D and McGrew, A (eds), Cambridge, Polity.

Herz, John H, 1976, *The Nation-State and the Crisis of World Politics: Essays on International Politics in the Twentieth Century*, New York, D. McKay.

Hickson, David J, 1997, *Exploring Management Across the World: Selected Readings*, edited by Harmondsworth, Penguin.

Hickson, Kevin, 2004, 'The postwar consensus revisited', *The Political Quarterly*, 75: 2, 142–54.

Hirakawa, Sukehiro, 1989, 'Japan's turn to the West', *The Cambridge History of Japan: Volume 5, The Nineteenth Century*, Jansen, M B (ed.), Cambridge, Cambridge University Press.

Hirschman, Albert O, 1982, 'Rival interpretations of market society', *Journal of Economic Literature*, 20: 4, 1463–84.

Hobbes, Thomas, 1981 [1651], *Leviathan*, Harmondsworth, Penguin.

Hobsbawm, Eric J, 1969, *Industry and Empire: From 1750 to the Present Day*, Harmondsworth, Penguin.

Hobsbawm, Eric J, 1983 'Introduction: inventing traditions', *The Invention of Tradition*, Hobsbawm, E and Ranger, T (eds), Cambridge, Cambridge University Press, 1–14.

Hobsbawm, Eric J, 1990, *Nations and Nationalism since 1780: Programme, Myth, Reality*, Cambridge, Cambridge University Press.

Hofstadter, Richard, 1955, *The Age of Reform: from Bryan to F.D.R.*, New York, Vintage.

Hollander, John, 1991, 'It all depends', *Social Research*, 58: 1.

Hollinger, Carol, 2001 [1965], *Mai Pen Rai Means Never Mind*, Bangkok, Asia Books.

Holmes, David, 1997, 'Virtual identity: communities of broadcast, communities of interactivity', *Virtual Politics: Identity and Community in Cyberspace*, Holmes, D (ed.), London, Sage.

Honneth, Axel, 1995, *The Struggle for Recognition: The Moral Grammar of Social Conflicts*, Cambridge, Polity.

Horváth, Ágnes and Szakolczai, A, 1989, 'A governmental technology resurrected by the party: the early modern police', *The Dissolution of Communist Power: The Case of Hungary*, London, Routledge.

Houseman, Susan and Abraham, K G, 1993, 'Female workers as a buffer in the Japanese economy', *The American Economic Review*, 83, 45–51.

Hsu, Francis L K, 1970, 'Iemoto', *Kodansha Encyclopaedia of Japan*, Tokyo, Kodansha; 260.

Hui, Lim Mah and Porpora, D, 1987, 'The political economic factors of migration to Bangkok', *Journal of Contemporary Asia*, 17: 1, 76–89.

Hume, David, 1987 [1777], 'Of the balance of interest', *Essays: Moral, Political and Literary*, Indianapolis, Liberty Fund.

Hunt, Michael H, 1988, *Ideology and United States Foreign Policy*, New Haven, Yale University Press.

Ishii-Kuntz, Masako, 1992, 'Are Japanese families "Fatherless"?', *Sociology and Social Research*, 76: 3, 105–10.

Itô, Kimio, 1998, 'The invention of *Wa* and the transformation of the image of Prince Shotoku in modern Japan', *Mirror of Modernity: Invented Traditions of Modern Japan*, Vlastos, S (ed.), Berkeley, University of California Press.

Jackson, Peter A, 1999, 'Royal spirits, Chinese Gods, and magic monks: Thailand's boom-time religions of prosperity', *South East Asia Research*, 7: 3, 245–320.

Jansen, Marius B, 1995 [1975], *Japan and Its World: Two Centuries of Change*, Princeton, Princeton University Press.

Jansen, Marius B, 2000, *The Making of Modern Japan*, Cambridge, Belknap Press.

Johnson, Chalmers, 1982, *MITI and the Japanese Miracle: The Growth of Industrial Policy, 1925–1975*, Stanford, Stanford University Press.

Jones, Eric, 1990, 'The real question about China: why was the song economic achievement not repeated?', *Australian Economic History Review*, 30: 2, 5–22.

Kantorowicz, Ernst H, 1981 [1957], *The King's Two Bodies: A Study in Medieval Political Theology*, Princeton, Princeton University Press.

Kedourie, Eli, 1994 [1960], *Nationalism*, Oxford, Blackwell.

Kemp, Jeremy, 1982, 'The tail wagging the dog: the patron-client model in Thai studies', *Private Patronage and Public Power: Political Clientilism in the Modern State*, Clapham, C (ed.), London, Frances Pinter.

Kemp, Jeremy, 1991, 'Process of kinship and community in north-central Thailand', *Cognation and Social Organization in Southeast Asia*, Husken, F and Kemp, J (eds), Leiden, KITLV Press.

Keys, J B and Miller, T R, 1998 [1984], 'The Japanese management theory jungle', *Japanese Business: Volume I*, Beechler, S and Stucker, S (eds), London, Routledge.

Kim, Kwang-Ok, 1996, 'The reproduction of Confucian culture in contemporary Korea: an anthropological study', *Confucian Traditions in East Asian Modernity: Moral Education and Economic Culture in Japan and the Four Mini-Dragons*, Wei-Ming, Tu (ed.), Cambridge, Harvard University Press.

Kimoto, Kimiko, 1997, 'Company man makes family happy: gender analysis of the Japanese family', *Hitotsubashi Journal of Social Studies*, 29, 1–17.

Kipnis, Andrew B, 1997, *Producing Guanxi: Sentiment, Self, and Subculture in a North China Village*, Durham, Duke University Press.

Klausner, William J, 2000, *Reflections on Thai Culture*, Bangkok, Siam Society.

Kondo, Dorienne K, 1990, *Crafting Selves: Power, Gender and Discourses of Identity in a Japanese Workplace*, Chicago, Chicago University Press.

Kopytoff, Igor, 1986, 'The cultural biography of things: commoditization as process', *The Social Life of Things: Commodities in Cultural Perspective*, Cambridge, Cambridge University Press.

Koselleck, Reinhart, 1988 [1959], *Critique and Crisis: Enlightenment and the Pathogenesis of Modern Society*, Oxford, Berg.

Kumar, Krishan, 1997, 'Home: the promise and predicament of private life at the end of the twentieth century', *Public and Private in Thought and Practice*, Weintraub, J and Kumar, K (eds), Chicago, University of Chicago Press.

Kuttner, Robert, 1997, *Everything for Sale: The Virtues and Limits of Markets*, New York, Knopf.

Kwon, Huck-ju, 1998, 'Democracy and the politics of social welfare: a comparative analysis of welfare systems in East Asia', *The East Asian Welfare Model: Welfare Orientalism and the State*, Goodman, R, White, W and Kwon, Huck-ju (eds), London, Routledge.

Laird, John, 2000, *Money Politics, Globalisation, and Crisis: The Case of Thailand*, Singapore, Graham Brash.

Landes, Elisabeth M and Posner, R A, 1978, 'The economics of the baby shortage', *Journal of Legal Studies*, 7.

Laslett, Barbara, 1973, 'The family as a public and private institution: an historical perspective', *Journal of Marriage and the Family*, August.

Laslett, Peter, 1977, 'Characteristics of the European family over time', *Family Life and Illicit Love in Former Generations*, Laslett, P (ed.), Cambridge, Cambridge University Press.

le Goff, Jacques, 1988, *Your Money or Your Life: Economy and Religion in the Middle Ages*, New York, Zone Books.

Lee, Mei-lin and Te-Hsiung Sun, 1995, 'The family and demography in contemporary Taiwan', *Journal of Comparative Family Studies*, 26: 1.

Lee, Sing, 1998, 'Higher earnings, bursting trains and exhausted bodies: the creation of travelling psychosis in post-reform China', *Social Science and Medicine*, 47: 9, 1247–61.

Leung, J, and Wong, Y C, 2002, 'Community-based service for the frail elderly in China', *International Social Work*, 45: 2, 205–16.

Li, Jiali, 1995, 'China's one-child policy: how and how well has it worked? A case study of Hebei Province, 1979–88', *Population and Development Review*, 21: 3, 563–85.

Li, Zhisui, 1996, *The Private Life of Chairman Mao*, London, Arrow.

Lidtke, Vernon L, 1985, *The Alternative Culture: Socialist Labor in Imperial Germany*, Oxford, Oxford University Press.

Lieven, Anatol, 2004, *America Right or Wrong: An Anatomy of American Nationalism*, London, Harper Collins.

Lin, G, 2002, 'Regional variation in family support for the elderly in China: a geodevelopmental perspective', *Environment and Planning*, 34:9, 1617–33.

Lincoln, James R, Olson, J and Hanada, M, 1978, 'Cultural effects on organizational structure: the case of Japanese firms in the United States', *American Sociological Review*, 43: 4, 829–47.

Lincoln, James R, Olson, J, Hanada, M and Kalleberg, A L, 1996, 'Commitment, quits, and work organization in Japanese and US plants', *Industrial and Labor Relations Review*, 50: 1, 39–59.

Lincoln, James R, Olson, J, Hanada, M and Nakata, Y, 1997, 'The transformation of the Japanese employment system: nature, depth, and origins', *Works and Occupations*, 24: 1.

Lindblom, Charles E, 1982, 'The market as prison', *Journal of Politics*, 44: 2, 324–36.

Lindblom, Charles E, 2002, *The Market System: What It Is, How It Works, and What to Make of It*, New Haven, Yale University Press.

Lipset, Seymour M, 1959, 'Some social requisites of democracy: economic development and political legitimacy', *American Political Science Review*, 53, 69–105.

Lipset, Seymour M, 1996, *American Exceptionalism: A Double-edged Sword*, New York, W.W. Norton.

Luttwak, Edward, 1999, *Turbo Capitalism: Winners and Losers in the Global Economy*, London, Orion.

Lyttleton, Chris, 1994, 'The good people of Isan: commercial sex in Northeast Thailand' *Australian Journal of Anthropology*, 5: 3, 261.

Mackie, Jamie, 1998, 'Business success among Southeast Asian Chinese: the role of culture, values, and social structure', *Market Cultures: Society and Morality in the New Asian Capitalisms*, Hefner, R W (ed.), Boulder, Westview.

Madrick, Jeff, 2001, 'Mr Fixit', *New York Review of Books*, July 19, 48: 12.

Magraw, Roger, 1989, 'Socialism, syndicalism and French labour before 1914', *Labour and Socialist Movements in Europe before 1914*, Geary, D (ed.), Oxford, Berg.

Maitland, F W, 1996, 'Introduction', von Gierke, O F, [1900], *Political Theories of the Middle Age*, Bristol, Thoemmes.

Marsh, Robert M, and Mannari, H, 1971, 'Lifetime commitment in Japan: roles, norms, and values', *American Journal of Sociology*, 76: 5, 795–812.

Marshall, T H, 2000, 'Citizenship and social class', *Citizenship and Social Class and other Essays*, Cambridge, Cambridge University Press, reprinted in *The Welfare State Reader*, Pierson, C and Castles, F G (eds), Cambridge, Polity.

Marx, Karl and Engels, F, 1985 [1848], *Communist Manifesto*, Harmondsworth, Penguin.

Marx, Karl and Engels, F, 1977 [1866–67], *Capital: Volume I*, New York, Vintage.

Mauss, Marcel, 1985 [1938], 'A category of the human mind; the notion of person; the notion of self', reprinted in *The Category of the Person: Anthropology, Philosophy, History*, Carrithers, M, Collins, S and Lukes, S (eds), Cambridge, Cambridge University Press.

Mayer, Michael and Whittington, R, 1996, 'The survival of the European holding company: institutional choice and contingency', *The Changing European Firm: Limits to Convergence*, Whitley, R and Kristensen, P H (eds), London, Routledge.

Mayr, Otto, 1986, *Authority, Liberty and Automatic Machinery in Early Modern Europe*, Baltimore, Johns Hopkins University Press.

McCormack, Gavan, 2002, 'New tunes for an old song: nationalism and identity in post-Cold War Japan', *Nations under Siege: Globalization and Nationalism in Asia*, Starrs, R (ed.), New York, Palgrave.

McLeod, Hugh, 1996, *Piety and Poverty: Working-Class Religion in Berlin, London and New York 1870–1914*, New York, Holmes & Meier.

McLuhan, Marshall, 1998 [1964], *Understanding Media: The Extensions of Man*, Cambridge, MIT Press.

Mead, George H, 1967 [1934], *Mind, Self, and Society: From the Standpoint of a Social Behaviorist*, Chicago, University of Chicago Press.

Meisner, Maurice, 1996, *The Deng Xiaoping Era: An Inquiry into the Fate of Chinese Socialism, 1978–1994*, New York, Hill & Wang.

Menger, Carl, 1981 [1892], 'On the origins of money', *Principles of Economics*, Dingwall, J and Hoselitz, B F (trans. and eds), New York, New York University Press; 257–85.

Merton, Robert K, 1938, 'Social structure and anomie', *American Sociological Review*, 3, 672–82.

Micklethwait, John and Wooldridge, A, 2000, *A Future Perfect: The Challenge and Hidden Promise of Globalization*, London, Heinemann.

Mill, John S, 1985 [1859], *On Liberty*, Harmondsworth, Penguin.

Miller, Alan S, and Kanazawa, S, 2000, *Order by Accident: The Origins and Consequences of Conformity in Contemporary Japan*, Boulder, Westview.

Mills, Mary B, 1998, 'Migrant labor takes a holiday: reworking modernity and marginality in contemporary Thailand', *Critique of Anthropology*, 19: 1.

Mills, Mary B, 1990, 'Moving between modernity and tradition: the case of rural-urban migration from Northeast Thailand to Bangkok', *American Studies*, 2, 52–70.

Miyanaga, Kuniko, 1991, *The Creative Edge: Emerging Individualism in Japan*, New Brunswick, Transaction.

More, Thomas, 1965 [1516], *Utopia*, Harmondsworth, Penguin.

Morone, James A, 2003, *Hellfire Nation: The Politics of Sin in American History*, New Haven, Yale University Press.

Muecke, M, 1992, 'Mother sold food, daughter sells her body: the cultural continuity of prostitution', *Social Science and Medicine*, 35: 7, 891–901.

Mulder, Niels, 1997, *Thai Images: The Culture of the Public World*, Chiang Mai, Silkworm.

Mulder, Niels, 2000, *Inside Thai Society: Religion, Everyday Life, Change*, Chiang Mai, Silkworm.

Murakami, Yasusuke, 1984, 'Ie society as a pattern of civilization', *Journal of Japanese Studies*, 10: 2, 281–363.

Murakami, Yasusuke, 1996, *An Anti-Classical Political-Economic Analysis: A Vision for the Next Century*, Stanford, Stanford University Press.

Nakai, Nobuhiko and McClain, J L, 1998, 'Commercial change and urban growth in early modern Japan', *The Japanese Economy in the Tokugawa Era, 1600–1868*, Smitka, M (ed.), New York, Garland.

Nakane, Chie, 1970, *Japanese Society*, Berkeley, University of California Press.

Nakane, Chie, 1970, 'Ie', *Kodansha Encyclopaedia of Japan*, Tokyo, Kodansha.

Nakanishi, Toru, 1996, 'Comparative study of information labor markets in the urbanization process: The Philippines and Thailand', *The Developing Economies*, 34: 4, 470–95.

Nartsupha, Chatthip, 1999 [1984], *The Thai Village Economy in the Past*, Baker, C and Phongpaichit, P (trans.), Chiang Mai, Silkworm Press.

Niehoff, Justin D, 1987, 'The villager as industrialist: ideologies of household manufacturing in rural Taiwan', *Modern China*, 13: 3, 278–309.

Noell, Edd S, 2001, 'In pursuit of the just wage: a comparison of reformation and counter-reformation economic thought', *Journal of the History of Economic Thought*, 23: 4, 467–89.

Nora, Pierre, 1988, 'Nation', *Dictionnaire critique de la Révolution française*, Furet, F and Ozuf, M (eds), Paris, Flammarion.

North, Douglass C, 1996 [1973], *The Rise of the Western World: A New Economic History*, Cambridge, Cambridge University Press.

North, Douglass C, 1981, *Structure and Change in Economic History*, New York, Norton.

North, Douglass C and Weingast, B W, 1989, 'Constitutions and commitment: the evolution of institutions governing public choice in 17th-century England', *Journal of Economic History*, 49: 4, 803–32.

Nozick, Robert, 1974, *Anarchy, State, and Utopia*, New York, Basic Books.

Oestreich, Gerhard, 1982, 'From contractual monarchy to constitutionalism', *Neostoicism and the Early Modern State*, Cambridge, Cambridge University Press.

Offe, Claus, 1984, 'Some contradictions of the modern welfare state', *Contradictions of the Welfare State*, London, Hutchinson.

Ogasawara, Yuko, 1998, *Office Ladies and Salaried Men: Power, Gender, and Work in Japanese Companies*, Berkeley, University of California Press.

Ogena, Nimfa B, and de Jong, G F, 1999, 'Internal migration and occupational mobility in Thailand', *Asian Pacific Migration Journal*, 8: 4.

Olson, Mancur, 1982, *The Rise and Decline of Nations: Economic Growth, Stagflation, and Social Rigidities*, New Haven, Yale University Press.

Ortega y Gasset, José, 1994 [1930], *The Revolt of the Masses*, New York, Norton.

Oxfeld, Ellen, 1993, *Blood, Sweat and Mahjong: Family and Enterprise in an Overseas Chinese Community*, Ithaca, Cornell University Press.

Parry, Geraint, 1963, 'Enlightened government and its critics in eighteenth-century Germany', *The Historical Journal*, 6: 2, 178–92.

Pateman, Carole, 2000 [1989], 'The patriarchal welfare state', *The Welfare State Reader*, Pierson, C and Castles, F G (eds), Cambridge, Polity.

Peng, Ito, 2000, 'A fresh look at the Japanese welfare state', *Social Policy and Administration*, 34: 1, 94–7.

Peracca, Sara, Knodel, J and Saengtienchai, C, 1998, 'Can prostitutes marry?: Thai attitudes toward female sex workers', *Journal of Social Medicine*, 47: 2, 255–67.

Persky, Joseph, 1997, 'Retrospectives: classical family values: ending the poor laws as they knew them', *Journal of Economic Perspectives*, 11: 1, 179–89.

Peukert, Detlev J K, 1991, *The Weimar Republic: The Crisis of Classical Modernity*, Harmondsworth, Penguin.

Phillips, Gordon, 1989, 'The British Labour movement before 1914', *Labour and Socialist Movements in Europe before 1914*, Geary, D (ed.), Oxford, Berg.

Phongpaichit, Pasuk, 1982, *From Peasant Girls to Bangkok Masseuses*, Geneva, ILO.

Phongpaichit, Pasuk and Baker, C, 1998, *Thailand's Boom and Bust*, Chiang Mai, Silkworm Press.

Phongpaichit, Pasuk and Baker, C, 2000, *Thailand's Crisis*, Chiang Mai, Silkworm Press.

Pierson, Paul, 1994, *Dismantling the Welfare State?: Reagan, Thatcher, and the Politics of Retrenchment*, Cambridge, Cambridge University Press.

Pirenne, Henri, 1947 [1933], *Economic and Social History of Medieval Europe*, San Diego, Harcourt, Brace.

Pizzorno, Alessandro, 1986, 'Some other kind of otherness: a critique of "Rational Choice" Theories', *Development, Democracy and the Art of Trespassing: Essays in Honor of Albert O. Hirschman*, Foxley, A, McPherson, M and O'Donnel, G (eds), Notre Dame, Notre Dame University Press.

Podhisita, Chai, Pramualratana, A, Kanungsukkasem, U, Wawer, M J and McNamara, R, 1994, 'Socio-cultural context of commercial sex workers in Thailand: an analysis of their family, employer, and client relations', *Health Transition Review*, 4.

Polanyi, Karl, 1957 [1944], *The Great Transformation: The Political and Economic Origins of Our Time*, Boston, Beacon Press.

Polanyi, Michael, 1958, *Personal Knowledge: Towards a Post-Critical Philosophy*, Chicago, University of Chicago Press.

Pollard, Sidney, 1968, *The Genesis of Modern Management: A Study of the Industrial Revolution in Great Britain*, Harmondsworth, Penguin.

Polo, Marco, 1993 [1298/1903], *The Travels of Marco Polo: The Complete Yule-Cordier Edition, Volume II*, New York, Dover.

Popkin, Samuel, 1979, *The Rational Peasant: The Political Economy of Rural Society in Vietnam*, Berkeley, University of California Press.

Popper, Karl R, 1964, *The Poverty of Historicism*, New York, Harper & Row.

Postman, Neil, 1987, *Amusing Ourselves to Death*, London, Methuen.

Potter, Jack M, 1976, *Thai Peasant Social Structure*, Chicago, University of Chicago Press.

Potter, Sulamith Heinz and Potter, J M, 1990, *China's Peasants: The Anthropology of a Revolution*, Cambridge, Cambridge University Press.

Putnam, Robert, 2000, *Bowling Alone: The Collapse and Revival of American Community*, New York, Simon & Schuster.

Pye, Lucian W, 1985, *Asian Power and Politics: The Cultural Dimensions of Authority*, Cambridge, Belknap.

Radin, Margaret Jane, 1996, *Contested Commodities*, Cambridge, Harvard University Press.

Raeff, Marc, 1983, *The Well-Ordered Police State: Social and Institutional Change through Law in the Germanies and Russia, 1600–1800*, New Haven, Yale University Press.

Ramseyer, J M, 1995, 'The market for children: evidence from early modern Japan', *Journal of Law, Economics, and Organization*, 11: 1, 127–49.

Rapson, Richard, 1965, 'The American child as seen by British travellers, 1845–1935', *American Quarterly*, 17, 520–34.

Redding, S Gorgon and Whitley, R D, 1990, 'Beyond bureaucracy: towards a comparative analysis of forms of economic resource co-ordination and control' *Capitalism in Contrasting Cultures*, Clegg, S R and Redding, S G (eds), Berlin, Walter de Gruyter.

Reich, Simon, 1990, *The Fruits of Fascism: Postwar Prosperity in Historical Perspective*, Ithaca, Cornell University Press.

Renan, Ernest, 1996 [1882], 'What is a nation?', reprinted in *Nationalism in Europe: 1815 to the Present*, Wolf, S (ed.), London, Routledge.

Richardson, Gary, 2001, 'A tale of two theories: monopolies and craft guilds in Medieval England and modern imagination', *Journal of the History of Economic Thought*, 23: 2, 217–42.

Rieger, Elmar and Leibfried, S, 2000, 'Welfare state limits to globalization', *The Global Transformations Reader*, Held, D and McGrew, A (eds), Cambridge, Polity.

Ringmar, Erik, 1996, *Identity, Interest and Action: A Cultural Explanation of Sweden's Intervention in the Thirty Years War*, Cambridge, Cambridge University Press.

Ringmar, Erik, 1998, 'Nationalism: the idiocy of intimacy', *British Journal of Sociology*.

Ringmar, Erik, 2001, 'Critical thinking as institutionalised practice: East and West compared', *Manusya*, 1–2, 61–79.

Ringmar, Erik, 2002, 'The institutionalization of modernity: shocks and crises in Germany and Sweden', *Culture and Crisis: The Case of Germany and Sweden*, Trägårdh, L and Witozek, N (eds), New York, Berghanh.

Ringmar, Erik, 2005, *The Mechanics of Modernity in Europe and East Asia: The Institutional Origins of Social Change and Stagnation*, Oxford, Routledge.

Robertson, H M, 1933, *Aspects of the Rise of Economic Individualism: a Criticism of Max Weber and His School*, Cambridge, Cambridge University Press.

Robespierre, 1965, *Discours et rapports à la convention.* Paris, Unions générale d'éditions.

Rodrik, Dani, 1998, 'Why do more open economies have bigger governments?', *Journal of Political Economy*, 106: 5, 997–1032.

Rosser, Gervase, 1997, 'Crafts, guilds and the negotiation of work in the medieval town', *Past and Present*, 154, 3–31.

Rueschemeyer, Dietrich, Stephens, Evelyne Huber and Stephens, J D, 1991, *Capitalist Development and Democracy*, Cambridge, Polity.

Ruggie, John G, 1982, 'International regimes, transactions, and change: embedded liberalism in the postwar economic order', *International Organization*, 36: 2, 379–415.

Rybczynski, Witold, 1986, *Home: A Short History of an Idea*, New York, Viking.

Rykwert, Joseph, 1991, 'House and home', *Social Research*, 58: 1, 51–62.

Sacks, R G, 1997, 'Commercial sex and the single girl: women's empowerment through economic development in Thailand', *Development in Practice*, 7: 4, 424–7.

Said, Edward W, 1995 [1978], *Orientalism: European Conceptions of the Orient*, Harmondsworth, Penguin.

Sangren, P S, 1984, 'Traditional Chinese corporations: beyond kinship', *Journal of Asian Studies*, . 43: 3.

Sarti, Rafaella, 2001, 'The material conditions of family life', *Family Life in Early Modern Times, 1500–1789*, Kertzer, D I and Bargagli, M (eds), New Haven, Yale University Press.

Scarbrough, Elinor, 2000, 'West European welfare states: the old politics of retrenchment', *European Journal of Political Research*, 38.

Schama, Simon, 1987, *The Embarrassment of Riches: An Interpretation of Dutch Culture in the Golden Age*, New York, Knopf.

Schlesinger, B, 1966, 'The family in Communist China', *Social Science*, 41: 4, 221–8.

Schrecker, John E, 1976, 'The reform movement of 1898 and the Ch'ing-i reform as opposition', *Reform in Nineteenth-Century China*, Cohen, P A and Schrecker, J E (eds), Cambridge, Harvard University Press.

Schulze, Hagen, 1994, *States, Nations and Nationalism: from the Middle Ages to the Present*, Oxford, Blackwell.

Schumpeter, Joseph A, 1976 [1942], *Capitalism, Socialism and Democracy*, New York, Harper.

Scott, James C, 1976, *The Moral Economy of the Peasant: Rebellion and Subsistence in Southeast Asia*, New Haven, Yale University Press.

Scott, James C, 1989, 'Everyday forms of resistance', *Everyday Forms of Peasant Resistance*, Colburn, F D (ed.), Armonk NY, M. E. Sharpe.

Scott, James C, 1998, *Seeing Like a State: How Certain Schemes to Improve the Human Condition Have Failed*, New Haven, Yale University Press.

Segalen, Martine, 1996, 'The Industrial Revolution: from Proletariat to Bourgeoisie', *A History of the Family: Volume Two – The Impact of Modernity*, Burguère, A, Klapisch-Zuber, C, Segalen, M and Zonabend, F (eds), Cambridge, Polity.

Sennett, Richard, 1986 [1974], *The Fall of Public Man*, London, Faber & Faber.

Sennett, Richard, 1998, *The Corrosion of Character: The Personal Consequences of Work in the New Capitalism*, New York, W.W. Norton.

Sewell, William H Jr, *Work and Revolution in France: The Language of Labor from the Old Regime to 1848*, Cambridge, Cambridge University Press.

Shapiro, Daniel M, Gedajlovic, E and Erdener, C, 2003, 'The Chinese family firm as a multinational enterprise', *International Journal of Organizational Analysis*, 11: 2, 105–22.

Shigetomi, Shinichi, 1992, 'From "Loosely" to "Tightly" structured social organization: the changing aspects of cooperation and village community in rural Thailand', *The Developing Economies*, 30: 2.

Shimizu, Akitoshi, 1987, '*Ie* and *Dozoku*: family and descent in Japan', *Current Anthropology*, 28: 4, 85–90.

Simmel, Georg, 1990 [1900], *The Philosophy of Money*, London, Routledge.

Singhanetra-Renard, A, 1981, 'Mobility in North Thailand: a view from within', *Population Mobility and Development: Southeast Asia and the Pacific*, Jones, G W and Richter, H V (eds), Canberra, Australian National University.

Siu, Paul C P, 1952, 'The Sojourner', *American Journal of Sociology*, 34–44.

Siu, Shu-hsien, 1996, 'Confucian ideals and the real world: a critical review of contemporary neo-Confucian thought', *Confucian Traditions in East Asian Modernity: Moral Education and Economic Culture in Japan and the Four Mini-Dragons*, Wei-ming, Tu (ed.), Cambridge, Harvard University Press.

Skinner, Quentin, 1978, *The Foundations of Modern Political Thought: Volume 2, the Age of Reformation*, Cambridge, Cambridge University Press.

Skinner, Quentin, 1989, 'The State', *Political Innovation and Conceptual Change*, Hall, T, Farr, J and Hanson, R L (eds), Cambridge, Cambridge University Press.

Skoggard, Ian A, 1996, *The Indigenous Dynamic in Taiwan's Postwar Development: The Religious and Historical Roots of Entrepreneurship*, Armonk NY, M.E. Sharpe.

Smart, Alan, 1993, 'Gifts, bribes and *Guanxi*: a reconsideration of Bourdieu's social capital', *Cultural Anthropology*, 8: 3, 388–408.

Smith, Adam, 1981 [1776], *An Inquiry into the Nature and Causes of the Wealth of Nations*, Indianapolis, Liberty Fund.

Smith, Anthony D, 1986, *The Ethnic Origin of Nations*, Oxford, Blackwell.

Smith, Michael A, 1983, 'Social usages of the public drinking house: changing aspects of class and leisure', *British Journal of Sociology*, 24: 3, 367–83.

Smith, Thomas C, 1959, *The Agrarian Origins of Modern Japan*, Stanford, Stanford University Press.

Smith, Thomas C, 1986, 'Peasant time and factory time in Japan', *Past and Present*, 111, 165–97.

Social Portrait of Europe 1998, Luxembourg, EU Statistical Office.

Spence, Jonathan, 1999 [1990], *The Search for Modern China*, New York, W.W. Norton.

Stevens, C M, 1995, 'The social cost of rent-seeking by Labor Unions in the United States', *Industrial Relations*, 34: 2, 190–202.

Stewart, Susan, 1993, *On Longing: Narratives of Miniatures, the Gigantic, the Souvenir, the Collection*, Durham, Duke University Press.

Stockman, Norman, 2000, *Understanding Chinese Society*, Cambridge, Polity.

Stone, Lawrence, 1991, 'The public and the private in the stately homes of England, 1500–1990', *Social Research*, 58: 1, 229–30.

Strange, Susan, 1995, 'The defective state', *Daedalus*, 124: 2, 55–74.

Strange, Susan, 1996, *The Retreat of the State: The Diffusion of Power in World Economy*, Cambridge, Cambridge University Press.

Streeten, Paul, 1996, 'Free and managed trade', *National Diversity and Global Capitalism*, Berger, S and Dore, R (eds), Ithaca, Cornell University Press.

Strong, Roy, 1984, *Art and Power: Renaissance Festivals, 1450–1650*, Woodbridge, Boydell.

Swedberg, Richard, 1991, *Schumpeter: A Biography*, Princeton, Princeton University Press.

Szporluk, Roman, 1988, *Communism and Nationalism: Karl Marx versus Friedrich List*, New York, Oxford University Press.

Taira, Koji, 1970, 'Factory legislation and management modernization during Japan's industrialization, 1886–1916', *Business History Review*, 44: 1, 86–97.

Taira, Koji, 1997, 'Japan: Labour', *The Economic Emergence of Modern Japan*, Yamamura, K (ed.), Cambridge, Cambridge University Press.

Talwar, Jennifer P, 2002, *Fast Food, Fast Track: Immigrants, Big Business, and the American Dream*, Boulder, Westview.

Tampke, J, 1981, 'Bismarck's social legislation: a genuine breakthrough?', *The Emergence of the Welfare State in Britain and Germany, 1850–1950*, Mommsen, W J (ed.), London, Croom Helm.

Tan, Eugene K B, 'Re-engaging Chineseness: Political, Economic and Cultural Imperatives of Nation-Building in Singapore,' forthcoming in *China Quarterly*.

Taylor, Arthur J, 1972, *Laissez-Faire and State Intervention in Nineteenth-Century Britain*, London, Macmillan.

Taylor, J L, 1990, 'New Buddhist movements in Thailand: an "Individualistic Revolution" reform and political dissonance', *Journal of Southeast Asian Studies*, 21: 1, 135–54.

Textor, Robert B, 1961, *From Peasant to Pedicab Driver: A Social Study of Northeastern Thai Farmers who Periodically Migrated to Bangkok and Became Pedicab Drivers*, New Haven, Yale University Press.

Thatcher, Mark, 2004, 'Varieties of capitalism in an internationalized world: domestic institutional change in European telecommunications', *Comparative Political Studies*, 37: 7, 1–30.

Their, Clifford F, 2000, 'The success of American communes', *Southern Economic Journal*, 67: 1, 186–99.

Thompson, E P, 1967 [1963], *The Making of the English Working Class*, Harmondsworth, Penguin.

Thompson, E P, 1967, 'Time, work-discipline, and industrial capitalism', *Past and Present*, 36.

Totman, Conrad, 1980, 'From *Sakoku* to *Kaikoku* : the transformation of foreign-policy attitudes, 1853–1868', *Monumenta Nipponica*, 35: 1, 1–19.

Totten, George O, 1999 [1974], 'Japanese industrial relations at the crossroads: the Great Noda Strike of 1927–1928', *Japan in Crisis: Essays on Taishō Democracy*, Silberman, B S and Harootunian, H D (eds), Ann Arbor, University of Michigan.

Toynbee, Polly, 2002, 'Introduction', *Nickel and Dimes: Undercover in Low-wage USA*, Ehrenreich, Barbara (ed.), London, Granta.

Trägårdh, Lars, 2002, 'Crises and the politics of national community: Germany and Sweden, 1944/1994', *Culture and Crisis: The Case of Germany and Sweden*, Witoszek, N and Trägårdh, L (eds), New York, Berghahn.

Tribe, Keith, 1984, 'Cameralism and the science of government', *Journal of Modern History*, 56: 2, 263–84.

Tsurumi, E P, 1984, 'Female textile workers and the failure of early trade unionism in Japan', *History Workshop*, 13, 3–27.

Tudge, Colin, 2000, *The Day Before Yesterday: Five Million Years of Human History*, Oxford, Oxford University Press.

Turner, Sarah and Seymour, R, 2002, 'Ethnic Chinese and the Indonesian crisis: the emergence of a new ethnic identity', *Nations under Siege: Globalization and Nationalism in Asia*, Starrs, R (ed.), New York, Palgrave.

Unger, Danny, 1998, *Building Social Capital in Thailand: Fibers, Finance, and Infrastructure*, Cambridge, Cambridge University Press.

Unger, Jonathan, 1993, 'Urban families in the eighties: an analysis of Chinese surveys', *Chinese Families in the Post-Mao Era*, Davis, D and Harrell, S (eds), Berkeley, University of California Press.

Unger, Roberto M, 1987, *False Necessity: Anti-Necessitarian Social Theory in the Service of Radical Democracy*, Cambridge, Cambridge University Press.

Ure, Andrew, 1967 [1835], *The Philosophy of Manufactures*, London, Frank Cass.

van Caenegem, R C, 1995, *An Historical Introduction to European Constitutional Law*, Cambridge, Cambridge University Press.

van Esterik, Penny, *Materializing Thailand*, Oxford, Berg.

van Wolferen, Karel, 1990 [1988], *The Enigma of Japanese Power: People and Politics in a Stateless Nation*, New York, Vintage.

Visser, Jelle, 'Why fewer workers join unions in Europe: a social custom explanation of membership trends', *British Journal of Industrial Relations*, 40: 3, 403–30.

Vlastos, Stephen (ed.), *Mirror of Modernity: Invented Traditions of Modern Japan*, Berkeley, University of California Press.

Vogel, Ezra F, 1979, *Japan as Number One: Lessons for America*, Cambridge, Harvard University Press.

Walder, Andrew, 1986, *Communist Neo-Traditionalism: Work and Authority in Chinese Industry*, Berkeley, University of California Press.

Walker, Dave and Ehrlich, R S, *'Hello My Big Big Honey!': Love Letters to Bangkok Bar Girls and Their Revealing Interviews*, San Francisco, Last Gasp.

Wallace, William, 1999, 'Europe after the Cold War: interstate order or post-sovereign regional system?', *Review of International Studies*, 35: 4, 201–23.

Waltz, Kenneth, 1986 [1979], 'Theory of international politics', reprinted in *Neorealism and Its Critics*, Keohane, R O (ed.), New York, Columbia University Press.

Walzer, Michael, 1983, *Spheres of Justice: A Defense of Pluralism and Equality*, New York, Basic Books.

Wang, Shuguang and Jones, K, 2002, 'Retail structure of Beijing', *Environment and Planning*, 38: 10, 1785–1808.

Wasserstrom, Jeffrey, 1984, 'Resistance to the one-child policy', *Modern China*, 10: 3, 345–74.

Watson, James L, 1993, 'Rite or beliefs?: The construction of a unified culture in late imperial China', *China's Quest for National Identity*, Dittmer, L and Kim, S S (eds), Ithaca, Cornell University Press, 1993.

Watson, James L (ed.), 1997 , *Golden Arches East: MacDonald's in East Asia* Stanford, Stanford University Press.

Weber, Eugene, 1972, *Peasants into Frenchmen: The Modernisation of Rural France, 1870–1914*, Stanford, Stanford University Press.

Weber, Max, 1996 [1920–21], *The Protestant Ethic and the Spirit of Capitalism*, London, Routledge.

Weber, Max, 1991 [1924/1948], 'The protestant sects and the spirit of capitalism', *From Max Weber: Essays in Sociology*, Gerth, H H and Mills, C W (eds), London, Routledge.

Weiss, John H, 1983, 'Origins of the French welfare state: poor relief in the Third Republic, 1871–1914', *French Historical Studies*, 13: 1, 47–78.

Weiss, Linda, 1993, 'War, the state, and the origins of the Japanese employment system', *Politics and Society*, 21: 3.

Weiss, Linda and Hobson, J M, 1995, *States and Economic Development: A Comparative Historical Analysis*, Cambridge, Polity.

Wellman, Bary and Gulia, M, 1998, 'Virtual communities as communities: net surfers don't ride alone', *Communities in Cyberspace*, Smith, M and Kollock, P (eds), New York, Routledge.

Welter, Barbara, 1966, 'The cult of true womanhood, 1820–1860', *American Quarterly*, 18, 151–74.

Whyte, Martin King, 'The Chinese family and economic growth: obstacle or engine?', *Economic Development and Cultural Change*, 45: 1, 1–30.

Whyte, William H, 2000 [1949], 'The Class of '49', *The Essential William H. Whyte*, LaFarge, A (ed.), New York, Fordham University Press.

Whyte, William H, 2000 [1956], 'From *The Organization Man*', *The Essential William H. Whyte*, LaFarge, A (ed.), New York, Fordham University Press.

Wilson, Edward O, 1980, *Sociobiology*, Cambridge, Belknap.

Wintrobe, Ronald, 1996, 'Some economics of ethnic capital formation and conflict', *Nationalism and Rationality*, Breton, A, Galeotti, G, Salmon, P and Wintrobe, R (eds), Cambridge, Cambridge University Press.

Wolin, Sheldon S, 1987, 'Democracy and the welfare state: the political and theoretical connection between *Staatsräson* and *Wohlfartsstaatsräson*', *Political Theory*, 14: 4, 467–500.

Wong, R B, 1997, *China Transformed: Historical Change and the Limits of European Experience*, Ithaca, Cornell University Press.

Wong, Siu-lun, 1985, 'The Chinese family firm: a model', *British Journal of Sociology*, 36: 1, 58–72.

Wood, Alan T, 1995, *Limits to Autocracy: From Sung Neo-Confucianism to a Doctrine of Political Rights*, Honolulu, University of Hawaii Press.

Woronoff, Jon, 1979, *Japan: The Coming Economic Crisis*, Tokyo, Lotus Press.

Wright, Gwendolyn, 1991, 'Prescribing the model home', *Social Research*, 58: 1.

Wyatt, David K, 1982, *Thailand: A Short History*, New Haven, Yale University Press.

Xu, Yuebin, 2001, 'Family support for old people in rural China', *Social Policy and Administration*, 35: 3, 307–20.

Yamamura, Kozo, 1997, 'Entrepreneurship, ownership, and management in Japan', in *The Economic Emergence of Modern Japan*, Yamamura, K (ed.), Cambridge, Cambridge University Press.

Yamamura, Kozo, 1999, 'The Japanese economy, 1911–30', *Japan in Crisis: Essays on Taishō Democracy*, Silberman, B S and Harootunian, H D (eds), Ann Arbor, University of Michigan.

Yang, C K, 1959, *The Chinese Family in the Communist Revolution*, Cambridge, MIT Press.

Yang, C K, 1975, 'The functional relationship between Confucian thought and Chinese religion', in *Chinese Thought and Institutions*, Fairbank, J K (ed.), Chicago, University of Chicago Press.

Yang, Dali L, 1996, *Calamity and Reform in China: State, Rural Society, and Institutional Change since the Great Leap Famine*, Stanford, Stanford University Press.

Yang, Mayfair Mei-hu, 1994, *Gifts, Favours and Banquets: The Art of Social Relationships in China*, Ithaca, Cornell University Press.

Young, S B, 1968, 'The Northeastern Thai Village: A non-participatory democracy', *Asian Survey*, 8: 11, 873–86.

Zhang, W, 2002, 'Changing Nature of Family Relations in a Hebei village in China', *Journal of Contemporary Asia*, 32: 2, 147–70.

Zylan, Yvonne and Soule, S A, 2000, 'Ending welfare as we know it (again): welfare state retrenchment, 198–1005', *Social Forces*, 79: 2, 623–52.

Websites

Asia Times, 'MITI Minister Speaks of Economic Future, US Relations', 14 January 1999, *www.atimes.com/japan-econ/AA14Dh01.html*

Atlasphere, The, *http://www.theatlasphere.com*

British Pub and Beer Association, *www.beerandpub.com*

Catholic Encyclopaedia, The, *www.newadvent.org*

Democratic Staff of the House Committee on Education and the Workforce, Report by the '*Everyday Low Wages: The Hidden Price We All Pay for Wal-Mart*', 16 February 2004.

Dickens, Charles, 'A Walk in a Workhouse', *Household Words*, *http://users.ox.ac.uk/~peter/workhouse/lit/walkinaworkhouse.html*, 25 May 1850.

Ferry, Jules François Camille, 'Speech Before the French Chamber of Deputies, 28 March 1884', Modern History Sourcebook, *http://www.fordham.edu/halsall/mod/1884ferry.html*

Guardian, The, 'Shanghai eases China's one-child rule', 14 April 2004, *www.guardian.co.uk/china/story/0,7369,1191213,00.html*

Luther, Martin. 'Martin Luther's Sermon on Trade and Usury', 1520, *www.reformation.org/luther-trade-usury.html*

Marx, Karl, *The Introduction to Contribution to The Critique Of Hegel's Philosophy Of Right*, 1844, *www.marxists.org/archive/marx/works/1843/critique-hpr/intro.htm*

Mill, John Stuart, *Principles of Political Economy*, 1848, *http://www.econlib.org/library/Mill/mlP13.html*

Nordisk Familjebok: konversationslexikon och realencyklopedi, *www.lysator.liu.se/runeberg/nf/*

Senior, Nassau, 'Three Lectures on the Wage Rate', 1830, *http://socserv2.socsci.mcmaster.ca/~econ/ugcm/3ll3/senior/wages.html*

Sieyès, Abbé Emmanuel Joseph, *Qu´est-ce que le tiers état?*, 1789, Modern History Sourcebook, *www.fordham.edu/halsall/mod/sieyes.html*

Wesley, John, *A Plain Account of Christian Perfection*, 1766, *http://gbgm-umc.org/UMhistory/Wesley/perfect.html*

Index

Anthem Studies in Development and Globalization

Other titles in the series: